Murder on the Sky Ride

By Joe B. Hewitt

Hewitt / *Murder on the Sky Ride*

Murder on the Sky Ride
Copyright 2012 Joe B. Hewitt
All rights reserved
ISBN-13: 978-1-4811831-7-8
LCCN: 2012923147

About the Author:

Joe B. Hewitt covered the Police Beat for an Ohio daily newspaper. *The Lima News*. He went under cover and did a series of articles on the underworld. He served as a special deputy sheriff in Auglaize County, Ohio.

He organized and led a raid on a clandestine illegal drugs, prostitution, and gambling house. Hewitt covered some spectacular murder cases often scooping the competition.

For this book he interviewed a Texas Rangers captain for technical details.

The author has been to every state in the United States, 21 foreign countries, and has a natural rapport with people of different cultures and ethnic backgrounds. One goal of this book was to paint a picture of the diversity of the people of Texas while telling a story of murder, mystery and action.

A published nonfiction author, Hewitt formerly used the pen name Alexander Whitehouse for his fiction. *Murder on the Sky Ride* is fiction. Settings are actual places. Historical figures are mentioned, but are not used as characters. The mammalian diving reflex that has a part in this story is factual, as are oilfield methods.

Chapter 1
A Sunday in August, 1978

Day Minus Two; Conspiracy for Murder

On Interstate Highway 35 near Clearwater Springs Amusement Park in San Marcos, Texas, a green Chevy's tires hummed on the hot pavement harmonizing with those of a yellow sailboat pulled behind. A faded red flag flapped on the end of the horizontal mast as if directing a concert of singing tires.

Five cars back, a black Mercedes followed. "Don't get too close, Ben," Johnny Diaz said as he affectionately polished a thirty-ought-six, bolt-action rifle with a telescopic sight and leather sling cradled in his lap.

In the green Chevy, Gar Garcia smiled with contentment and squeezed his wife Liz who sat as close as possible. "I'll be glad to get that boat in the water, and sails in the wind," Gar said. "But first and most of all I'll be glad to get in bed with you tonight. It's been over two weeks. Not my fault."

"I know. Mine either. It was Reynaldo Diaz's. If he hadn't switched from politics to dope, maybe I could stay closer to home. And maybe our love life wouldn't have suffered so much lately. But . . . ," he paused and grinned, taking in a whiff of perfume. ". . . it's over now, and we can look forward to two uninterrupted weeks."

"With Diaz safely in jail," she said with finality.

"Well, not exactly."

"What do you mean?" Startled, she pulled her arm away and sat upright.

Gar let out a big sigh.

"He surely didn't raise that million-dollar bail?" she asked.

"His friends from *La Gente Unida* raised it for him. But Diaz won't cause us any trouble. I don't think he would cross his party by jumping bail." Gar went over in his mind the case against Reynaldo Diaz. Two eyewitnesses said they saw him supervise receiving a plane load of marijuana from Mexico. Gar had arrested him without incident. *I've got a good solid case. No problem. Two solid witnesses. We can enjoy our vacation. So why then do I feel uneasy about it? Diaz didn't seem to be the kind of person who would jeopardize a successful law practice to do stupid crimes.*

Back in the Mercedes, Johnny acted jumpy. "I'm afraid he'll lose us in traffic.

"Don't worry. That big, yellow boat is easy to see, but this car looks little in a rear view mirror," Ben Diaz paused and looked at his brother. "You know I don't know you and Reynaldo as well as you do each other, since I came along ten years later."

"Yea. You were just a baby while we were big boys. People used to think Reynaldo and me were twins."

"I've been around Reynaldo more lately," Ben said. "Helped him in his campaign for governor."

"That was a lost cause if there ever was one."

"Well, we made a statement."

"What statement? Chicanos are losers?"

"No, Chicanos can go to law school and run for

governor and organize."

"And educated Chicano former candidate for governor can get arrested on phony charges and go to jail," Johnny said with disgust.

"We'll fix that Ranger," Ben said with his eyes intently on the yellow boat ahead.

"I'm gonna kill that *cabron*, and I'm gonna enjoy it." Johnny caressed the rifle in his lap.

"He needs to be killed, but be calm. No point in us going to jail too," Ben said. "And when the time comes, you better let me do the shooting. I'm used to that rifle and scope."

Several cars passed the black Mercedes. "Looks like Gar and us are the only people on the road going the fifty-five speed limit," Johnny mused, and continued to fondly rub the rifle.

Meanwhile at Clearwater Springs Amusement Park in San Marcos, colorful cable cars rode a large, black cable across the clear, cold water of the San Marcos River and up to a wooded hill.

"I want a word with you, please," a man in a suit said with authority as he stepped out of a red cable car. He whipped out a wallet with a plastic laminated card bearing his picture, a gray seal, and "FBI," and thrust it into the startled face of Steve Pierce who had just opened the cable car door for him.

"I'm Don Thomas, with the FBI," his commanding voice rose above the squeaks, clanks, slamming steel doors of cable cars, and footsteps on the plank floor. "What's your name, son?"

"Steve Pierce." Fear made the words lodge in his

throat. Steve had been in trouble with the law and had been sensitized to men with authority who grab and give orders.

Another cable car swung into place, ready to be unloaded. Steve handed a well-worn door handle to another young man. "Take over here, Larry."

With a small package under his arm, Thomas took Steve's elbow and guided him toward a corner of the terminal.

"Are you in charge here?"

"Just at this end."

"That's what I mean," Thomas continued, "I'm here on some vital government business, and I'm going to ask you to cooperate with me, fully and confidentially," he raised his voice, talking over the noise of the machinery and excited voices of amusement park visitors getting on and off the cable cars. Thomas glanced around as he spoke. This raised a clanging mental alarm amid red flags that surfaced from Steve's subconscious mind, but he couldn't identify what had caused the deep seated fear. He recalled that the same kind of alarm had arisen when Steve, at age thirteen, met a bully he didn't recognize.

"Yes, sir." Pushy police authority added to the stress caused by some unknown danger. Emotional trauma brought beads of perspiration out through the pores of his skin to join those brought on by the August heat.

"You may not understand why I ask you to do certain things, but you must do them without hesitation, and without question. Do you understand?"

"Yes, sir."

The two walked down a narrow asphalt path, under a canopy of black oak trees, to a wooden veranda built on the side of the hill. They sat on hard bench seats of a heavy wooden table and looked over the park's varying shades of green and the transparent water of the San Marcos River welling up out of the ground, clear and cold.

Thomas opened a cigar box and showed a gray lump of clay. "This is modeling clay," Thomas pressed a thumb into it to demonstrate its resiliency. "After the sky ride closes down tonight, I want you to take this up to the main wheel that carries the cable, and press it into the groove. I want an impression of the cable itself, and the groove of the wheel that it rides in. Do you understand?"

"Yes, I understand," Steve said, trying to make his voice sound strong and hide his fear.

"Put it back in this box. Take the box to the parking lot out front. You'll see a green Plymouth Fury there. Here's a key to the trunk." Thomas handed Steve a single key. "Leave the key and box of clay in the trunk. Got that?"

"Yes, sir."

"Okay," Thomas snapped the box lid shut. "Will you be here and on duty Tuesday at one-thirty?"

"Yes."

"Good. I'll need your help at that time, so be sure you're here," Thomas said. "Now remember: this is secret business. Don't say anything about it to anybody. Got that?"

"Yeah. I've got it. I won't say anything."

Thomas intently looked beyond the outdoor refreshment stand and studied the brightly-colored cars on the sky ride, gliding on a heavy black cable, crossing over the river and manicured lawns and gardens of the park. It seemed to Steve a strange mix: a beautiful place of family fun being stirred up by a spooky cop.

Thomas reached into his coat pocket and withdrew

several twenty-dollar bills. "Here's a hundred dollars for your trouble. There'll be another hundred for you in the car trunk."

"Oh, you don't need to do that," Steve protested. "I'm glad to help."

"Take it. It's okay. Just be sure you don't say anything to anybody about it. "This is a secret project," he cautioned.

Steve watched Thomas go, and remembered that intelligence operatives are usually pretty average so they won't stand out in a crowd. This one was average in every way except that he sweltered in a dark business suit. Among the families dressed in colorful shorts and summer shirts, this one stood out like a cigar in a banana split.

In the green Chevy, Liz stretched to see the back seat. "He's still out."

Eight-year-old Enrique, Junior, snoozed. The boy had his mother's blond hair and blue eyes, and his father's high cheekbones. All three wore blue jeans and matching white t-shirts with blue sailboats and the message, "Druther be Sailing."

A green sign with white letters proclaimed, "San Marcos City Limits."

"How many times have we passed Clearwater Springs at San Marcos, but we have never visited. I've heard it's really beautiful," Liz said.

"We don't see the tourist attractions close to home," Gar said with his mind more on the shape of his wife's t-shirt.

The hot sun glinted off a gold Texas and "Department of Public Safety" seal on a passing patrol car.

As they passed the patrolman driving commented, "Nice rig."

"Looks familiar." The Sergeant beside him turned for a better look. As they came abreast of the green Chevy, his face brightened with recognition. "Hey, that's Gar Garcia, the highway cop that made good." He smiled and waved. Gar waved back.

"You know, I had just as much experience and education as Gar did when he was appointed a Texas Ranger," the Sergeant said.

"He was in Narcotics, wasn't he?"

"Yes, Narcotics, and I was in Patrol. Guess that made the difference. Or maybe it was 'equal opportunity' and his Spanish surname."

"Do you really believe that?"

"Naw, not really," the Sergeant said. "Gar's a good man. A smart man. Doesn't make mistakes. I guess he deserved to be a Ranger." Then he laughed, "But I deserved it more. My wife and I both agreed on that."

The officers gradually advanced ahead and passed. A nostalgic note touched Gar's heart. He had served two years in a similar black patrol car with its red and blue "bubble gum machines" on the roof, and a traffic radar unit protruding from the rear side window.

The elevated highway over Austin allowed a clear view of the Texas Capitol Building. The pink granite building, just a few feet higher than the United States Capitol in Washington, rose majestically out of a green salad of giant pecan trees. Then the Lyndon B. Johnson Library came into view, a white stone cube, monument to the former president.

As the car and boat rig neared Waco, Enrique woke, looked around. Excited, he reminded his father of a promise to visit the Texas Rangers Museum. Soon Enrique read exit signs aloud, "Baylor University, Fourth and Fifth Streets. Fort Fisher, Next Exit. That's it, Dad."

As they exited the highway, the Baylor University campus spread out to the right. Nostalgia gripped Gar as he looked at the stately old red brick buildings that surrounded the silver-domed, 'Old Main' administration building, and lawns garnished with great magnolia trees whose large dark green leaves allowed no sunlight to bare ground below.

Liz lowered her window. "Smell that romance?" The sweet odor of white magnolia blossoms the size of ruptured softballs came in the open car window. Thick, dark branches of live-oak trees reached out like mighty arms to hold multitudes of dainty leaves that would continue to face the sun all winter.

Liz read aloud a sign at the university entrance, "Baylor University; Chartered by the Republic of Texas, 1845," then added, "Our dear old alma mater. I think that translates 'soul mother.' It's also where I found my soul mate."

Surge brakes on the trailer made a crunching sound as Gar slowed for the exit.

"You are my soul mate, aren't you?" she asked.

"Sure, baby," Gar answered, as if he hadn't really listened while maneuvering the car and boat in heavy traffic. Liz dropped her hand to his crotch and pinched.

The car and boat trailer coasted heavily up the drive and into the parking lot of Fort Fisher, a rough-hewn, native limestone building on the Brazos River. As soon as the car stopped, excited Enrique jumped out and ran up to the porch. He had clomped the length of the plank-covered porch before his stiff parents got all the way out of the car.

Enrique bounced into the museum foyer where another family bought tickets from a Daughters-of-the-Texas-Revolution-type matron. Her diamonds suggested she worked more for patriotism than salary.

A boy, a head taller than Enrique, waited with two little girls near the entrance. Enrique held his hands around his eyes and peered through the glass doors. "O boy. I can't hardly wait. I've been wanting to come here for a long time, ever since my dad became a Texas Ranger."

"Is your dad really a Texas Ranger?" the biggest little girl asked with awe.

"Yes, he is. He's coming in now," Enrique said. His disheveled parents entered. The three children inspected them.

"I know all the Texas Rangers, and I sure never seen him before," the boy remarked, looking Gar up and down. "What position does he play?"

Enrique's parents started toward the doors, Enrique darted in ahead of them, surveying the hundreds of pistols, rifles, badges, and other Rangers' memorabilia.

The bigger boy motioned for his sisters, "Hey, here are the guns that killed Bonnie and Clyde," and pointed to two Remington automatic rifles lying in a glass case. Enrique stood on his tiptoes to get a better look.

"What's your name?" the biggest girl asked Enrique.

"Enrique García."

"Henry-Kay García. That's a funny name."

"Not Henry-Kay, En-ri-que. It's a Spanish name.

It's really Enrique Krause Garcia. Kids at school call me 'Ki-ki', but my folks don't like it. I was named after my Dad, and my Mom's last name was Krause. My Dad was named after my great, great, grandfather, who fought at the Alamo. If you go to the Alamo, read the plaque that has the names of the men who died there, and you'll see my great, great grandfather's name, 'Enrique Garcia.'"

The boy came to the aid of his sister, "I didn't know they had the names of the enemy."

"He wasn't the enemy," Enrique protested.

"He was a Mexican, wasn't he?"

"He was a Texan. Lots of the Texans who died at the Alamo had Spanish names," Enrique explained.

"Yea," the boy said skeptically. He took a sister with each hand and moved ahead toward his parents.

Enrique's countenance fell. He turned and hurried to join his parents. He reached for his Dad's hand, which automatically closed around his. Gar heard the exchange between the kids and feared that Enrique's enthusiasm had been quenched. Enrique looked up at his father with pride in his eyes. His enthusiasm had returned.

In the parking lot outside the stone museum building, Ben and Johnny Diaz parked on the far side.

"That's his car, Ben. They must be inside the museum." Johnny studied the building, "I'll nail him as he comes out. He'll never know what hit him."

Ben shook his head. "No, no, Johnny, there'll be a dozen witnesses."

"You'd just let him get away with ruining our brother, wouldn't you?"

"No, but I don't plan to go to jail either. We've got

to be careful, not only for our sake, but Mama's. Daddy getting killed, then Reynaldo getting arrested. . . If anything happened to one of us, it would be the end of her." He jerked his head toward their car. "Come on. We'll follow them to where they're going, some lake, I guess, and find a nice, quiet place for him to just disappear."

"I wish we could let him know why he's dying." Johnny climbed into the driver's seat of the black Mercedes and slammed the door. Hate boiled out of his mouth: "Here's for persecuting Reynaldo Diaz, you traitor." He pointed a finger toward the museum, and said, "Pow."
Ben shook his head. "That's a luxury we can't afford. We'll have to be satisfied with killing him."

Inside the museum, the Garcia family viewed displays of weapons and gear used by the Rangers. The family entered a large, circular room with a ceiling dominated by a forty-foot Texas Ranger badge that appeared to have been carved out of stone. On the badge, the words "Texas Ranger" circled a Texas star. Pictures depicting Rangers and their exploits covered the room's walls. A hundred visitors found places to sit on the carpeted floor and faced three white projection screens.

Enrique tugged on his Dad's hand, guiding his parents to an empty spot in the middle of the room. As they sat cross-legged on the floor, the lights dimmed and music filled the room. The voice of a male vocalist sang about the Rangers. Pictures flashed on three screens to illustrate a narration.

The amplified voice of the narrator enveloped the audience, telling the history of the Texas Rangers, beginning when Stephen F. Austin established them in

1823.

"In order to become a Ranger today, you have to be thirty-years-old, and no older than fifty. You must have completed sixty college hours and have served eight years in some kind of law enforcement. You also have to own, or have access to a horse, because Rangers still use them today, along with helicopters, in rough country."

"I hope I can be a Texas Ranger," Enrique said.

His mother shushed him.

The narrator continued. "There are only ninety-seven Texas Rangers, divided into six companies. Company "F" is located next door to us in the same building as the museum. There are now six-hundred men on a waiting list who have applied to become Texas Rangers."

After an hour in the museum, the Garcia family stepped out of the cool building into the 99 degree heat.

"Hot as Texas in August," Gar said.

The August heat radiated from the parking lot. Gar made a quick check of the tangle of stainless steel cables suspended from the boat's mast that lay flat on the boat, and the open cockpit filled with boxes of supplies. The family got in the hot car and drove back onto the Interstate highway.

The Diaz brothers followed several hundred yards behind. The brothers drove quietly for a few minutes, then Ben Diaz spoke: "I don't understand how Garcia could frame Reynaldo like that. He claimed he had witnesses that saw Reynaldo bringing in dope from Mexico."

"I know. It just ain't right," Johnny shouted. His hands gripped the steering wheel until his knuckles turned white. "His witnesses were liars." The intent gaze of his black eyes shot forward toward Gar.

"I'm sore enough at Gar to shoot him, but don't have a fraction of your hate. Has he done something else you hate him for?"

Johnny's face reddened; looking straight ahead he muttered a string of Mexican cuss words.

"Reynaldo was the best of the litter. He never got into any trouble like you and me did," Ben said as if to relieve his brother's anguish.

"*Si hermano.* It just ain't right." Johnny calmed himself. "But we're gonna make it right by killing that *cabron.*" He cocked his head and paused. "We might should do those two eyewitnesses too."

"Even if we kill Garcia, Reynaldo will still be in trouble. He'll have to go to trial."

"Yea, but with that Ranger dead we'll feel better about it. And he won't be around to testify." He paused, and added more calmly, "We just need to kill him, that's all. Then we need to find out who his two witnesses are and pop them too." The black Mercedes continued north, keeping several cars between it and the yellow boat ahead.

Two hours later Gar's car and boat topped a rise, and a great expanse of Lake Texoma's blue water suddenly appeared. Gar squinted at the yellow light of the evening sun that glinted off the rippling waves. Gar, Liz, and Enrique flexed their numb and fatigued bodies.

Leaving the concrete dam and spillway on their right, the rig turned onto a park road, and through a rustic stone entrance into Eisenhower State Park on the lake shore.

The Diaz brothers parked on the road above the boat ramp. Through binoculars, Johnny watched Gar back the boat into the water. Ben Diaz cradled the rifle on a rock as big as a Buick and waited for Gar to get out of the car. As Gar raised the mast, he moved so fast and so often that Ben Diaz couldn't get a shot. When he found Gar in the scope, Gar moved, Finally Gar, Liz and Enrique got into the boat's cockpit.

"Shoot," Johnny ordered.

"Can't. The wife and kid are in the way."

"Shoot anyway. You got plenty of shells. Kill them all," Johnny shouted under his breath.

"No way. Johnny, you sound crazy." Ben Diaz stood, pulling the rifle back off the rock.

"Okay. Have it your way," Johnny said with resignation, and then watched the yellow sailboat motor out into the lake and fade into the dusk. The buzz of the outboard motor grew faint in the distance. As night descended, blackness surrounded the boat, visible only as a green light fore, and a white light aft. Finally the boat's white stern light disappeared in the darkness.

"Forget what I said about killing the wife and kid. I'll be satisfied to kill the *cabron.*"

"I'm glad. If I thought you wanted to kill them too, I wouldn't have bought into this project." He handed the rifle to Johnny. We'll rent a boat tomorrow and find them. I can pick him off from three-hundred yards easy."

Bright moonlight outlined rustling leaves of tall cottonwood trees covering a small island on the Oklahoma side of the lake. "This'll be home for the next two weeks," Gar announced as the boat's bow slid smoothly to a stop on the sandy beach. "And it looks like we're the only ones here."

After pitching the tent and bedding down, Gar's libido had not diminished. But as he snuggled close to her, sleep interested Liz; and talking interested Enrique.

"Why doesn't Uncle Joe like you, Dad?" Enrique's voice seemed loud on the quiet island.

"What makes you think he doesn't like me? . . . Don't you want to go to sleep?"

"The way he talks. He says you trample on people's rights to smoke grass. What's smoking grass, anyway?" Enrique asked.

"Grass is just a slang word for marijuana. It's a drug. Makes people drunk. Joe seems to think it ought to be legal."

As the boy spoke, Gar caressed his wife lying next to him. She pushed his hand away.

"What's the matter?" he whispered in her ear.

Liz flicked Gar's ear with her tongue. "Wait until he's asleep."

"Should it be?" Enrique asked, unaware of the private mouth-to-ear exchange.

"Should what?" Gar asked.

"Should marijuana be legal?"

"I don't think it should be. Anyway it's not legal. Part of my job is to try to stop the marijuana trade. Joe disagrees. He'll change his mind when he gets a little older. Remember, he's only eighteen. That's young."

"That's young?" Enrique echoed. "He's grown up, isn't he?"

"Thinks he is. Let's go to sleep now," Gar said with authority. Enrique took a deep breath and got quiet. As soon as the quiet settled, Enrique asked another question.

"Hush, now and go to sleep," Liz said.

After a few minutes Gar squeezed Liz's hand. No response. She was sound asleep.

"Good night, Dad," Enrique said softly.

"Good night, Son."

Gar listened to the breeze blowing through the cottonwood trees, and remembered back to the last time he had made love to Liz, a wonderful satisfying experience. It had been two weeks ago. *Since then something always happens*, he thought: being out of town on the Diaz case, finally getting home and having an opportunity for good sex. Then like a sentence being ended, that opportune time slammed to an abrupt stop by a period.

But, tomorrow is another day. The period is well over. There would be a good opportunity for love-making. The longed-for vacation actually happened. So why did he feel uneasy, as if something might happen to his family, but like a bad dream, he couldn't bring the fear to the surface.

Chapter 2
MONDAY, Day Minus One

The Setup

The soft soles on Steve's shoes gave a muted clang as he climbed the steel framework of the still dark sky ride. Distant park lights shone through Steve's blond hair and cast dark shadows on the wall as he pushed modeling clay into the space where the black, greased steel cable entered the groove on the five-foot diameter wheel. He pulled the clay out, and holding it up in the faint light, examined the impression. Satisfied, he put the clay into the cigar box and climbed down.

In the parking lot Steve found a green Plymouth Fury parked alone under a light. He inserted the key Thomas had given him. It fit. He opened the trunk. The blue-white light from a pole above illuminated a trunk, empty, except for a neat stack of five twenty-dollar bills. Steve dropped the key into the cigar box with the clay, and closed the box's lid. He set the cigar box gently into the trunk, scooped up the money and slammed the trunk lid with a "thump" that echoed off the building and across the parking lot. As he walked to his own car in the employee parking section, he squeezed the wad of twenties in his pocket and grinned.

At mid-morning Monday, the excited voice of a young woman ended the quiet dignity of Carson's Jewelry Store in downtown San Marcos.

"Oh, Steve. Can we really get it today?" Her large

brown eyes, crowned with naturally long, black lashes, looked squarely into his blue eyes. Steve saw in her eyes an unspoken message of intense love. With a toss of her hand she flipped straying strands of long black hair over her shoulder's smooth skin the color of caramel. Steve and Anita Ramirez had been involved in an uphill engagement for three months. Anita's mother didn't like the part of town Steve lived in, that he was not Anita's *kind of people*, and especially she didn't like Steve having a criminal record.

Smiling broadly, Anita held her left hand above a square pad of black velvet that accentuated a bright gold ring with a small, brilliant diamond.

"Do you want it today?" Steve asked, not taking his eyes from hers, and ignoring the nattily dressed salesman trying to be attentive.

"Oh, yes. Can I have it now?" she asked with growing excitement.

"I think so," Steve said. Then turning to the salesman, asked, "How much do I still owe you on it?"

The salesman picked up a small, brown envelope with several notations in different shades of blue ink. "Let's see. You've paid a total of a hundred and sixty-nine dollars. There's a balance of a hundred and seventy." His eyes lifted from the envelope to Steve.

Steve reached into his pocket and pulled out a wad of twenty-dollar bills. He counted out nine of them.

"When's the happy date, Anita?" the salesman asked, handing Steve his change and a receipt.

"We haven't set it yet," Anita answered, with less excitement.

"We still have a hurdle to cross," Steve said.

"Is that hurdle's name Mama Ramirez?" the salesman asked with a grin.

"Could be." Steve returned the grin.

Outside, Steve and Anita walked briskly on the downtown San Marcos sidewalk with her left arm looped through his. In the other hand she held a small paper bag containing an empty, velvet ring box. Each few steps she held her left hand up to look at the diamond, glinting brightly in the sunlight. Steve looked proudly from her to the ring, and back to her.

"Where did you get the money?" she asked, still excited.

"I've been doing a little moonlighting."

Gar, Liz, and Enrique enjoyed a totally different world. Soft white Dacron halyard lines hanging from the top of the now erect mast swayed in the breeze and hit against the hollow aluminum pole, banging out a muted E above High C. The scarred wooden rudder moved from side to side with the waves, causing the tiller to jerk back and forth as if guided by an invisible hand.

The breeze powered the boat into the vast lake. Gar held the varnished wood tiller in his left hand, reached around the bare shoulders of his wife, in a one-piece green swimsuit. He pulled her to him. Liz snuggled in close.

"This is the life, huh, Baby?" Gar gave her a peck of a kiss on the forehead.

"Let's don't ever leave here," she sighed. "Let's just stay here forever."

Gar took a deep breath. "Smell that fresh air." The gentle breeze carried an occasional hint of wood smoke from a distant cooking fire. "Makes me hungry." After a day of sailing and swimming, they returned to their private island. Gar assigned Enrique to gather wood for a fire. Liz wrapped fresh corn on the cob and potatoes in foil with salt and butter. Gar pushed the foil-wrapped packages down into the hot coals and ashes. Soon the aroma of cooking steak covered the area.

"I'm about to die of starvation," Enrique said.

"You can make it until I get dinner ready," Liz said. Gar chuckled at the boy's impatience, and remembered himself as an eight-year-old.

Like many Texas families, the Garcias enjoyed many different cuisines. Liz had learned German cooking from her mother and grandmother, being descended from the colony established by Prince Carl of Solms-Braunfels in the Republic of Texas in 1845, at what is now New Braunfels. Gar had brought a tradition of what outsiders called "Mexican food," but it had been influenced for so many generations by *Tejanos*, Mexican-Americans living in Texas, that they called it "Tex-Mex," and, like most other Texas families, the Garcias had a liking for Southern cooking, and relished things like okra and black-eyed peas, strange fare for Northerners.

Meanwhile the Diaz brothers, tired from searching the lake all day, docked their rented motor boat at Eisenhower Marina. Johnny carried the rifle, clumsily wrapped in a burlap bag and hidden among fishing rods. His brother carried a picnic cooler.

"I don't know where they could be." Johnny deposited his burden in the trunk of the Mercedes. "Fine *asesinos* we turned out to be."

"It's a big lake." Ben shrugged.

"We'll find him tomorrow." Johnny looked intently across the wide expanse of water.

Chapter 3

Orange

Busy making the bed on the tent floor, Liz called out to Gar. "Did you get the towels?"

"Yes, and got a good deal on them too."

"Good. I brought only a few old towels and wash cloths."

"They were closing out one color. I got them at half price." Gar entered the tent, reached into a duffel bag, and withdrew a plastic-wrapped package of orange-colored towels, proud of his ability to find a bargain.

"They're orange."

"That's the color they were selling at half price," Gar said.

"Orange." Enrique opened the package and withdrew a bright, orange towel.

"Orange is okay. Why not? We'll keep them with our camping gear," Gar said.

After dinner, Gar gave Enrique a bar of soap and ordered him to the beach to bathe.

"I'm afraid someone will see me," he protested.

"Go ahead. I'll keep watch," his father assured him. "Want to take one of the new wash cloths?"

"I already have an old one." While standing in knee-deep water, the boy washed himself cautiously at first, as if afraid he'd get wet. Then he got with the program and jumped and splashed.

"Let's try to get Enrique to sleep in the boat," Gar suggested.

"I wouldn't sleep out there all alone."

Stepping carefully in flip-flop sandals, Enrique made his way from the water's edge to the tent.

"Mom's got your sleeping bag ready in the tent, but wouldn't you rather sleep in the boat?"

"No, Dad. I want to sleep with y'all."

Darkness settled over the beach. Gar and Liz, both wearing white terry cloth robes, stepped to the edge of the lake where gentle waves lapped the sand.

"You make absolutely sure the coast is clear," Liz admonished.

"Okay." Gar looked every direction. He hung his robe on the back of a lawn chair, scooped up the soap and splashed noisily into the water.

The farther he went away from the bright light of the Coleman lamp hanging by the tent, the darker the water appeared.

Waist deep in the water, Gar dipped his close-cut black hair into the water and soaped his scalp, releasing the soap's pleasant odor. Then, using one of the new orange wash cloths, he briskly washed his face, neck, and body. Liz stood in her white robe beside the lawn chair. Gar almost finished bathing before Liz believed no one could see. She took off the robe, draped it over Gar's on the lawn chair, stepped out of her thongs and carefully tiptoed into the water. Gar suddenly stopped washing, and stared at her as she waded toward him.

Away from the harsh lantern light, the moonlight had an even more softening effect on her beauty, which Gar regarded with relish. Her swimsuit had left her breasts and abdomen creamy white in delicate contrast to her lightly tanned skin.

"It's cold." She carefully stepped in the water up to her ankles.

"Come here, and I'll warm you up." Gar stood still and kept his eyes on Liz. "Grr," his growl came from down deep. He watched every slow step with relish until she reached him. Then he put both arms around her, pressed her bare breasts to his chest and caressed her. Starting on her shoulders, he gently worked his way down to her buns while holding her close.

"Enrique might be able to see us," she cautioned.

"He can't," Gar said under his breath. "He can't see beyond that light." He nodded toward the white light of the lantern near the tent.

Hearing Liz's breathing added impetus to his.

Liz turned her back. "Wash my back," she said, handing him a white wash cloth.

Gar soaped the wash cloth and began washing her back. The soapsuds smelled even better on her. He reached around and washed her breasts with his bare hands, slowly and deliberately.

"Maybe he'll go sound asleep," Liz suggested.

"I hope so," Gar moaned.

With her husband's eager help, which majored on caressing and minored on washing, Liz completed her bath.

The two white-robed figures walked hand in hand back to the tent and quietly slipped into bed.

"Y'all sure took a long time." Enrique's small voice shattered the stillness like broken glass.

"I was extra dirty," Gar said the first in a series of short answers to long questions. Once again fatigue overtook desire, and Liz went limp and sound asleep. Gar lay awake for an hour, frustrated as a celibate priest in a convent.

Chapter 4

The *Asesinos*

Meanwhile the Diaz Brothers continued their search. Ben yawned. "I'm tired; let's go back to the motel."

"Let's check one more marina," Johnny said, and steered the boat with its outboard motor along the coast toward a cluster of lights.

"What makes you think he's in a marina?"

"If he was on the coast, we would have seen him by now unless he went twenty miles. Then he would have driven closer to where he was going," Johnny said. "I see a yellow sailboat. Look."

Ben Diaz peered through binoculars. "It's twice bigger than Gar's. Let's go. We'll have all day tomorrow.

On the island in Lake Texoma, Gar lay quietly, listening to Liz and Enrique's quiet breathing. Again, sexual frustration overwhelmed Gar. *I feel like a eunuch in a harem.* As sleep eased into his mind, he felt uneasy. *No reason. Just a feeling, like something had gone terribly wrong and danger lurked near.*

Chapter 5

Tuesday, Day Zero

Murder on the Sky Ride

The sun cast short shadows Tuesday noon at Clearwater Springs amusement park when a green Plymouth Fury's front tires gently bounced from the curb in the parking lot. Thomas emerged from the driver's side, but rather than his previous clean-cut appearance he wore a full black wig covering his ears and with bangs over his forehead. Dressed in a business suit, his bushy black eyebrows, long, shaggy black sideburns, and a drooping black mustache made him a standout among the amusement park crowd in light colorful clothing.

From the right front seat another man, slight of build and a narrow face with a long thin hawk nose emerged and looked around. He had the same kind of hair as Thomas: over the ears, bangs, bushy eyebrows, sideburns, and drooping mustache.

A handsome man in his early forties, with dark skin, and high cheekbones came out of the back seat and followed the other two.

"He'll meet us in the restaurant, Mr. Diaz, Thomas said, and led the way into a restaurant filled with diners.

"There'll be four of us," Thomas told the hostess. With large, shiny, red menus under her arm, the hostess led the men to a table next to a window, which offered a panoramic view of the park.

The three men sat quietly, looking alternately at the

menus, and then through the window. A sidewalk, surrounded by lush green grass, and an occasional palm tree, led to the lower sky ride terminal. Brightly colored cars glided one after the other on the steel cable across the park, over the San Marcos River and to the other terminal on the side of a steep, tree-covered hill.

At the table, a smiling, well-scrubbed high school girl in starched uniform, greeted the trio, and took their orders. When the waitress left, Diaz spoke. "I don't understand what the FBI's interest is in this, Mr. Thomas."

Thomas glanced around and answered. "I can't give you all the details, Mr. Diaz. Let's just say that we want to make sure you have every opportunity to have a good defense. You know, the Bureau has had quite a bit of bad press lately. We've been accused of helping kill President Kennedy and Martin Luther King, among other things. If you can hire the best lawyers, and really have a good defense, whether you win or lose, they won't be pointing a finger at us for crucifying Reynaldo Diaz and trying to ruin your *La Gente Unida* Party.

"What's that in English, 'Mexican-American Political Party?'" the skinny guy with the hawk nose asked. Thomas looked impatient.

Diaz took a deep breath. "That's what it is all right, but *La Gente Unida* just means 'The United People.' The Texas Rangers are sure trying to destroy us," he said. "Especially one Gar Garcia. I don't know why he's got it in for us." Diaz's voice calmed. "You know I was framed on that marijuana smuggling deal, and Garcia did it. I think he was responsible for that million-dollar bond too. It was a miracle our people ever raised it."

"If Mr. Peters agrees to back your defense fund,

you'll be able to get the best lawyers in the country," Thomas said.

"I don't understand what his interest is. He's not a member of the party. I don't think he has ever made campaign contributions," Diaz said.

"I don't know either. I suppose he's got good reason to put that much money into your defense," Thomas said.

"I'm due for some good luck," Diaz said. "My father was killed in a car accident two weeks ago. On the day of the funeral I was arrested on a trumped-up charge of importing tons of marijuana, and it took a week to make bond."

"I'll guarantee this day is the day your life will turn around." Thomas stopped speaking abruptly and stood to his feet. He half raised his hand, beckoning to a tall man who had just come into view, carrying a cane and a briefcase.

The tall man stood head and shoulders above than the other three. Diaz smirked a smile and quickly sobered up as if he had to control himself to keep from laughing as he looked over the newcomer: His light complexion accentuated a heavy black mustache with drooping ends, and a black wig, identical to Thomas and his colleague. Like Thomas he wore a dark business suit and tie in the ninety-five degree weather.

"Mr. Peters, this is Reynaldo Diaz," Thomas said. Peters and Diaz shook hands. "And you know John Grimes," Thomas said as he motioned with an upturned palm toward Hawk Nose.

"Hot outside, isn't it," Diaz commented with a straight face. Peters blotted sweat from his forehead with a white handkerchief. "But it's nice in here. You'll soon cool off," Diaz said reassuringly.

Over lunch while each one had difficulty maneuvering food around the drooping moustaches, Diaz and Peters had a long discussion of famous lawyers and their fees. Peters continued to sweat throughout the meal, and dabbed his face with a handkerchief.

At the far end of the restaurant, seated at another table at another large window, a young couple held hands under the tiny table for two.

"Do you feel married now?" He looked deeply into her eyes.

"After last night, I'd better." Her voice trailed off into a tiny giggle.

"Did you like last night?"

"Uh huh," she said softly. Then seeing the waitress approach with their lunch, she released his hand and sat back in her chair.

At another table, a fiftyish, shapely woman looked through another window. "I wonder what that big castle-looking building is way up there on the mountain side, sticking up through the trees?" She spoke to a man across the table from her. Full gray hair covered his head, and smile line-wrinkles pointed to his mouth and eyes.

"Sweets, that's not a mountain. It's a hill."

"It looks like a mountain to me," she said defensively.

"In Arkansas, it'd be a mountain, but here in the Hill Country of Texas, it's a hill."

"All right," she said with mock impatience. "What is that castle-looking building up there on the side of that hill?"

"I think it's a university," he said, and after reflecting a moment, "Yes. It's a school. It's where Lyndon Johnson went to college before he became a school teacher."

"I thought he was a president. Do you mean the same Lyndon Johnson who was president?"

"Yes, Sweets," he smiled. "He taught school first and here's where he learned how."

"Are you making fun of me?" With a spoon in her hand, she slowly reached across the table, and gently wrapped him on the knuckles.

"No, my dear. You are the most intelligent, and the most beautiful woman in this place, if not in this entire county..."

"You are making fun of me," she interrupted, and again half smiling gently bounced the rounded bottom of the spoon off his knuckles.

"Well, anyway, you're the most beautiful," he said with a wink.

"I love you in spite of your blindness," she said.

"Have I wished you a happy Thirtieth Anniversary?" she asked.

"Only thrice, but you can do it again," he said eagerly. "I'm already as happy as an ant in a sugar bowl."

Rows of square windows on each side made the white glass-bottom boats look like floating trolley cars. The bright sun made ghostly bright reflections on the cold, clear water of the San Marcos River.

A message written in chalk on a black sign proclaimed that a boat at the dock would leave in ten minutes. Two fortyish women in pants and tops that might have come from Niemen Marcus occupied the otherwise empty boat.

Two black vinyl-covered benches, one on each side ran the length of the boat. Between the benches the glass bottom rose up to knee level, like a long, glass-covered coffee table full of water with an aquarium below.

The two women sat on one of the benches, and looked through water as clear as air down 40 feet to the bottom of the river. A few small fish lazily swam by.

"I don't hate him anymore, Bernice," one woman said with resignation. Each of her golden blonde hairs occupied its place like disciplined soldiers. Brilliant diamonds set in yellow gold loaded her fingers and neck.

"I don't think you ever really hated him, did you, Clara?"

"Yes I did. I hated him from my very soul. I had two years to practice hating him while he was gone off to South America leaving me with two teen-age boys to raise in their most difficult teen-age years." Her voice grew louder and she spit out the words. "Every time those boys drove me to tears, I hated him more."

"Don't get upset now, Clara." Bernice gently patted her companion on the shoulder.

"And now, with one son dead, and the other in a mental institution with a drug-fried brain, I blame him." Clara took a deep breath. "I'm sorry," she said, calming down. "I'm over it. I don't hate him anymore. I just don't have any feeling at all. I know he's your brother, and you love him. And I don't think my feelings for you could ever change." Her perfectly painted lips formed a warm smile. "You know, we've been sisters-in-law for over twenty years, and we're still friends."

"And we always will be," Bernice said.

A group of children bounded onto the boat, followed by several adults.

"I really think he feels the same way I do," Clara said in a quiet voice. "We have had no words for three months. He bought me a new car. And he insisted that I come here today and relax. He doesn't know I invited you to come. I wouldn't have enjoyed it alone."

"Where is he to meet you?" Bernice asked.

"At the little snack bar on the hill, just below where the sky ride goes," she said, pointing behind them and across the river. Then looking at her watch, she added, "He said he'd be there at one-thirty. When we get through with this boat ride, it will be just about the right time to take the sky ride over there."

"I'm curious to know what he and his lawyer want to talk to you about."

"He's just setting up some separate investments for me so I'll have my own income. I can go my way, and he can go his," Clara said. Then with a puzzled look, added, "But I don't have the foggiest notion of why he chose this place for us to conclude the business." She paused. "But, it's fine with me. This is a beautiful place, and a beautiful day." She let out a deep breath. "You know, Bernice, I feel as if this might be the day of a new beginning for me."

The glass-bottom boat filled with people who leaned over the glass "table." With heads bowed they peered into the water, looking like a congregation praying.

As the boat left the dock, a uniformed young man stood in the bow, and began his often- practiced lecture on the river and its inhabitants. He held a single control handle, which controlled the propeller and rudder, enabling him to turn and stop the heavy boat over spots of interest. He called his "congregation's" attention to a group of Rio Grande River perch, each from six to ten inches long. He explained that although related to the ferocious Amazon piranha, the perch didn't bite.

The boat passed over dark green aquatic plants gently waving in the current. The boatman pointed out an alligator gar, a primitive fish with long tooth-filled snout, eighteen inches long. The fearsome looking fish waited almost invisibly in the vegetation for prey. The fish ignored the boat and sixty eyes peering through the glass bottom.

The water became deeper as the boat continued. Every few yards a white clearing appeared among the aquatic plants with a crater, one to three yards wide. The boatman explained that the cold and clear underground water came up into the river through the craters. He stopped over one large, white crater, and pointed out a fifty-pound catfish, forty feet below.

"That's old Felix," the boatman said. "As far as we know, he's been there in that same hole ever since the park was built twelve years ago. He stays right there, feeding on microscopic aquatic life that comes up with the water. Since there's no fishing allowed here, old Felix has never been disturbed.

"The water emerging here is sixty-eight degrees, year round. Over at the submarine, where you watch the underwater show, it has warmed to about seventy degrees, but it's never any warmer than that," he paused.

A woman sitting between two little girls asked, "Weren't you in the underwater show this morning?"

"Yes, Mam, I was," he said. "All the people who

work on the water are in the show. We have to switch off and do other jobs to get warm after the water show."

The three shaggy-haired men with drooping moustaches and Reynaldo Diaz left the restaurant and walked two abreast down the long sidewalk toward the sky ride. Hawk Nose carried the attaché case Peters had brought into the restaurant.

Visitors bought commercial fish food from coin dispensers, and from a wooden dock, dropped pellets to the fish in the clear water. Male Mallard ducks, with their shiny, green heads, and females of mottled brown, quacked and paddled on the surface, splashing to get some of the food before it sank to the fish.

The four men walked leisurely past a rusty ship's anchor stuck into a spit of sand, and a leaning palm tree. Thomas hung back, took Diaz by the arm, and spoke quietly. "Peters is just a little eccentric, I guess, wanting us to meet these other people on the other side, but let's go along with whatever he wants, okay?"

Diaz shrugged his shoulders. "Why not?"

At the sky ride, a red cable car swung on its pendulum rod as the car stopped. A uniformed young man inserted a door handle into the square hole, and deftly turned the handle, opening the door. A man stepped out, carrying a toddler. A sighing woman followed, leading a small child.

Peters and Hawk Nose entered the red car, and the young man slammed the door shut. Thomas and Diaz entered a blue cable car. When the door slammed shut, Diaz remarked to Thomas, "Reminds me of a cage I just got out of. It's rightfully called 'the slammer.'" He paused a moment, then remarked, "You know, Agent Thomas, it's obvious you three guys are in disguise. I just wonder if all that is necessary."

Thomas smiled. "You'll understand perfectly very soon, Mr. Diaz," he said reassuringly.

Rollers on tracks carried the car, hanging by its pendulum bar, while inside the terminal building. When the car exited, its entire weight rested on the inch-and-a-half steel cable. The car climbed to forty feet above the ground, and rode the cable from support tower to support tower, across the park and then over the river. The occupants looked down into the clear water as they passed directly over old Felix the Catfish's hole.

"Seems strange to see the end of a river," Diaz said, half to himself.

"It's not the end. It's the beginning," Thomas said. "Water comes up out of the ground here, and it's the beginning of the river."

"The beginning is one end of it," Diaz countered.

As the cars swung into the high terminal on the side of the hill, Steve inserted his door handle and opened the door of the red cable car. Peters had to turn sideways to get his broad shoulders out.

The blue cable car swung to a stop. Steve opened the door. Thomas came out first. Steve did a double take when he saw Thomas with the shaggy, black hair and drooping mustache. He spoke to Steve. "Steve, get ready."

"I didn't recognize you, Mr. Thomas."

"I didn't either," Diaz said with a grin, as if going along with a silly joke.

"Aren't you Reynaldo Diaz?" Steve began.

"We're here on important government business,"

Thomas interrupted. "Remember, follow instructions exactly."

Steve handed his door handle to Larry Wilkins, about Steve's age, and dressed in the same kind of starched-and-ironed uniform. "Take over, Larry."

As Diaz came abreast of Steve, he put a hand to his mouth and spoke, with a grin, confidentially to Steve. "Yes. I am." Then he quickened pace to catch up with Thomas.

Hawk Nose took binoculars from the attaché case, and went to the opening where the cable and cars passed through. Through the binoculars, he studied each car as it approached.

Out of the way of people entering and leaving the cars, Peters, Diaz, and Thomas stood together in the corner of the building.

Steve examined the three strange *clowns,* dressed in suits and ties in the August heat. It didn't add up. The red flags again popped up from his subconscious.

"You wait here with Mr. Peters, Mr. Diaz. I'll be right back," Thomas instructed.

Taking Steve aside, Thomas barked instructions. "I want you to stand by to stop the sky ride. When I give you the signal, stop it immediately, and don't start it again, no matter what happens, until I tell you." Steve looked puzzled. "I'll say, 'Now,' and when I do, you throw the switch. Got that?"

"Yes sir."

At the other end of the sky ride, Clara and her sister-in-law, Bernice, boarded a red cable car. The door slammed shut. The heavy latch vibrated the sheet metal of the car's door like a drum as it clicked into a locked position. The car swung gently on the cable and moved up and away.

The minister and his wife, celebrating their thirtieth wedding anniversary, boarded the next cable car, a yellow one. As it swung away, a green car took its place. The young couple who had not yet been married twenty-four hours stepped aboard green cable car as it swayed slightly on the heavy cable.

All together eighteen cable cars occupied the sky ride, three on each end, and twelve in transit, six going one way, and six the other.

The red cable car, containing Clara and Bernice passed over river's center.

"Old Felix the Catfish is down there somewhere, but I can't see him," Bernice said.

Behind them, the yellow cable car had just reached the edge of the river. The minister and his wife both looked down to the river toward the white boats floating on the transparent water.

In the green cable car, crossing over the wide, concrete sidewalk. In a tight embrace the bride and groom kissed with their eyes closed.

Hawk Nose peered intently through the binoculars. He raised his right hand into the air, "Get ready," he shouted.

Thomas motioned to Steve, and ordered, "Get ready to stop the sky ride."

Steve stood by an electrical panel, and held his hand over a large red button.

Hawk Nose dropped his hand.

"Now," Thomas ordered. Steve's hand immediately pressed the button and the whir of the large gray electric motor stopped. Cars inside the terminal clanked to a halt and swung quietly back and forth.

Larry, the attendant, poised with handle in hand to receive a car that stopped three feet short of the unloading spot, looked toward Steve. "What happened?"

"What happened?" also echoed from voices within the cars in the terminal.

Steve projected his voice in the direction of the questions, "We've had to stop just for a minute. Everything's all right. Just stand by for a moment."

Hawk Nose's footsteps echoed off the thick wood planks of the floor as he ran back toward Peters and Diaz. When Diaz saw Hawk Nose running toward him, he turned to face him. Unseen behind Diaz, Peters raised his fist and hit Diaz squarely in the back of the neck. Stunned, Diaz fell forward. Hawk Nose locked both hands into a double fist and, with the full force of his body, hit Diaz in the back of the neck. Diaz hit the wooden floor with his face.

Steve's body froze in shock and surprise. "Hey. What's going on?" he shouted to Thomas.

Hawk Nose fell on Diaz with both knees. Withdrawing a roll of nylon strapping tape from his pocket, Peters grabbed Diaz's right hand and drew it to the middle of his back. Hawk Nose did the same with Diaz's left hand. Peters deftly wound several layers of the tough tape around the dazed man's wrists and ankles. Memory of a rodeo and a calf tied by a cowboy flashed by Steve's mind. They had tied Reynaldo Diaz as tight as a calf for branding.

Hawk Nose peeled a six-inch length of white adhesive tape from a roll, grabbed Diaz by the hair, jerked his head up, and pasted the wide, white tape over his mouth.

Steve shook himself from his frozen posture by the

emergency stop button and ran toward Thomas.

The scuffle on the far side of the building alarmed visitors who stood in line to board cars. Those caged in the cable cars beat on the metal walls and shouted. A woman screamed. A man beat on the heavy, steel screen of his cable car, stomped his feet and shouted, "Let me out of here."

"It's all right, folks," Thomas shouted, holding up his FBI identification. "We're with the FBI, and we're just taking a man into custody." He paused, and a chorus of mixed sighs of relief from the adults, and "wows" from the children arose from the dozen people who had witnessed the precision hog-tying of the unsuspecting Diaz.

"We're going to question this man for just a minute," Thomas continued, waving his hand toward the heavy steel framework that of the sky ride. ". . . then the sky ride will start up again, and we'll be on our way."

Steve had a strong urge to jump in and try to help Diaz, but a severe beating from a prison guard conditioned Steve not to raise a hand against legal authority, While Thomas spoke, Peters threw Diaz over his shoulders and carried him like sack of potatoes. Hawk Nose followed, carrying the attaché case and Peters' walking stick.

Peters' burden began to struggle. The big man dropped Diaz to the floor near the opening through which the large black cable passed.

Bewildered, Steve asked Thomas again, "what's going on?" Thomas ignored him. To Steve it was all unreal, like a crazy dream. He watched Peters climb up the steel girders past a Volkswagen motor on standby in case electricity failed. Six feet above the floor a large grooved wheel carried the cable that stretched across the river.

Peters forced a double-edged steel axe head onto the *walking stick*. Standing on the girder near the sheave wheel, he withdrew a block of wood that had been carved to a peculiar shape, and a coil of three-quarter-inch, nylon rope. He quickly threw one end of the rope down to Hawk Nose. The heavy end hit the floor and revealed a carefully-prepared hangman's noose.

Diaz's eyes opened wide in alarm. He bowed his back and straightened his legs and body with great force. He strained at the strapping tape holding his wrists and feet. He kicked, twisted and grunted in panic, but the nylon strapping tape held him tight.

Hawk Nose calmly stepped over Diaz and wrapped the rope six times around the heavy, sticky-with-grease, black cable and tied the rope in a double, half-hitch. The hangman's noose end he pulled tight around the neck of the wide-eyed, terrified, and writhing Diaz.

Meanwhile above on the steel framework, Peters put the block of wood into the groove of the sheave wheel. The wood fit perfectly, *the same shape as the modeling clay*, Steve thought.

Hawk Nose put a foot on Diaz's neck and held the rope taut. High above, Peters settled both feet on a girder, picked up the axe, raised it high, and with the power of his entire large body, brought the sharp, hard steel axe blade down onto the steel cable again and again. Sweat ran down Peters' face and dripped off his square chin. Perspiration got into his eyes. He reached for a handkerchief and hurriedly wiped his eyes. One of his black eyelashes fell unnoticed to the steel beam on which he stood.

In the red cable car, stopped over the river, the sisters-in-law continued their chat. "I wonder why we stopped," Bernice said.

"I don't know," Clara replied. "It'll just give us more time to enjoy the view."

In the yellow cable car, stopped at the edge of the river, the white-haired minister patted his wife's hand. "You know, Sweets, we're going to have to do things like this more often."

"I've heard that before," she chided.

In the green cable car, the honeymooners parted lips and opened their eyes. "Hey, we're stopped," the new husband said.

"I wonder what happened," the bride said in a voice filled with alarm. She turned her head to see ahead of the car and began to cry.

The big man again shifted his weight and lifted the axe. He kicked the unseen, black eyebrow from the steel beam. With all his strength, Peters brought the axe down again. The cable parted, and as fast as a bullet, the severed end went through the opening.

The rope that Hawk Nose had tied to the cable held its grip and, pulled by the suddenly released cable, jerked Diaz through the opening. His shoes came off, and fell to the wood floor. Halfway through the opening, the force of the cable jerked Diaz's head from his body, leaving a red stump in the middle of his shoulders like that of a chicken with its neck wrung. Diaz's head shot two-hundred yards into the treetops before it fell out of the hangman's noose.

The body came crashing down through the trees in front of the terminal building. A spray of blood covered the floor, the steel girders, the snack bar, and tree leaves.

Peters grabbed the attaché case, hit the end of the axe handle on the girder, loosening the axe head, dropped it into the attaché case, clicked shut the latches, and jumped to the floor and ran toward the entrance of the terminal building.

Steve and Larry stood like statues with their mouths open. Women screamed. Children cried. Men shouted, "What's going on?"

"*Vamos, Muchachos,*" Peters shouted, and ran through the door. The knot of people in the doorway parted.

Steve, who had stood catatonic during the ninety-second action, came alive. "You're no FBI man," he said, and grabbed for Thomas.

Thomas reached under his coat and withdrew a dark blue, short-barreled .38 revolver. He pointed it in Steve's face. "Do as I say, and quickly, or you're dead." Just then the two shaggy accomplices, one tall and one short, ran past. "Follow him, and be fast," Thomas waved the .38 toward Hawk Nose.

Steve ran behind Hawk Nose, closely followed by Thomas with the menacing .38.

When the cable parted, the red cable car suddenly jerked backward with a force that stunned both women. The pendulum bar jumped off the cable, which continued its springing, backward travel. The red car splashed into the center of the river.

The car entered the silent world of clear, cold water, and slowly descended forty feet to the bottom. Old Felix the Catfish, startled by the huge, shiny red object falling into his hole, whipped his tail, and darted away. The red cable car settled on its side. Inside the car, the cold water aroused Clara. Her blonde hair now waved in the water like the aquatic plants. She tried to reach her hand through the door's window, but the wire mesh was too fine. She pushed the still form of her sister-in-law aside, and bracing her back on the opposite side of the car, pushed against the door with both feet.

Growing weaker, she pushed again, but the latch held the door solidly. She slumped to the floor, and desperately held her nose and mouth with both hands. Her sister-in-law still didn't move. Then Clara's eyes closed, her head fell to one side. Her relaxed hands fell from her face, and great bubbles of air left her lungs. The bubbles, like little quicksilver umbrellas, floated easily through the wire mesh, hurrying to the surface.

Meanwhile the yellow car jerked backward and fell to the grass. Force of the impact sprang open the door, and the woman fell out of the door in a heap. The minister crawled out on hands and knees. His white hair soaked up blood as it oozed out of a wound on the right side of his head.

"Oh, God," he choked. His wife lay beside the car on her side, her left arm grotesquely twisted under her body. Her left leg was drawn up to her chest, and the right extended. "Oh, God, please help her," he prayed aloud, over and over again, as he gently rolled his unconscious wife onto her back and freed the twisted arm.

When the cable snapped the green car backward, the bride sprawled over her husband. As the car fell, she uttered a piercing scream, which continued all the way down. The car's convex sheet metal bottom crumpled upward as it hit the concrete sidewalk. The door sprang open. The bride crawled out, gasped her lungs full of air and screamed again and again in hysteria.

    The lower half of her new husband's body lay in the seat, but the top half of his twisted body lay on the floor. With eyes open, his hands moved to his hips. Then he patted his legs, as if feeling for something. His legs did not move. He said nothing. His wife continued to scream.

    Park visitors and staff ran to aid the injured. They checked the other cars and found them to be empty.

    On its regular tour, a glass-bottom boat approached the deepest part of the river when the red car fell into the water. The boat operator proceeded on at top speed, no faster than a crawl, to the spot over old Felix's hole. The young man, stopped the motor, and kicked off his shoes and stepped to an open window. The visitors suddenly hushed. "I'm going to try to help," he said. "Don't go away." He dove into the cold, clear water. The spectators leaned over the long glass "coffee table" and watched as he swam forcefully, straight down toward the shiny red cable car settled forty feet below in Felix's hole.

    Sticking his fingers through the wire mesh of the red car's door, the boatman pulled his body to the bottom. His sandy hair waved weightless in the current of the cold water. He allowed a few bubbles of air to escape his mouth. Bright silver, and trembling, the bubbles rose to the surface. He braced a foot against the side of the car, and with the fingers of both hands in the wire mesh, he pulled with all his strength. The door held tight. He reached into his pants pocket. As he did so his body tried to float up. He held on to the red car with the other hand, and his body floated upward, suspending him upside down. He fished in his pocket.

    He found his pocket knife, wrapped his legs around

the pendulum rod of the cable car to keep from floating away, and opened the knife blade. He pulled himself back down to the door and stuck the knife blade into the door handle hole. He let out a few more bubbles of air, and turned the knife.

The blade broke. He dropped the knife, and released his hold on the red cable car. Shiny silver bubbles of air left his mouth in a small stream as he floated and swam rapidly to the surface.

He gasped air as his head broke the surface of the water. Eager hands of two men pulled him aboard the glass-bottom boat. A buzz of questions and wonder filled the boat.

"I couldn't get the door open," the boatman gasped. "We've got to get a door handle or something to get the door open."

A small motor boat approached with a young staff member at the outboard motor, Jim Bradshaw, assistant manager of the park, in a loud Hawaiian shirt, and two divers in wet suits, with air tanks on their backs.

"We've got to have a handle to the cable car door," the wet and gasping boatman shouted toward the motor boat.

Bradshaw waved acknowledgment and spoke into a walkie-talkie radio.

A diver lazily fell over backward into the water and dove toward the red cable car.

The motor boat continued to the other side of the river and brought back a cable car door handle. The second diver grasped the door handle and eased himself backward into the water.

Arriving back at the glass-bottom boat, Bradshaw

called over the sound of the idling outboard motor to the wet and shivering boatman. "Tie on to us here," then to the visitors aboard the glass-bottom boat, he shouted "we're going to need a couple of you men to help."

The motor boat bumped gently on the side of the larger craft. A volunteer tied the two boats together. Just then first diver surfaced and grabbed the side of the small boat. "Need some needle nose pliers," he said, holding his mouthpiece in one hand and holding on to the boat with the other.

"Needle nose pliers," the outboard motor operator repeated like a nurse in surgery, and opened a tool box.

"There's something stuck in the door handle hole," the diver said.

"It's my knife blade," the wet boatman explained.

With a pair of needle nose pliers in his hand, the diver descended again to Felix's hole and the red cable car.

Bradshaw stood on the bow of the glass-bottom boat. "Folks, I'm Jim Bradshaw, assistant manager of Clearwater Springs." He was a golf pro type, with a deep tan. "There are several people seriously hurt. Our people are administering first aid, and the fire department and ambulances are on their way," he projected his voice into the boat. "In the meantime we have to do what we can to help the people in the water."

"It's been at least ten minutes. Won't they be dead?" one asked.

"Probably so," Bradshaw answered. "But there is a chance. People in the boat hushed, and he raised his voice so they could all hear. "Since the water is so cold, sixty-eight degrees, it is possible that an automatic reflex action took over. It's called the 'mammalian diving reflex.' It causes the heartbeat to slow, to restrict blood flow to muscle tissues, and take what oxygen is available in the blood to the brain. It works for air-breathing seals and porpoises. They can stay submerged for up to thirty minutes. Sometimes it works for humans, and sometimes it doesn't."

The people watched as the two divers, each with the limp body of a woman, came to the surface. Volunteers and staff members pulled the women's wet bodies aboard, and rolled them onto their stomachs. Bradshaw pushed on Clara's rib cage. With each stroke, water came out of her mouth. The wet boatman pushed on Bernice's rib cage, but no water came out.

Bradshaw started cardiopulmonary resuscitation (CPR) on Clara. Her chest rose as her lungs inflated.

The boatman started CPR on Bernice. "We got no water out of her," he called to Bradshaw.

People in the boat stayed quiet as observers in a surgical theater. The bride continued to scream in the distance.

"She may not have had any water in her," Bradshaw gasped between blasts of breath into Clara's lungs. "Continue with CPR," he ordered. "How could that cable have broken?" He asked no one in particular.

"I'm a nurse. Maybe I can help." A short, middle-aged woman with frizzy hair shouted through the window to Bradshaw.

"Come on," Bradshaw gasped between breaths. "Take this one's pulse."

The nurse held Clara's wrist for a moment. "No pulse," she said officially.

Sirens wailed in the distance.

"Check the other one," Bradshaw gasped.

The frizzy-haired nurse went to Bernice and held her wrist. "This one has a faint pulse."

A cheer went up from the audience in the glass-bottom boat.

The black steel cable, that minutes before had been so deadly, lay still on the green lawn like a dead snake. Colorful sky ride cars littered the ground like broken Easter eggs, two of which had spilled bleeding contents.

A wailing siren grew louder and a red fire department rescue truck drove onto the grass, followed by three square, white and gold ambulances festooned with an array of flashing lights of red, blue, and bright white.

The bride's hysterical screaming had continued from the moment the cable snapped, and although bystanders tried to comfort her, the screams continued until paramedics arrived at her side. But seeing her relatively good condition, they turned their attention to her husband.

"We were afraid to move him," a man visitor said, then added, "He can't feel his hips or legs."

The paramedics carefully extricated the groom from the car, strapped him to a backboard and loaded him into an ambulance.

As two paramedics raced to the fallen car nearest the river, they found the minister, cradling his wife's head in his right hand. Blood oozed from her nose and ears. With a finger and thumb, the minister held the tip of his wife's tongue half out of her mouth.

"Oh, God, please help her," he continued to pray. Tears wet his cheeks. He looked up toward the two men with a stretcher rushing toward him. "She's unconscious.

She was swallowing her tongue," his voice cracked.

The glass-bottom boat with Clara and Bernice docked. Two fire department paramedics, panting from the long run, set their black cases of equipment on the wooden dock.

"How long do you think they were under?" one asked.

Between blows of air into Bernice's lungs, Bradshaw answered, "No more than fifteen-minutes."

"Slim hope, I'd say," the paramedic said, and reached a hand to Bernice's carotid artery. "Hey. This one has a pulse."

"She's breathing on her own," one of the men working on Bernice announced. The people on the boat again applauded.

The paramedics forced oxygen into Clara's lungs, and with fist-sized electrodes tried to shock her heart into action.

"I'm afraid she's had it," a paramedic said.

"Let's not give up," Bradshaw said.

All the way to the ambulance the paramedics continued CPR on Clara.

As the last ambulance sped away with its lights flashing, red, blue, and bright white, and its siren wailing, a uniformed police lieutenant approached Bradshaw.

"We need to get across the river, and see if we can find out what caused this," the lieutenant said.

"We'll take my boat," Bradshaw said, as he walked toward the dock. "We've received conflicting reports from up there," he said, motioning with his radio toward the hillside terminal of the sky ride. "One man reported that the cable broke, hit a man and cut his head off."

Another officer caught up with the pair and began taking notes.

"The other report said four Mexicans got into a fight. One of them got his throat cut, and somehow in the fracas, they cut the cable," Bradshaw continued. "In any case, they tell me there's blood all over the place. And to make it even more confusing, both reports say an FBI man was involved."

Chapter 6

Confusion

Steve slumped in the corner of the back seat of the green Plymouth. "Be careful. These little towns have speed traps," Thomas said. He sat beside Steve, resting Thomas' .38 in his lap, but the barrel still pointed toward Steve. Hawk Nose drove between 55 and 60 with the flow of traffic, south on Interstate 35 toward San Antonio.

Thomas had dropped out of law school in New York City to serve three years in prison for beating a fellow student half to death. He started in a country club, minimum security, facility because of his youth. After assaulting a guard with a dining spoon whose handle had been sharpened by scraping it on a concrete floor, prison officials transferred Thomas to Attica. There he met people who liked violence as much as he did. Thomas joined their tight circles. They spent hours planning jobs and dreaming of what they would do when they got out. Murderers, rapists, armed robbers, and embezzlers shared their trade secrets with Thomas, and he gave them legal advice. In addition to getting his unofficial master's degree in criminal behavior, Thomas also did valuable networking.

Hawk Nose had been serving a life term for killing his wife in a jealous rage. He had been inside for ten years when Thomas arrived. Hawk Nose got out on parole the same day that Thomas got discharged. They went west together and robbed their way across country until they got to Dallas. There they found their niche: doing the dirty work for smarter people who could pay well.

Continuing down I-35, Hawk Nose's eyes darted around. Steve felt the same alarm rise up from his subconscious he had felt when Thomas looked around suspiciously at the amusement park. Thomas had glanced around while he talked, just like Hawk Nose. Now, Steve realized that convicts made those antsy moves, not FBI agents.

Hawk Nose reached to his head and pulled off a wig, revealing closely cropped black hair. He peeled away the heavy black mustache under his hawk nose, revealing a closely-trimmed shorter mustache. He pulled off the black, shaggy fake eyebrows. Following his lead, Thomas pulled the black wig from his head to reveal brown hair with premature gray temples and sideburns. He removed his drooping mustache that had covered a smooth upper lip.

They crammed all the phony hair into a used hamburger sack and ditched it in a roadside park trash can. Hawk Nose opened the car's trunk and took out two sports jackets. He tossed one to Thomas.

Back on the highway, each withdrew a brown envelope from his jacket's inside pocket. Thomas opened his envelope and fanned the ends of a quarter-inch thick stack of hundred-dollar bills.

"Is yours all there?" Hawk Nose asked.

"Seems to be. How about yours?"

"Seems to be," Hawk Nose said. His grin turned into a big smile. "Ya-hoo. We're in the chips now."

"In the chips now," Thomas echoed, and laughed. Then turning to Steve, "Hey. You're in the chips too, partner." He reached into another inside pocket of the coat and withdrew another brown envelope. Handing it to Steve, he said, "You're in this with us, you know."

"No, I'm not," Steve shook his head.

Thomas laid the envelope on the seat between them.

Hawk Nose began to sing, "We're in the chips now. We're in the chips now. . ." to the tune of *The Farmer in the Dell*. "Hi ho, the scary ho, we're in the chips now."

Thomas joined in and they sang together, "We're in the chips now. We're in the chips now. Hi ho the scary ho, we're in the chips now."

"You might as well take it, kid. The cops will be looking for you, and you'll never be able to convince them you weren't in on it from the beginning," Hawk Nose advised looking intently at Steve.

"I wasn't in on it. I don't want your money. Just let me out," Steve demanded.

"Can't get out, partner," Thomas said. "Let me tell you what will happen if the cops catch you," he pointed a finger toward Steve. "They're going to say. . . ." Thomas snarled, "'You ever been arrested before, boy?' and you're going to say, 'Oh, just twice, once for possession of grass, and once for robbery,' and that's the last thing you say that they'll believe." He paused, then sighed and continued. "Yep. They won't believe another thing you tell them because you're an ex-con." He sat back in the seat, stretched his legs, locked his fingers over his chest, and took a deep breath. "You're an ex-con. Once a criminal, always a criminal," he said cynically. "Face it, partner. You don't have a chance."

Steve reached to the car seat, picked up the envelope, then hesitated. Thomas turned toward him, watching, but didn't speak. Steve opened the end flap of the envelope. Dry rubber cement strung from the flap down across the opening. Steve raked away the rubbery glue with a finger, and pulled out an inch of the bill ends. He fanned through them. "Five hundred dollars. That's not much to give for ruining a person's life."

Hawk Nose's head jerked around. The little man had a deep voice. "Your life's not worth anything, Kid. That's just a bonus."

Steve tossed the envelope containing the twenties into the front seat. Thomas reached for his gun, then relaxed.

"You guys can have this. Just let me out, and we'll forget the whole thing," Steve bargained.

Thomas shook his head. "No chance," he said with finality.

Chapter 7

Authority

Colonel Woodrow Lance, commander of the Texas Rangers stepped confidently up the steps of the Texas State Capitol building in Austin. The soft brown leather of his western boots flexed easily as he strode up gray stone steps that had been perfectly hand-hewn by proud artisans nearly a hundred years before.

Pink granite stones, half the size of cotton bales, had been expertly cut and fitted to form a monument to a proud and determined people. The Capitol rose to a pink dome patterned after the United States Capitol in Washington, D. C.

On his right hip, Lance wore a pearl-handled, .357 Magnum revolver in a brown, tooled leather holster. His khaki military shirt displayed a round gold Texas Ranger badge. Full colonel, gold eagle pins adorned his shirt collar. A white western hat of soft felt shaded his tanned face that showed fifty-eight years of sun, cuts, and various scrapes in and out of the line of duty.

Inside the building he passed by the single elevator, and walked into the rotunda. The sound of his heels on the shiny marble around the Great Seal of Texas that decorated the floor, echoed off the cylindrical walls.

At a counter in a hallway off the rotunda, two young men, dressed in dark blue trousers, white shirts and red ties, watched Lance as he passed. Leaning on the counter with a sign announcing "Capitol Tours," the older of the two college students spoke. "That's Colonel Woodrow Lance, commander of the Texas Rangers. You won't see him often."

"I remember hearing about him when I was a little kid. He's been the commander forever, hasn't he?"

"You can't use terms like that when you're conducting a tour. I'm supposed to be training you, so pay attention. You can't be vague or use exaggerations when you answer questions on a tour. You might say, 'Colonel Woodrow Lance has been the commander of the Texas Rangers through the administrations of three governors.' That sounds better."

"Here's what my dad said I could say about Lance," the student began, lowering his voice to sound like his father, "'More than being a good policeman and efficient administrator, Lance has the quality of being completely apart from state politics, even though he reports to politicians and is forever worried by the erratic actions of a Legislature made up, for the most part, of young lawyers trying to make a name for themselves.'"

"Stop," the instructor warned. "You'd have the whole Legislature down your throat if you said that.

"My Dad's a smart man."

"That's beside the point. You're hired here to conduct tours, not make political speeches. You've got to stay neutral, and make everybody happy."

"How about the Governor? My Dad helped me with some information about the Governor, and it's complimentary," the student asked eagerly.

"Okay. Let's hear it, but not too loud."

The trainee lowered his voice again. "Although Governor Ralph Bridger has been governor for nearly eight years, he ran for governor three times before winning election. Governor Bridger does not consider himself a politician. His self-image is that of a rancher who wanted to take his turn at helping his state. He ran on a platform of 'no new taxes' and stuck to it. Even after losing his party's nomination, as a 'lame duck' governor, he called a special session of the Legislature, and succeeded in reducing taxes. His fiscal conservatism got him in trouble with the free-spending, liberal national party leadership. They also considered him a rancher rather than a politician, and abandoned him in favor of his opponent, who was a politician who also ranched."

"Stop. Stop," the instructor protested. "We're going to have to make a lot of changes in that spiel."

At the top of a wide staircase, Colonel Lance passed ten-foot high office doors with door facings richly carved and adorned with brass hardware bearing the state seal and the word "Texas." At the end of a wide hall, glass etched with elaborate, decorative patterns and the words, "Office of The Governor" decorated the larger door's top half. Lance opened the door and walked in. At a large desk facing the door, an aide who could have modeled men's suits, stood to his feet.

"The Governor is expecting you, Colonel. Please go right in." The aide motioned to his right, and pressed a button on his desk.

The second door opened into an expansive office with curved, brocaded, French provincial furniture. A large unoccupied desk dominated the center. On the desk a curved wooden name plate with white, Old English letters announced "Ralph Bridger, Governor."

Standing just inside the door, another aide, dressed in a dark blue, vested, pin-stripe suit with knife-sharp creases, greeted him, "Hello, Colonel. The Governor will see you in his inner office."

Lance passed through the large, ceremonial office and into a smaller office occupied by a secretary and yet another male aide. The aide opened the door of the Governor's private office. Overstuffed chairs and a long sofa covered with dark brown leather contrasted to the bare ceremonial desk in the larger office. Books, papers, files, and memorabilia covered the governor's working desk.

A round, little boy face, frequently covered by a wide smile, seemed somehow out of place on the Governor's tall, slender body. "Come in, Colonel Lance," the Governor said as he stood and came around the desk with outstretched hand. "Thank you so much for coming," he said enthusiastically, and shook Lance's hand firmly.

"Glad to come any time, Governor."

"Let's sit here." The Governor motioned toward the plush leather sofa. "Would you like a cup of coffee or something?"

"No, thank you. I just had some." The Ranger commander sat down, hat in hand. The Governor settled back on the sofa beside Lance, and the solicitous smile left his face.

"Colonel, I'm concerned about this terrible tragedy at San Marcos. Can you tell me what you know about it, and what's being done?"

"Yes, sir. Eyewitness reports are quite contradictory. I talked on the phone just a while ago to the police chief there. After preliminary investigation, this is what he thinks probably happened: At about one-thirty this afternoon, three Mexican subjects took Reynaldo Diaz to the sky ride at Clearwater Springs, tied him up with strapping tape, tied a hangman's noose around his neck, and the other end of the rope around the sky ride cable. They cut the cable, and when they did, the force of the cable jerked Diaz's head off. Of course the cable cars on the sky ride fell to the ground. Two cars fell into the water. One fortunately was empty. In the other car were two women. One was drowned and the other is still in a coma, not expected to live. And if, by some miracle she does live, she is expected to have severe brain damage.

"In the other cars that fell, several people were injured. Two are in critical condition.

"We have no line on the three men," Lance continued. "Composite drawings are being made now from the witnesses' stories. They all agree that the perpetrators had long black hair with bangs, and long, black mustaches. One of them claimed to be an FBI agent.

"A subject who worked at the sky ride ran off with them, probably their inside man. He has a record, possession of illegal drugs, and robbery. He's our main lead, and there's an all-points bulletin out on him now." The colonel paused.

"Have you assigned a Ranger to the case?" the Governor asked.

"As a matter of routine, in a case of this size, Captain Summers of Company 'D' in San Antonio would assign a Ranger. But Chief Bryan at San Marcos has requested that no Ranger be sent. At the moment, we're honoring that request," Colonel Lance said.

The Governor cleared his throat and straightened in his seat. "As much as we wish to not interfere in a city jurisdiction, I'm afraid you're going to have to send a Ranger. This is a hot tamale, Colonel," the Governor continued. "Rumblings are coming from all over the state, phone calls and telegrams from *La Gente Unida* groups and other people demanding something be done quickly.

"It's a potentially explosive situation. The *La Gente Unida* troublemakers have really got fuel for their fire. On top of their campaign to encourage more illegal immigration from Mexico and swell their party numbers, and their *police brutality* publicity campaign, some of their more radical elements are, as you well know, getting involved in violence. I don't want to see them start pulling heads off of Anglos, and then a bunch of Anglo idiots doing worse."

Colonel Lance nodded.

The Governor continued, "Colonel, I don't know if you can believe this or not, but I really do love the people of this great state, the Mexican-Americans and the Anglos alike, as well as others of many racial origins. I don't want this criminal, Diaz, to become a martyr. And I don't want the good people in *La Gente Unida* thinking we're coming down hard on them. We can't let the disease of racial violence get worse." The Governor paused, then frowned. "Why do you suppose the chief of police doesn't want a Ranger?"

"He didn't say, but I *suppose* it might have something to do with Bryan's being considered for the chief's job in Dallas."

"I can understand why he would want the publicity," the Governor said. "But this thing is too big. I want you to send a Ranger to take charge of the investigation." The Governor paused, then spoke in measured tones, "and I want you to send a particularly qualified Ranger, one who can really do the job."

"They're all qualified, Governor," Lance answered quickly as if the Governor had touched a nerve. "The Rangers are the best of the best."

"Yes, I understand," the Governor said with a hint of impatience. "Do you have a Mexican-American Ranger you can send?"

"We have several, but they're all tied up on important cases, except one, the man who made the case against Diaz, Gar Garcia. He's on vacation."

"Yes," the Governor's big smile returned. "I remember Garcia. He handles the press well too. . ."

"They all do," Lance interjected.

"Yes. Yes, of course," the Governor conceded. "I hate to interrupt a man's vacation, but this is vital. Get Garcia from wherever he is, at whatever cost, and get him on it."

Chapter 8

Meanwhile Tuesday Evening, Day Zero

Hot Shot

Heat radiated up from the asphalt parking lot as Hawk Nose parked the green Plymouth Fury in front of Room 129 at the San Antonio Rose Motel. He and Thomas jerked Steve out of the car and toward a door with peeling, gray paint. They half drug him around an old hedge that needed trimming between the narrow sidewalk and the off-white stucco building. Just above the level of the hedge a wood-framed window had been painted shut.

A bare yellow light bulb sent harsh shadows beyond the hedges and behind the car. A window air conditioner whirred noisily and blew even hotter air over the hot sidewalk.

Shoved along by Thomas and Hawk Nose, Steve could see bright little points of light through the hedges as cars passed on the street. Traffic noises and the smell of exhaust smoke followed the hot night air through the hedges.

Inside the motel room the two men shoved Steve onto a sagging bed. In frustration, he wanted to cry, but that wouldn't do any good. He felt trapped, and looked anxiously for a way out. A corroded brass lamp with a yellowed shade cast dim light from a small table beside the bed. Between Steve and the outside door, Thomas and Hawk Nose sat on worn occasional chairs with bare wood arms.

Thomas leaned forward, looking intently at Steve. "Listen, Steve, you're in this thing whether you like it or not. We don't want to hurt you, kid. Take the money and run." Thomas tossed the envelope of twenties on the bed. Steve picked up the envelope and tossed it back. Hawk Nose snatched it out of the air. He reached back to his jacket hanging on the chair back and dropped the envelope into an inside pocket.

"I gave you two hundred bucks. What did you do with that?" Thomas asked accusingly.

"I spent a hundred and seventy of it." Steve withdrew a wallet from his pocket and opened it. He took out a ten and a one and threw them toward Thomas. Still bent from hours in the wallet, the bills fluttered forward and fell to the floor. "Here. That's all I've got. I don't want your money."

"We don't want your money, kid," Thomas protested. "We just want to give you. . ." He paused and watched Hawk Nose pick up the ten and one from the worn red carpet. ". . .some more." Thomas' voice trailed off.

Hawk Nose dropped the bent ten and the one into his own coat pocket. "Let's get on with it," he said impatiently, and stood to his feet. He reached into a bulging front pocket and withdrew two car keys on a ring, a pocket knife, the motel room key on a green, plastic, oval tag, and another key ring with several keys and laid them on the chair seat. He reached deeper into the same pocket and withdrew a red, imitation leather manicure case. He snapped the red case open and laid it on the table.

Steve watched apprehensively.

A hypodermic syringe, a spoon with a bent handle, a bundle of kitchen matches tied with a red rubber band, a length of white cord, and several white papers folded in inch squares lay snug under red elastic straps.

Thomas beckoned to Steve and the outfit. "You know how to shoot up, don't you, kid?"

"Why do you want me to shoot up?" Panic in Steve's voice made it a shout.

"We've got to go, and we want leave you relaxed and as happy as a flea in a kennel," Thomas said.

"Look, I never messed with any heroin," Steve protested.

Hawk Nose picked up the kit and began to open a white paper packet. "One fix won't hurt you, kid."

Steve watched wide-eyed as Hawk Nose dumped white powder into the spoon. Thomas stood to his feet as if on guard.

"It's a hot shot. It's a hot shot." Steve's mental red flags flew and alarm took over his thoughts. He sprang to his feet and lunged forward. He reached out with his open hand and pushed Thomas' face backward. Hawk Nose fumbled with the heroin outfit. Steve's lunging body glanced off Hawk Nose, knocking him backward. Hawk Nose dropped the white powder and spoon. Steve took giant strides, scooped up the car keys, and dived through the window. *No use in trying to open it,* Steve thought. Glass shattered and exploded out before him. His face and chest landed on the prickly top of the hedge, and his right leg scraped over a sharp glass point in the window. He kicked the window facing and fell over the hedge and onto the hot sidewalk, still grasping the keys.

Hawk Nose lunged out the window after Steve. Thomas fumbled with the motel room door lock, then the chain lock. As Steve ran toward the car, he felt for the diamond-shaped key that would fit the door. He quickly turned the key in the door lock. He fell into the front seat and found the ignition key. Hawk Nose got to his feet outside the hedge.

Thomas finally got the motel door unlocked and bounded out just in time to run into Hawk Nose. They both fell to the ground cursing.

Steve inserted the ignition key. Just then Hawk Nose, scratched and bleeding, reached for the door handle. Steve slapped down the door lock. Hawk Nose pushed impatiently on the door handle button. Then Steve realized that the car window had been open all the time, and frantically began cranking it up.

Hawk Nose reached through the now half-closed window, grabbing for the keys. Steve grabbed Hawk Nose's arm and held on. With the other hand Steve continued to crank up the window. On the other side of the car Thomas struggled to get a door open. Finding that side of the car locked tight, he ran back around to the driver's side.

With all his strength, Steve cranked up the window. It caught Hawk Nose under the right armpit and over his right shoulder. Steve fought off the flailing arm with his left hand and turned the ignition key with his right. The starter whined, and the motor started.

Thomas pulled his .38, but before he could bring it to bear, Steve pulled the shift lever into reverse and stomped down on the accelerator. The car jerked backward, dragging Hawk Nose off his feet.

Steve put the car into *drive* and jammed down the gas pedal. The tires squealed and the car lurched forward. Hawk Nose's body, jerked by the car, hit Thomas, knocking him to the sidewalk.

Hanging from the window Hawk Nose kicked and jerked. He lost his footing, but still grabbed for the keys with his captive arm inside the car.

Thomas ran back inside the motel room and grabbed Hawk Nose's jacket off the chair. He ran back outside. The green Plymouth, lighted by a street light, bounced out the driveway and onto the street, dragging Hawk Nose by its side.

The tires squealed again as Steve accelerated and turned sharply to the right onto a busy street. Thomas ran behind, carrying the jacket in one hand and the .38 in the other. As the car turned, the centrifugal force of Hawk Nose's body broke the window. His body flew, spread-eagled into the lane of oncoming traffic. Nine wheels of an eighteen-wheeler ran over him.

Thomas leveled the .38 toward the fleeing Plymouth, and fired three shots in quick succession. Tires squealed as drivers coming from both directions slammed on their brakes. The gunman, standing in the motel drive, with a smoking pistol in one hand and the jacket in another, looked around to see astonished drivers and their passengers staring at him.

The drivers then frantically tried to drive away, but found themselves in a traffic jam.

The owner and operator of the San Antonio Rose Motel ran outside. Her curves bulged a tight red dress as she ran and blonde hair caught the wind. She ran into the drive. "What's going on here?" she screamed through heavily painted lips.

Thomas ran toward a side street. Just as he rounded the corner, a black and white San Antonio Police car sped straight for him. He quickly raised the .38 and fired. The startled officer in the front passenger seat flinched. The bullet cut a round hole surrounded by lacy cracks in the safety glass. The bullet crossed harmlessly through the car and exited through the rear window. Thomas fired again. The second bullet hit the officer squarely in the forehead. He slumped.

The third bullet hit the rear view mirror and sent a shower of silvery splinters over the car's interior. Fine sharp pieces of glass hit the driver's face. His glasses saved his eyes. He braked to a stop, slamming his partner's body forward. The body draped over the seat belt like wet clothes on a line. The driver opened his door, and with a smooth motion, pulled his .38 service revolver. He calmly leveled the pistol on the car top, cocked the hammer, and holding the gun with both hands squeezed off a shot at the fleeing man. The bullet hit Thomas' left arm, and turned him half around.

Thomas ran back around the corner. His bleeding hand dropped the jacket, and he disappeared into the darkness. The officer holstered his weapon. He grabbed his partner by the collar and pulled the limp body upright and checked for a pulse.

Steve drove in a panic. He took the route of least resistance and wound his way to the middle of downtown San Antonio. He could hear sirens wail in the distance. A police helicopter sent a piercing flood of light into the streets. Red and blue flashing lights came to meet him. He swerved the green Plymouth into a side street just as a crowd of laughing conventioneers spilled off the sidewalk to cross the street in his path. An ambulance, with lights flashing and siren wailing, roared past.

Hewitt / *Murder on the Sky Ride*

Seeing the crowd of laughing men, Steve stomped the brake pedal and held it down. With the wheels locked, the car went into a skid, bounced over the curb, onto the sidewalk, and into a heavy concrete bridge railing. The group of men exploded in every direction. The front end of the car crumpled. The hood sprang open and a geyser of water shot up from the ruptured radiator. The car looked like a big-mouthed, green dragon, spewing hot water above, and bleeding green blood below. Exclamations from the crowd of men provided lyrics to a spewing tone coming from the radiator. Sirens in the distance provided the counterpoint. The smell of antifreeze and hot motor oil permeated the warm air.

Steve bailed out of the car and flew down the steps to the San Antonio River below.

Only thirty feet wide at that point, with sidewalks on both banks, the San Antonio River had long since been lined with concrete and meticulously landscaped with plants, flowers, and decorative shrubs. Palm trees, live oaks, and pecan trees provided a canopy above. Mercury vapor lamps lighted the River Walk, showing the colors of delicate flowers and many shades of green.

At the base of the stairs, Steve dived into thick shrubbery, crawled in deeper, and lay on the damp ground, panting like a wounded dog. Scratches on his face hurt. Bursting through the motel window scratched his chest and legs. Blood oozed from a 12-inch cut on his right leg. Steve hurt all over. He laid his head on his right arm, and slowly began to relax. His breathing slowed. Tears filled his eyes. His chin quivered. He covered his mouth with both hands to muffle the sound of sobbing.

Chapter 9

Recall

Tall cottonwood trees on the island cast long shadows over the beach and yellow sailboat. Liz worked over a folding metal table outside, chopping lettuce, tomatoes and onions surrounded by taco shells and picante sauce. Heat from the fire further warmed a gallon jar of sun brewed amber tea.

Ground beef, with small bits of potatoes and onions, sizzled in a black, cast iron skillet that flavored the still air. Halyard lines hung slack against the boat's mast.

"I see a yellow sail boat." Ben Diaz, on his knees in bow of the motor boat, looked through binoculars.

Johnny shouted from his aft seat by the motor. "Where?"

"It's beached on that little island. It's the only yellow sailboat we've seen. That must be it." Ben stretched back and handed the binoculars to Johnny. Ben reached the rifle lying in the bottom of the boat with tangles of fishing equipment. "We got to get a lot closer before I can get a shot."

A mile west of the little island, aboard a Bell Ranger, Texas Department of Public Safety (DPS) helicopter, Phil, a veteran Texas Highway Patrol officer, scanned the lakeshore below. In the distance an Oklahoma Bureau of Investigation helicopter, flying at 200 feet altitude. It too followed the beach and wooded edge of the water on the Oklahoma side of the lake.

Phil picked up binoculars, peered ahead, and spoke into a microphone. "There's a little island ahead on your side. I can make out a boat on the beach. Could be him."

"Ten-four, Texas." A voice came over the radio. "I'll check it out."

The Diaz brothers' motor boat sped toward the island. Ben Diaz settled on his knees, and looked through the telescopic sight of the rifle. "I can't even find the boat in the sight, we're bouncing so much. Get closer. We'll have to stop to get a shot." Johnny twisted the throttle to idle and put the motor in neutral. The boat settled to a stop and rose and fell with the waves. Ben Diaz stood and twisted his right arm through the rifle sling and continued to peer through the telescopic sight. "I see a tent." Then the up-and-down motion of the boat brought the sailboat into view and swept past Gar. Ben brought the cross-hairs to Gar's body, and then on past him.

The approaching Oklahoma helicopter's rotors slapped the stillness.

"Helicopter," Ben shouted. "How'd they know we were here?" The Oklahoma helicopter hovered 200 feet over the yellow sailboat.

"There's another one coming," Johnny shouted, and pointed to the Texas helicopter heading straight for the island.

"Let's get out of here." Johnny twisted the throttle wide open, and turned the boat abruptly. His brother lost his balance and went backward into the water. Sinking head-first in the deep water, he paddled with his hands, trying to right himself and swim, but the heavy rifle, its sling twisted around his right arm, pulled him down. He kicked and flailed his arms, but continued to sink.

Johnny made another sharp turn back to the place where Ben Diaz had fallen overboard. He throttled back, put the motor into neutral, and peered into the deep water. He saw nothing but the reflection of light in every direction from the little wavelets on waves on bigger waves.

In the deep water below Ben continued to twist, kick, paddle, and fight the rifle sling. Earth's gravity pulled him downward. The water became gradually darker. Eighty feet below the surface the rifle rested on the muddy bottom. Large bubbles of air escaped his mouth and ascended like a collection of bright jewels to the surface. On the surface, Johnny sobbed, and continued to peer over the side of the boat, downward, into the deep water.

On the island, Enrique ran excitedly onto the beach and looked up at the helicopter hovering directly above and another flying at only a hundred feet above the surface of the water.

The Texas helicopter circled around the island and landed on the sandy point. As the helicopter blades swished to a stop, Phil got out and ran toward the tent. Liz stood in awe, looking at the two helicopters, and then to the running officer.

Phil gave a thumbs-up sign to the Oklahoma helicopter, which zipped away northward.

Phil greeted Gar, dressed in patched, cutoff blue jeans, t-shirt and sandals with two days of black whiskers shaded by a white terry cloth floppy hat. "I've got a message for Garcia."

Gar menacingly raised the long sharp blade of a machete. "If it's what I think it is, I'm gonna cut your head off."

"If you do, it'll mean the end of our friendship," the officer said. "And besides, I'm just the messenger."

Gar tossed the machete into his left hand and reached out his right, "Hi Phil. What's up?"

"Good God Gar." Phil stared at Gar's face. It was the color of an over-ripe orange. "Are you sick?"

"No. Not sick."

"You look like your liver died," Phil said emphatically.

Gar explained the bargain, orange towels and wash cloths, and that the dye had stained his skin. "I scrubbed my face with soap. It just won't come off. So what's up?"

"It's a big one, in San Marcos. You're to come now. We have a helicopter for you."

"Even if I'm orange?" Gar asked.

"Orders are straight from the Governor. He said you are to come immediately at any cost. He didn't mention any exceptions, like being orange."

The two friends walked down the sandy incline toward the tent. "I'll stay here and see to it your boat gets taken care of and that your family gets home okay," Phil said, then smiled, "And all the expenses are on the DPS."

"I'm glad they sent a sailor."

"Your boat will be in good hands, Captain of the Horse Marines."

"What is it?" Liz shouted as her orange husband approached.

"I don't know the details, Honey, but it's a big one in San Marcos."

Liz burst into tears, and put her face in her hands. Gar held her in his arms. "We can't help it, Baby." She wept for a full minute. Gar held her close.

Liz caught her breath and stepped back. "I'm okay," she said.

"Phil will take care of things. I'll call you at home tomorrow." Gar held her again, and kissed her long on the mouth. Enrique ran to his side. Gar bent down and hugged the boy. "Take care of Mama."

"Okay, Dad," Enrique said, with a tremble in his voice.

"Bye, Honey. Bye, Pardner." Gar hurried to the helicopter. The engine started with a roar, and the blades began their swish.

"What about supper?" Liz called.

"Got to go, Honey," Gar called back over the roar of the helicopter's engine. "I'll help with that too," Phil called to him, but Gar didn't hear, over the helicopter's lift off.

Johnny put the idling motor back in gear and slowly circled the spot where his brother went down. He wept. He covered his eyes with the crook of his left arm and let out long, mournful sobs, wetting his shirt sleeve with tears. He shouted and screamed. He pleaded with God, and cursed "that *cabron*, Gar Garcia."

"Look, Mom, that boat out there is going in circles," Enrique said.

Liz watched the helicopter disappear. "Maybe he lost something."

"He's leaving now," Phil said, watching Johnny's distant motorboat pick up speed and head for the Texas side.

Chapter 10

Ranger on Duty

Twenty minutes after leaving the island the helicopter noisily settled down on a concrete tarmac at Dallas-Fort Worth Regional Airport where the Governor's Lear Jet stood by. Still in his beachcomber clothing, Gar ran to the plane and up the steps. Colonel Lance and Gar's commanding officer, Captain Ben Summers waited in the plane. Gar noticed Captain Summers' scarred face that, like Colonel Lance's, reflected many years and many battles. *I wonder how many battle scars would be necessary for me to be promoted to captain.* As soon as Gar boarded, the steps moved up into the plane's belly to the tune of a whirring electric. The jet engines whine increasing louder and the plane began to move.

    Gar removed his floppy hat to reveal uncombed hair and an orange face. The powerful acceleration pressed his body back in the seat as the jet took off. He sat awkwardly in the seat, holding the terry cloth hat, feeling the eyes of his superior officers from across the aisle. He again regretted buying orange towels and wash cloths. The air conditioner blew cold on his uncovered skin. His superior officers strained to get a better look at him.

    As the plane gained altitude, lights below twinkled in the dusky light. Rows of street lights, blinking advertising lights, and car lights grew smaller as the jet flew higher. And soon the ground below became black, with only an occasional glittering splash of light marking a small town.

"The Governor insisted on getting you on this case no matter what. But . . . but are you sick?" Captain Summers asked as if in pain.

"I've never seen anyone as jaundiced as you, Gar," Lance said.

Once again Gar had to explain the bargain towels and wash cloths.

"After I became orange, I dropped one of the wash cloths into a wash basin and it turned the water orange. It even turned the wash basin orange. A little bit of that dye goes a long way. But I'm sure it'll wear off, "Gar said, and his voice trailed down. "Eventually."

Colonel Lance and Captain Summers explained all they knew about the murder in San Marcos.

After the briefing, a plainclothes DPS officer handed Gar a small suitcase. "Hope we got everything, Gar."

Gar withdrew underwear, socks, a pair of beige slacks, and a light brown, western shirt with pearl snaps. He squeezed into the tiny lavatory, dressed and pulled two matching Colt .44s tooled leather holsters from the bag.

"Did you bring my hat?" Gar asked.

"It wasn't easy," the officer replied, reaching to an overhead rack. "We like to have never found all this stuff," he said, handing Gar the tan, Western hat with a silver Texas Ranger badge.

"How did you get in?" Gar asked.

"We got the key from your Dad."

The *Fasten Seat Belt* light came on. Gar and the officer took a seat. Holding the cartridge belt and pistols in his lap, Gar fastened his seat belt. "I don't know why you bothered.

I was comfortable the way I was dressed."

"Wouldn't that fix the Texas Rangers' image," the officer grinned.

Colonel Lance leaned in his seat toward Gar and said, "In every case, you not only have to do a good job because that case is important, and justice must be served, but you also carry the responsibility of upholding the Rangers' tradition." The Colonel paused. Then the dead seriousness of his face became a smile. "But then, you understand all that, don't you Gar? You've heard it before."

"Yes, sir, many times," Gar acknowledged, then added, "Of course, I agree completely."

"Yes. They all do," Colonel Lance said proudly to no one in particular.

The plane touched down smoothly at the well-lighted San Marcos airport, and as the sleek jet taxied toward the terminal, Colonel Lance said, "Oh, yes, Gar, one more thing. Chief Carl Bryan is under consideration for the chief's job in Dallas. If you can give him a little boost without sacrificing efficiency, do it, will you?"

"Sure."

"We want to maintain good relations with the local departments and fellow officers," Lance added.

Under the San Marcos Airport terminal building's bright lights, a black, unmarked police car waited. When the jet stopped, two men got out of the car and walked toward the plane.

The orange Ranger descended the steps, buckling on his cartridge belt, heavy with the two pistols, ready to tackle the case that the Governor had ordered only four-and-a-half hours earlier.

Chief of Police Carl Bryan's weather beaten face

with large skin pores indicated excess sun and cigarettes. His bulbous nose indicated excess alcohol. When his mouth shut without a cigarette, his thin lips met flat together looking more like a slit in his face. Slightly overweight and apparently in his early fifties, he seemed an unlikely candidate for one of the most prestigious jobs in law enforcement.

His resonate voice came from deep down. "Hello, I'm Chief Bryan," he said, extending a hand toward Gar. "This is Chief of Detectives Roy Sherman." The Chief motioned toward a man slightly younger with red hair mixed with gray, a red face, and pale blue eyes.

"I'm Enrique Garcia," Gar said, shaking hands with each man. "Gar for short," he added.

"I appreciate that," Sherman said with a chuckle.

Gar slid his body over the tough plastic covered back seat of the car. Chief Bryan got in the front right, and Sherman took the wheel. A 12 gauge pump shotgun stood like a sentinel in the center of the front seat, locked in a stand, pointed straight up. The bored voice of a female dispatcher came smoothly from the radio, dispatching cars to answer complaints. A burst of static came at the beginning and end of each transmission. To Gar the car smelled like the inside of a dirty ash tray.

As the car drove away, Chief Bryan turned and laying his arm on the back seat, turned to face Gar. "I guess you were briefed about the case, weren't you?"

"Yes. Is there anything new?"

"Not much. We've got a little more on the white male subject who ran the sky ride. He's got a record. Just been out of Huntsville for a year. He was convicted of possession with intent to sell, and while he was out on bond, he was arrested for armed robbery. He and some other punks got high on grass and stuck up a grocery store. He got a slap on the wrist, five-year sentence, and was out in two.

"He came up with a lot of money just the day before the killing. He's engaged to be married to a local Mexican girl, and he shelled out a hundred and seventy dollars cash to pay off an engagement ring. He still had quite a bit of money left." Chief Bryan paused, and stuck the wet end of an almost-flat cigarette between his lips.

"How about the other three subjects?" Gar asked. "Anything new on them?"

"They've all just vanished into thin air. Here are the composites." Chief Bryan grunted as he strained over the seat and handed Gar three photographs of three drawings.

Sherman switched on the bright, harsh light of the bare-bulb dome light. "We put some temporary names on them based on the witnesses' descriptions. One of them was extra tall. Nobody knew how tall, but they agreed he was taller than the rest. A waitress overheard the others calling him Peters, so we're calling him *Peters*. He's the one on the left. Then the next one . . . several witnesses said he had a long, thin nose, or a hawk nose, so we're calling him *Hawk Nose*. The third one, who posed as an FBI man, was overheard being called Thomas."

Chief Bryan handed Gar another photograph. "This is Steve Pierce, the subject who was an employee at the park." The mug shot showed a younger Steve Pierce with shoulder-length shaggy hair, dark shadows under his eyes, and a numbered tag hanging around his neck.

"Did either of you, personally, question any of the witnesses?" Gar asked.

"I did," Sherman answered. "I questioned most of them."

"What do you think about the size of this tall subject?"

Sherman chuckled. "One of the witnesses actually thought he was seven feet tall. Some thought he was six-two, and one old lady said he was five-eleven, because she knew he wasn't any bigger than her late husband." Sherman paused, and added, "You know how witnesses are. They see different things. I'm impressed, though, that he was really tall, so tall he'd stand out in a crowd, probably six-five and weighing two-seventy to three-hundred pounds."

"That ought to narrow the search," Gar mused. "How was the cable cut?"

"Apparently with an axe. Nobody saw it, but it looks like it was done with an axe. The tall man ran out carrying a stick, which could have been an axe handle, and a briefcase."

"I'd like to go to the scene first thing in the morning," Gar said.

The Chief turned again, exhaling a lung full of smoke. "We've got a room reserved for you at the Clearwater Springs Inn. The park itself is closed, and will be until we finish the on-the-scene investigation." He handed Gar a file folder, thick with pink blurry carbon copies of investigators' reports. "You might want to look at these reports."

"Yes. Thanks. Who'll be my liaison?"

"Sherman here will work with you, and the entire department is at your disposal," the Chief said.

"Thanks, Chief," Gar said, then to Sherman, "You

can just drop me at the Inn, and I'll meet you at the scene in the morning."

"What about the press? They'll be waiting at the station about now wanting to interview you," the Chief said.

"Okay, let's go meet them."

In the San Marcos Police Headquarters a sergeant peered through a glass with a half round hole like a theater ticket counter and nodded to the trio. The worn plank floor creaked with each footstep in the old, red brick building with the words "City Hall" cut into a large lintel stone over the entrance. Years of use had polished the brass door knobs and dark, stained wood furniture.

"I thought you were just dark complexioned, Gar. But here in the light, you look orange. Are you sick?" Chief Bryan asked.

"Orange," Sherman added.

"It's dye. Came off of some bargain wash cloths I got to take camping. The stuff won't wash off. But I'm not sick, just embarrassed."

Sherman chuckled. "I'm glad you're not sick." He chuckled some more.

At the end of a long hall the three men entered a briefing room filled with news men and women.

The crowd of news people parted as Chief Bryan entered, followed by Gar and Sherman. Chief Bryan strode to a slightly elevated rostrum. "Gentlemen and ladies. . . This is Texas Ranger Gar Garcia, who will be coordinating the investigation."

Bright lights from three television cameras made Gar's face even a brighter orange. "Ranger Garcia is not sick." Chief Bryan briefly explained Gar's dilemma.

A black newsman spoke up. "So now we have a *colored* Texas Ranger." A chorus of chuckles arose from the crowd.

"There are several black Texas Rangers. I'm the only orange one," Gar said.

Gar explained to the news people all he knew so far about the case. Chief Bryan then answered questions from the floor.

A plain young woman with yellow teeth held a notebook up to get attention. "Mister Garcia."

Gar nodded in her direction.

"Mister Garcia, are you here because you don't have confidence in the San Marcos Police Department to handle this investigation?"

Gar stepped quickly to the lectern. Chief Bryan stepped down. Gar paused a moment while cameramen positioned their lights brought to bear. Chief Bryan shifted his weight from one foot to the other and cleared his throat.

"I have confidence in this department. Otherwise, I would conduct the investigation independent of this department," Gar said. Chief Bryan's face brightened, and he reached into his shirt pocket for a cigarette. "Chief Bryan and his department are conducting an efficient investigation," Gar added. Chief Bryan shook a short Camel cigarette out of a crumpled pack and rolled the cigarette between the palms of his hands until tobacco spilled out each end.

A round-faced newsman stuck a gray microphone toward Gar. "Ranger Garcia, who do you think is behind this killing?"

"That's what I'm here to find out. And we need your help. If you will publicize these pictures, you will be helping a great deal," Gar said.

Chief Bryan stuck the mutilated cigarette between wet lips and lit it.

"Do you think it might be *La Gente Unida?*" the round-faced newsman asked.

"I'm not going to speculate on that," Gar answered.

"Do you think it might have been Mexican Federal Police doubling as gang enforcers?" the newsman asked.

"I'm not going to speculate on that either," Gar answered.

A high-voiced young man in the back of the room stretched to tiptoes and shouted, "Why did they send only one Ranger?" A subdued chuckle arose from the rest of the news gatherers.

"One is enough," Gar responded soberly. Then in a low voice he spoke to Sherman. "Let's go." He shook the Chief's hand, and said, "Thanks, Chief. I'll see you tomorrow."

Gar and Sherman left the room. The Chief continued answering questions.

Chapter 11

Day Zero Continued

Johnny drove his brother Ben's car to their mother's house. Driving around the driveway full of cars he went over the curb and parked on the grass. His footsteps echoed off the planks of the front porch as he ran.

His mother met him at the door. "Johnny. What's the matter?"

"Oh, Mama." Johnny embraced her. "It's Ben. He's dead." His tears flowed again as they had while he searched the water for his brother.

Weeping Mrs. Diaz guided Johnny into the house. Johnny sat on the couch, surrounded by family members. "You kids go play," Mrs. Diaz ordered. Several small children scampered into the back of the house. "Now, tell us what happened," she ordered.

Johnny had to stop occasionally in his story because of the shrieks and sobs of Maria, Ben Diaz's girlfriend.

"Ben and me went to Lake Texoma to kill Gar Garcia, that *cabron*, turncoat, traitor, who had framed Reynaldo."

"You shouldn't do that," his mother interjected.

Johnny continued, "We didn't know it, but while we were trying to get the boat close enough for a shot, Garcia had spotted our boat. He must have had a radio because in just a few minutes a Coast Guard Auxiliary boat full of DPS officers got there and tried to arrest us. Ben put up such a fight, all the cops struggled with Ben, so I got away. I hid in my boat behind some trees on the little island and watched the cops take Ben and his rifle back to the island. They beat him up good and put him in a helicopter."

Maria cried, "Then he's alive, just beat up?"

"I watched them, Mama. They flew up to about a thousand feet and dropped Ben. They had tied Ben's rifle to his arm, so when he hit the water he sank out of sight." Johnny's voice trembled with emotion. "There was nothing I could do."

Back under the dark shrubs on the San Antonio River, total exhaustion took over and Steve fell asleep. In a few minutes the distant sound of a girl laughing jarred him awake. Alarmed, he opened his eyes, started to rise, then lay back down on the damp, bare earth under the thick shrubbery. Pain seared his wounded leg. He reached a hand to feel it. Blood still oozed from the long cut, and the flesh felt hot.

A girl's voice grew nearer, then a man's chuckle. Steve lay dead still as the voices came within three feet of his hiding place under the hedge.

"Did you see that car?" the girl asked.

"He kinda missed the street, didn't he?" the man chuckled.

"I bet it hurt him, or her, whoever was driving," the girl said.

"Yea, he kinda came to a sudden stop when he hit that bridge railing. A guy up there said they couldn't find the driver."

"Suppose he flew over the railing into the water, and drowned?"

"Naw. He probably went home to tell his brother-in-law somebody stole his car." The man chuckled again, and grew silent.

Tense and stiff with fatigue and pain, Steve tried to remain invisible and totally silent under the bushes.

The girl uttered a low moan, as if it had been squeezed out of her.

The man said softly, "Give me another taste of those sweet lips."

A feminine, satisfied sigh followed. "Let's go rent a paddle boat," she said with a giggle.

"They're across the river, and you can't get there from here," he said. Neither spoke for a moment, then Steve heard soft, passionate moans from both.

Steve lay still on the dark, damp ground.

"We can go up the steps there," she giggled, "Then go across the bridge there," she giggled again. "And then go down the steps there."

"Okay, in just a little while," he said anxiously.

Steve tensed even more at the sound of feet breaking twigs, and bodies brushing against the shrubbery. Steve took shallow breaths afraid of making a sound.

"Oh, don't," she invited.

"Uh, huh," he responded with relish.

"Hey." An authoritative voice broke the spell. "Excuse me, but have you seen a man, or two men, come down here from the street?"

"No, we haven't seen anybody," the man's voice replied.

"How long have you been here?"

"Oh, a long time, officer," the girl giggled.

"Suppose you've been here twenty minutes?"

"Oh, yes, at least," she said.

"Thank you. Sorry to disturb you." The officer's

voice faded in the distance.

"Let's go get a paddle boat," the girl said. Bodies again made noises against shrubbery.

"In a little while."

Shrubbery rustled not far away. Even Steve's heartbeat seemed loud enough for them to hear. He didn't want to be discovered and blamed for crimes he didn't do, a fear he had lived with since getting out of prison. Finally the couple finished their groans and sighs. Steve heard irregular footsteps grow progressively softer. Then, exhausted, he became relaxed as a wet sock, and went back to sleep.

Chapter 12

Tuesday Night, Day Zero

The Clearwater Inn had been designed to show up day and night and gleamed white in bright floodlights. The white, two-story stucco set like a giant pearl at the edge of a great spring pool called the San Marcos River. Lights on the long veranda at the water's edge reflected off the still water, and touched gently on the trees, fan palms, live oak, and bell-bottomed, lacy-leafed cypress trees.

In the lobby, Gar picked up a copy of the *San Antonio Light*, and checked the time of sunrise and sunset.

"Call me at six," he told the desk clerk, and went to his room. Tomorrow would be a big day.

Wednesday, Day One

Rising above the trees, a big, red sun warmed Clearwater Springs and turned the motel building to gold. Gar left the coffee shop, walked out a rear door of the Inn and into dense woods toward the sky ride's hillside terminal.

Sunlight formed dancing patterns through the leaves of the oak tree canopy over the narrow asphalt sidewalk. At an intersection of the walk, four empty, wooden benches sat across from each other as if involved in a silent, early morning conversation. Gar took the right turn and followed the steep walkway upward.

He left the asphalt sidewalk and squeezed through the steel I-beam framework of the sky ride terminal. Below he saw a large spot of dried blood and above spatters of blood on tree branches and leaves.

Inside the wood plank building, he climbed the steel framework and examined the large spoked sheave wheel, its groove around the circumference now empty of the sky ride cable. He looked out across the park to the terminal on the other side of the river, then eyed the irregular line of the cable, lying like a great, limp, black snake on the grass, and the brightly colored cable cars scattered like broken toys.

Descending to the ground, he viewed the imaginary line where the cable had been. He found a block of wood the size of a cigar box lying on the ground. The block of solid wood had been carved to a peculiar point on one end. Debossed in a rounded groove in the block he saw thin, black lines, the pattern of the greasy twisted wires of the cable.

Gar left the block of wood in its place and continued down the hill. Soon he came to the end of the inch-and-a-half thick cable. He picked it up, and examined the shiny steel of the cut end. Then he walked, zig zagging through the trees until he found the other end, lifted it from the ground, and examined its cut end. Near the end a nylon rope had been wrapped tightly around the cable six times and tied and on the other end of the rope a bloody hangman's noose.

He recognized Chief of Detectives Roy Sherman' deep voice filtering through the thick trees.

"Is that you, Sherman?"

"Yes. Right here," Sherman called back.

"Come on down," Gar called.

Sherman and another detective made their way through the trees to where Gar stood, examining the rope knot on the cable. "This is Detective Sam Arnold. Sam, this is Ranger Gar Garcia," Sherman said.

Arnold shook hands with a firm grip. A toothpaste smile dominated his round face. He had apparently taken great care combing his graying hair forward over his forehead and down over his ears. He wore a matching mustache, a dark blue blazer with brass buttons and dark blue and white checked slacks. He carried a walkie-talkie radio in a black leather case with a chrome antenna extended.

Sherman wore the same dark gray suit as the previous night, but this time a gray straw hat with a wide black band covered his graying red hair.

"I told you not to stare," Sherman said to Arnold.

Arnold chuckled. "I'm not staring, Chief. But that really is an interesting shade of orange."

"It's beginning to wear off," Gar said, rubbing his cheek. "What do you think of this knot?"

"I've never seen one like it before," Sherman answered. "How about you, Sam?"

"Me neither," Sam said in a voice as high pitched as a woman's, but not soft.

"We may be looking for a sailor, or someone who has been a sailor," Gar said.

"Shall we check the Navy?" Sherman asked.

"Send the request to the DPS in Austin. They'll relay it on to the Navy Department," Gar began. Arnold took a well-worn notebook from his pocket and started making notes. "We'll want the Navy computer to tell us about all men from Texas who have served since, say, nineteen forty-five, who were over six feet-two. That should narrow it down some," Gar continued. Then get Austin to send the same request to the Coast Guard. We'll need information for their personnel and the Merchant Marine. Then let's get a bulletin out to all Texas yacht clubs and sailing clubs. Our man may be a sailor just for pleasure. Also get bulletins out to all the Texas maritime unions and longshoremen's unions."

Gar held up the steel cable and examined the knot. "Do we have some good pictures of this knot?"

"Yes," Sherman answered.

"Let's get copies out to the news media. We can get the Chief to show the knot for a picture. Maybe the public will recognize the knot and tie it in with someone who's big and tall," Gar paused, and then, half to himself, commented, "If we throw out enough hooks, maybe we'll catch something." Gar dropped the heavy cable end to the ground with a dull thud.

"There's a block of wood up there that I think they used to chop against when they cut the cable. See to it that it's dusted for prints, photographed in position, and its position measured and diagramed."

"Okay," Sherman replied.

"After all that's done, I want the block. And get me a good axe too, and a railroad tie. We'll do an experiment," Gar said.

"I'll get this started," Arnold said in his high voice while tapping the notebook with his ball point pen. He stepped back and gave instructions via the hand-held radio.

"Did you ever cut a cable with an axe?" Gar asked Arnold.

"I never cut a cable with anything. But I think if I were going to try, I'd use a torch. That stuff's hard."

"The witnesses said they heard hammering. They could have heard chopping. And the cable looks like it was cut in two by a sharp blade," Gar said.

Half an hour later a uniformed sergeant approached with a double-bladed axe, followed by two officers carrying a heavy railroad tie.

"I don't see how an axe blade can cut a bundle of steel wires that are harder than the blade," Arnold said.

"Well, a soft, lead bullet can go through steel," Sherman said.

"A plain piece of wheat straw shot through a tree trunk in a tornado. Maybe an axe will cut a cable," Gar speculated.

"Ready," Arnold replied.

Gar settled his feet like a weight lifter and got a good grip on the axe handle.

Arnold stepped back. "I'm going to get back out of the way of flying pieces of axe."

Gar raised the axe and swung it down with all his strength. The blade hit the cable solidly against the heavy railroad tie. Arnold rushed to examine the cut. The axe had cut a fourth of the way through the cable.

"Well, we know an axe will cut a cable, don't we?" Gar said.

Ten minutes later the cable had been hacked in two. "That's seven hits to get it severed, and twelve misses," Arnold grinned.

"And a dulled axe," Gar commented. He handed the axe to Arnold. The other end's your turn."

"Thanks a lot," Arnold said.

While Arnold hacked away with a dull axe at the other end of the cable, Gar closely examined the end of the cable he had just cut off. "It looks to me like he cut this thing in two with three strokes. He must have been big."

Gar reflected a moment. ". . .powerful, and experienced. Yes. He must have cut a cable with an axe before. What do you think?"

"Nine. Ten. Yes," Arnold gasped. "I think so. Eleven. I don't think. . . Twelve. . . that Sam Arnold here is experienced. Thirteen," he continued hacking, panting, and counting.

Back at the Inn, Gar went to his room and dialed his home telephone number. It rang once.

"Hello," Liz answered quickly.

"Hello. I'm glad you're home. Did everything go okay?"

"Oh, yes. The boat's in a slip at the Eisenhower Yacht Club. We just left all the camping gear on board, in the cabin, just in case we get to go back. The car is stored at D.F.W. Airport," Liz said. "Where are you?"

"I'm in Room One Twenty-Four at Clearwater Springs Inn."

"You're there without me," she said in a pouting voice.

"Not by choice. Listen, see if Dad and Mom can take care of Enrique for a few days, and you can come here," Gar said.

"Enrique would love that. I'll see what I can do, and call you this evening." She paused, then changed the subject, "I see you're on that sky ride murder case."

"Yes, I guess you read about it."

"It was horrible. We saw it on the news this morning too," Liz said, and then added, "Whoever did that has to be a maniac."

"I think you're right, but he's a smart one."

"Do you have any good leads?"

"Some promising, but we've just scratched the surface." He changed the subject. "I wish you could come up this evening." Then he abruptly changed it again. "Say, ole Phil behaved himself after I left didn't he?"

"Phil is a gentleman," Liz answered.

"Most philanderers are," Gar countered.

"Well Phil was perfectly nice, and besides that I had my little Enrique sticking by me every moment. If he had been inclined to make a pass, he wouldn't have done it in front of an eight-year-old who tells everything he knows," Liz said. "Besides, Phil isn't that kind. He's happily married to a wonderful girl."

"I never had any doubt," Gar said.

"Sure.".

"I'd sure like to get you alone," Gar whispered.

"I'll let you know," she said musically.

"I'll tell the desk clerk to be expecting you tomorrow. Let me say hello to my little pardner."

"Oh, he's gone. Out playing," Liz said.

"Tell him 'hi,'" Gar said. "I love you."

"I love you. Hope to see you soon," Liz said.

Gar hung up the phone, but before he could get his hand off, the phone rang.

"Hello."

"Mr. Garcia, this is Jim Bradshaw, assistant, I mean, manager of Clearwater Springs. I understand that you are in charge of the investigation now."

"That's right."

"I'd like to meet with you for just a few minutes."

"I was just going to the coffee shop for lunch. Would you care to join me?" Gar asked.

"Yes. I'll be standing with the hostess when you come in. How will I know you?" Bradshaw asked.

"I'll be armed, wearing a Texas Ranger's Badge, and have an orange face."

"Oh, uh, okay. See you in a minute," Bradshaw said.

Chapter 13

Witnesses

At the restaurant hostess counter a petite redhead with nose freckles asked sweetly, "One, Sir?"

"I'm meeting someone," Gar said, looking around.

Jim Bradshaw arrived. "Here you are." He extended a hand toward Gar. "Jim Bradshaw," he said.

"Gar Garcia." Gar shook hands with the shorter, more tanned man.

"This way, gentlemen," the redhead called. Carrying the large, shiny red menus, she led the way to a table, stealing glances at Gar's complexion. Turning to Bradshaw as they walked, the hostess said, "Congratulations on your promotion to general manager."

"Thanks," Bradshaw responded, then turning to Gar, said, "Our general manager for the past ten years decided this would be a good time to retire." Bradshaw looked intently at Gar. "Say, you weren't kidding about the orange face. There was a sidebar in the paper about the *Orange Colored* Ranger this morning. Now I believe it."

"Hope it isn't too much of a distraction," Gar ventured, half cynically.

"Not at all," Bradshaw said. "I'm not bigoted against people because of their skin color, not even orange."

The two men followed the hostess. Both men watched her rhythmic hips in a tight, short black skirt over long, shapely legs. Gar interrupted his study long enough to size up Bradshaw in his Hawaiian shirt with brilliant, large, red flowers.

"Here you are, gentlemen," she said, handing each a menu.

"You weren't hard to spot even without the orange face," Bradshaw said, looking at the menu. "Do all Texas Rangers wear two guns?"

"You don't exactly fade into the wallpaper," Gar answered with a smile.

"Well, you see, I try to encourage our visitors to dress comfortably, relax, and have a good time. My appearance rather reflects the nature of my business."

"So does mine"

"I see. So it does. What I wanted to talk to you about is: We would like to start cleaning up that mess out there and get the park ready to reopen. We want to cooperate fully, but I hope you understand that every day we're closed, we're losing a lot of money. May I suggest that you cut off whatever portions of the cable you need as evidence, and let us begin repair operations."

"Sure."

"Good. When will you have what you need of the cable?"

"We've got it now. You can do whatever you like at any time, except I'll need the rest of today on the hillside terminal building."

"Well, that's wonderful. Thank you," Bradshaw released a quiet sigh. "We have an engineer on his way here now from Switzerland to take charge of the repair."

"Now, Mr. Bradshaw, I'd like for you to start from the beginning, and tell me what you saw."

Chapter 14

Gathering Evidence

Sherman drove Gar across town in the black car that smelled like an ash tray. In a quiet residential neighborhood, the two lawmen walked up a sidewalk that curved its way from the street through a lush green lawn to a white brick home. Gar pushed the doorbell button and waited.

"Yes." The matron at the door wore combed but not coiffed hair, apparently settled on being middle aged.

"Mrs. Wilkins?" Gar asked.

"Yes, I'm Mrs. Wilkins."

Gar introduced himself and Sherman. "We'd like to see Larry Wilkins. Your son, I believe?"

"Yes. Larry is my son. Won't you come in?" They stepped into an entry of shiny terrazzo tile. She led them into a living room with plush beige carpet and early American furniture all in earth tones. Gar could see through an open door a den with well-worn furniture and a television set flashing colors.

"I'll get him," Mrs. Wilkins said.

Larry's beachcomber attire contrasted sharply with his neat and well decorated surroundings. He pulled up a shiny maple occasional chair and bent his long body to fit it. The group formed a circle in the living room.

"Tell us what happened, will you Larry?" Gar said.

"I already told another detective. And I told everything on the television's evening news. Do you want to hear it again?"

"I saw the television interview. You apparently remembered everything."

"Well, now they refer to me as the 'chief witness'," Larry said.

"Yes. Just begin at the beginning. Take your time," Gar said.

Larry had been on duty at the hillside terminal when Steve assigned him to open cable car doors while he went with Thomas on Monday. Then Larry described from his viewpoint the bloody Tuesday afternoon when Reynaldo Diaz got his head pulled off.

"Do these drawings look like the men you saw?" Gar asked, extending drawings of the three suspects.

"Yes, pretty much," Larry answered.

"How about the tall one. How tall would you say he was?" Gar asked.

"I'm six-two, and I had to look up to him. I'd say he was at least six-four or five," Larry said.

"Anything else you noticed that might distinguish these men?" Gar asked.

"Well, the little guy had a long, sharp nose, and a deep voice. The phony FBI man had a Yankee accent," Larry said.

"I hadn't heard that before," Gar said.

"Me neither," Sherman agreed.

"I've met lots of people at the park during the last three months, people from all over the country. I'd say it was kind of like a New York accent. This phony FBI man did most of the talking." Larry reflected for a moment. "He sounded real Yankee."

"Did you hear any of the people speak Spanish?" Gar asked.

"Only when they left. The tall guy said *vamos muchachos*."

Mrs. Wilkins interrupted, "Is he the one with cuts on his face?"

Gar and Sherman perked up. "Cuts?" they said in chorus.

"Yes, Larry said he had cuts all over his face," Mrs. Wilkins said.

"No, Mom, I didn't say he had cuts. I said he had bandages," Larry said.

"Oh," she said, "he had bandages all over his face."

"How many bandages?" Gar asked.

"Several," Larry answered.

"Where on his face?"

"Well," Larry ran his forefinger under his shaggy mustache. "One was on his chin."

"Where on his chin?"

"Right here." Larry put a finger in the middle of his chin.

"Where was another Band-Aid?" Gar asked.

Larry thought a moment, caressed his mustache some more, and answered. "One was right here." He put a finger on his right cheek. "Right in the middle. And the other one was on the other cheek, right in the middle."

"Where was another one?"

"That's all."

"You mean there were only three?"

"Yes. I hadn't really thought much about it. It just seemed like a bunch, but when I think back over it, there were three," Larry said.

"Were the two on the cheeks symmetrical?"

"What's that?"

"Were they exactly on the opposite sides of his face?"

"Yea. Yea, they were, exactly opposite of each other," Larry said.

"And the one in the middle of his chin was it exactly in the center?" Gar asked.

"I didn't study him, as I said, but I think so. Right in the middle," Larry thought a moment. "That's all I can think of."

"You've been a great help, Larry," Gar said, and rose to leave. As they walked toward the front door, Gar asked, "How long have you lived around here, Larry?"

"All my life."

"Do you speak Spanish?"

"A little."

"Do you know what *vamos muchachos* means?" Gar asked.

"Sure. 'Let's go, boys.' My friends say *vamos* about as much as they say, 'let's go,'" Larry said.

"Could you tell if there was any other Spanish spoken?"

"I couldn't hear what was said, but I know they were speaking English the rest of the time," Larry said. "And except for that Yankee, phony FBI man, and Reynaldo Diaz, who spoke with a Tex-Mex accent, I didn't hear any distinctive accents."

Sherman backed the smelly car down the driveway, straining to look back. "I think that eliminates Mexicans, or Mexican-Americans as the perpetrators, don't you?"

"I think so. Do you think it was a political killing?"

"It was dramatic enough," Sherman said. "If I were

a paranoid, Chicano activist, I'd probably think the Anglo political establishment did it to get rid of Diaz."

"People do things for the reaction too," Gar said.

"You mean they'd kill one of their own just to get both sides to over react and cause a real fuss?"

"It happens."

"What do you think about the possibility of a drug organization's execution of a double-crosser?" Gar asked, then added, "You know we've got the goods on Diaz. He's dirty as can be into drug dealing. I've got two eye-witnesses who'll testify that they saw him bringing in grass by the plane load."

"Possible," Sherman said.

"It may be the farthest thing from the obvious," Gar said. "You know those bandages opened up a new can of worms. Either it was just part of his disguise, or he had been in a fight and had some wounds, or he was trying to cover up something." Then as he picked up the photo from the car seat, added, "we've got to find a giant who knows how to tie knots and chop cables."

"Or a little guy with a hawk nose," Sherman chimed in.

"We might find an average size guy with an MO of impersonating an FBI agent too," Gar tapped the middle drawing on the picture, "Or a young man named Steve Pierce."

Chapter 15

Anita

On the other side of town Sherman drove into a gravel drive with grass growing between the ruts. The two lawmen walked over the uneven surface of dry, sparse Bermuda grass in front of a square, frame house. Weathered wide boards set vertically formed the walls, with narrow boards nailed over the cracks. The old, weathered boards had recently been covered with thin white paint that had soaked in, leaving a grayish white color. The house set on stacks of bricks, like short, skinny legs, and beyond them under the house: darkness.

As they approached worn, wooden steps, a deep growl came from the darkness under the house. A large mongrel dog with short gray hair splotched with dirt showed his teeth and snarled.

"Hello, dog. Be a good boy, now," Gar said soothingly. The dog growled louder. Gar pointed back toward Sherman, "If you've got to bite somebody, bite him." Gar quickly stepped up on the porch.

"I don't think he understands English," Sherman said, as he reached the porch and kept an eye back toward the menacing dog. "*Buen Perro*," Sherman said. "He doesn't understand Spanish either.

Gar's knocks made a slapping noise as the loose screen door hit the facing. "What's her name?"

"Mrs. Ramirez, and her daughter, Anita," Sherman added quickly under his breath. "Anita's engaged to Steve Pierce.".

"Yes, who is it?" A female voice with a Mexican accent came from behind the door. Her "yes" sounded more like "jess."

"Police, Mrs. Ramirez. We'd like to ask you some questions," Sherman answered through the closed door.

A white glass door knob turned loosely in the thin, paneled wood door by a plumpish, big-busted woman with a pretty face.

"If it's about that no-good Steve Pierce, I don't know nothing. I mean, I *still* don't know nothing about him. If I did, I would tell you. I think he should be in jail." She looked Gar up and down. "A Texas Ranger, huh?" She smiled. "I saw you on TV, orange face and all."

"Mrs. Ramírez, I'm Enrique García. This is Chief of Detectives Roy Sherman of the San Marcos Police Department." Gar again wished he had never become involved with orange wash cloths.

She smiled and opened the sagging screen door. "Come on in."

They stepped onto a clear plastic runner that formed a path over thick, red, shag carpet to an overstuffed couch and chair of red fabric, accented by silver threads. Shiny white Formica covered a coffee table and end tables. Mrs. Ramirez invited the men to sit on the couch. They followed the plastic runner to the couch and sat down. Mrs. Ramirez took a seat in the matching red chair, and folded her hands in her apron.

A large picture of the Virgin of Guadalupe, dressed in red and gold, dominated the opposite wall. On another wall a large picture, also with a red theme, depicted Jesus with exposed sacred heart. Red window curtains billowed with the flow of cold air from a large window air conditioner. Aluminum foil covered the west window and subdued the light. The cool room smelled of fresh fruit in contrast to the hot and dusty outside with its growling dog.

"Is Anita home?" Gar asked.

"No, she's working."

"Mrs. Ramirez, do you have any idea where we might find Steve Pierce? Do you know where he might have gone?"

"I don't have no idea about that boy. I don't like him. I told Anita not to see him, but she sees him anyway."

"Why don't you like him?" Gar asked.

"He's got a record. I found out he's been in the pen. He was a dope head, and robbed a grocery store. I don't want my daughter mixed up with him." She emphasized her point by bouncing her clasped hands on her lap. "There are lots of nice boys around here from good Catholic families. They like Anita, and would give her a good home and a good family. I don't know what she sees in that Steve."

From the back of the house another screen door slammed. Mrs. Ramirez stood, and turned toward the sound. "That must be Anita, home early. We live here alone, you know. Her Daddy died."

"Who's here, Mama?" a girl's voice came from the kitchen. "I thought I heard you talking to someone." She stepped through the door into the living room. "Oh," she said, and stopped. She held a fat brown wallet and a jangling set of keys in one hand and a wadded tissue in the other.

"Why are you home so early, Anita?" her mother asked.

"I just couldn't work, Mama." Her skin flushed red around dark tear-filled eyes. "I'm so worried about Steve."

After her mother introduced the officers, Anita sat on another red overstuffed chair, leaned back, and dabbed her nose with the tissue. "Are you looking for Steve?" she asked with resignation.

"Yes, we are," Gar answered. "Do you know where he might be?"

"I don't know." Anita leaned forward and covered her face with both hands. A small diamond glittered from her finger. "I don't know. I wish I knew," she said softly.

"Don't cry over him, Baby. He's a criminal," Mrs. Ramirez said.

"He's not." Anita shook her head without removing her hands from her face.

Sherman cleared his throat and leaned forward. "Anita, you're going to have to face this. Steve has a record."

"I know. But he hasn't done anything since he got out of Huntsville." She dropped her hands, and looked the veteran detective straight in the eye.

Sherman looked right back. "Remember why he went to Huntsville," Sherman said, leaning forward. "He was caught in possession of a kilo of marijuana, which is a felony. He got out on bond, and while he was out on bond, he was caught with some other guys right after a grocery store holdup. He had some of the money taken in the robbery in his possession. These are very serious offenses. He even pleaded guilty. I'm surprised he got out as soon as he did." Sherman sat back.

"He was stoned out of his mind on grass when he did all that . . . ," Anita began.

"That's no excuse," her mother interjected.

Anita gave her mother a brief scowl, and continued.

"He got his head straight in prison. He realized how stupid he had been. Those things he did were completely out of character. He realized he was somebody else when he was high on drugs, so he decided he would never use drugs again. And besides that, he became a Christian when he was in Huntsville."

"Jailhouse religion," Mrs. Ramirez muttered.

Anita caught her breath and began again. "He got into a rehabilitation program. He finished high school and a year of junior college before he got out. While he was still in prison, he went around with a group to high schools and churches all over the state, telling kids how they got messed up with drugs and how it hurt them. Steve has done a lot of good, even when he was in the pen," Anita said, her voice rising. "He went back to school at the university here, and has made good grades for the past two years. In only one more year he'll get his degree."

"People have a way of getting back on drugs," Sherman said.

"Not Steve," Anita shook her head. "I know Steve."

"Love is blind," Mrs. Ramirez said.

"Nobody is saying you shouldn't love Steve," Sherman began.

"I am," Mrs. Ramirez said, bringing another disapproving look from her daughter.

Sherman continued, ". . .but if you know where he is, you should tell us."

"I don't have any idea," Anita said with finality.

The air conditioner whirred steadily. Anita sobbed softly. No one spoke. Suddenly a beeper sounded angrily from Sherman's belt and destroyed the quiet.

Chapter 16

Hawk Nose and the Eighteen-Wheeler

"May I use your phone? Mrs. Ramirez," Sherman asked, shutting off the beeper.

"Sure," Mrs. Ramirez said, pointing to the phone on an end table.

Sherman punched seven buttons in rapid succession, requested his message, and listened for several minutes, only occasionally acknowledging with a muted "uh huh."

He hung up the phone and sat back down. "Well we've got some news about Steve."

Anita sat straight up.

"The San Antonio Police Department found his fingerprints on a rental car that had crashed into a bridge railing in downtown San Antonio last night." Looking intently at Anita, Sherman asked, "What do you suppose he was doing in San Antonio, driving a rented car?"

"I don't know." Anita again put her face in her hands, her long black hair falling around them.

"The San Antonio Police also found his fingerprints in a north side motel room." Sherman leaned forward to emphasize the next statement. "And they found a heroin outfit and some heroin in that same motel room."

Anita began to sob. Her mother went to her, put an arm around her, and gently patted her. Sherman leaned back, and self-consciously moved a hand over his face. The whiskers made a faint brushing sound. Gar sat silently, holding his hat in his hands. He looked awkwardly at the plastic runner over the thick, red carpet, then at the brokenhearted, weeping girl.

Anita's tissue became a small, white ball. He mother reached into an apron pocket and withdrew a fresh one. "Here, Baby," she said, handing the tissue to Anita. Mrs. Ramirez crossed back to her chair. Anita dabbed her eyes and looked up.

"Anita," Gar began softly, then lifted his head and looked at her. With her complete attention, he continued. "We don't want to hurt Steve. We don't want to hurt you. But two people have been killed, and more are in critical condition, and might die. We've got to find out why. Do you understand that?"

"Yes," she nodded.

"Steve won't gain anything by running. If you learn where he is, or if you hear from him, you must let us know. If you talk to him, please tell him I want to talk to him. If he's clean, he has nothing to fear. Tell him I want to talk to him personally." Gar stood and walked across the room.

Anita looked up to the man towering above her. On either side of sharply creased tan slacks bulged fearsome silver-colored pistols with white handles. With his hat in one hand he gently touched her shoulder. "Tell him, I'll personally guarantee a fair shake," he said softly.

"Okay." She forced a small smile.

Outside the Gar and Sherman descended the squeaky porch steps. Mrs. Ramirez stood on the porch, watching. A throaty growl came from under the porch.

"You know, Mrs. Ramirez," Sherman began as he stepped off the steps behind Gar. "That dog has to be kept . . ." Suddenly the snarling animal came out from under the steps and lunged. The dog came to the end of his chain and stopped abruptly, just short of Sherman's leg. ". . . up."

"He's chained, and licensed," Mrs. Ramirez said. Then she shouted, "Chico. Shut up." She pointed a finger at the dog. He muttered a low growl as if to have the last word, and disappeared in the darkness under the house.

"Ever been dog bit?" Sherman asked as they slammed shut the car doors.

"Oh, yes," Gar said, wincing a smile. "You?"

"Oh, yes," Sherman replied. "Guess it goes with the territory." He drove on down the street. Stopped at a red light, a pedestrian and Sherman exchanged waves. "I got some more news on the phone I didn't mention in there."

"Oh."

"Yes. It looks like Hawk Nose got it in San Antonio last night. He was involved in a traffic accident. Witnesses said he flew out of a car window onto the street and was run over and killed by an eighteen-wheeler. Anyway, the deceased subject fits the description of Hawk Nose."

"Reckon Peters threw him out of the window?"

"He was probably big enough to do it." Sherman again stroked his whisker stubble. "Along about the same time a man fitting the description of Thomas shot and killed a San Antonio Police officer. His partner was wounded by flying glass. According to his partner, they were on patrol when they heard three gunshots ahead of them. Then they saw this guy, matching the description of Thomas, standing on a sidewalk holding a pistol and a jacket. The subject then fired three shots into the windshield of the patrol car, killing one officer. The other officer got a shot at the subject, but he got away. Thinks he hit him. The subject was wearing a sport jacket and carrying a second one. He apparently dropped it. There was blood on the jacket, so

Thomas, if that was him, was probably hit."

"Did they recover anything out of the pockets of the jacket?" Gar asked.

"No. The pockets were empty. But what might tie the two subjects together is the fact that the jacket he was carrying was a perfect fit for the Hawk Nose subject. Also the jacket was dropped in front of the San Antonio Rose Motel where the heroin outfit and Steve Pierce's fingerprints were found," Sherman said.

"So we have possible Hawk Nose, a possible Thomas, and a sure thing Steve Pierce in San Antonio after the killings," Gar said. "Looks like Pierce and Thomas just dropped out of sight."

Chapter 17

Mrs. Pierce

Sherman stopped the car at a two-story, early Fifties style, red brick apartment building whose wood window frames peeled white paint. "Steve's mother is supposed to be at home about now."

"Is her name still Pierce?" Gar asked.

"Yes. She's been married a couple of times since Steve's Dad died, but she goes by Pierce again."

They entered the building through open, wood framed, glass, double doors held open with wedges. The men followed a worn path in the thin, red, carpeted hallway. Sherman knocked on the Pierce door.

Mrs. Pierce's forty years had left no tracks except for a small *V*-shaped scar high on one cheek that served rather as a beauty mark. Golden blonde hair and pale pink lipstick that matched her pants suit accented her mildly tanned skin. The second and third buttons of her silver satin blouse strained to hold her breasts. "Yes?"

"Mrs. Pierce, this is Texas Ranger Gar Garcia. I'm Chief of Detectives Roy Sherman. You'll remember that I talked to you yesterday."

"Yes," she repeated in a low voice. "Was there something you forget to ask me?" The question sounded seductive.

"I'd like to ask you a few questions, Mrs. Pierce," Gar said.

"Come in," the low, feminine voice said. She led them into a living room with well-worn furnishings and air heavy with tobacco smoke.

"I hope you'll excuse this mess. I just got off work, and was just reading the paper before trying to do something with this house."

Gar and Sherman sat on the divan, and Mrs. Pierce sat on a worn out recliner. She relaxed and drew her knees up to her chest showing shapely legs through the pink pants. Behind her, a two-foot high, home-made gate of wood lath barred the kitchen door. Two Chihuahua dogs whined eagerly, and scratched at the gate.

Mrs. Pierce turned toward the scratching. "You babies don't need to come in here. Just be still." Then turning to her guests, "They want to come in to see who's here."

"Have you heard from your son?" Gar asked.

"No, the last I saw of him was yesterday morning when he went to work. Have you heard anything about him?"

Sherman told her what the San Antonio Police had discovered the night before. Then he added, "He's in serious trouble, Mrs. Pierce."

She showed no emotion. With long and slender fingers, decorated with the same color as her lips and pants she reached a package of cigarettes on the end table. A tiny gold chain dangled from her wrist as she shook out a cigarette. "Would you like a smoke?"

"No, thanks," both men answered at once.

"I thought you smoked, Roy?" she said. The end of the unlit cigarette in her mouth danced with each syllable.

"Not any more. I quit a month ago."

"Why?"

"The doctor told me I had the first signs of

emphysema."

"My doctor told me the same thing. But I feel fine. I think he don't know what he's talking about," she said.

"Mrs. Pierce, do you know where Steve might have gone?" Gar asked.

"No. I don't. He'd go to Anita before he'd come here. He's pretty crazy about her, you know." With a deliberate motion outward, she struck a paper match, and lit her cigarette. "Of course, Anita's Mama ain't too crazy about Steve, so maybe he wouldn't go there."

"Does he know anybody in San Antonio?" Gar asked.

"Not that I know of."

"Has Steve had any extra money lately?" Gar asked.

"You asked that one," Mrs. Pierce said, gently jabbing pointed fingers toward Sherman. A trace of a smile showed in the corners of her mouth. "Yes," she turned to Gar. "He finished paying off Anita's engagement ring. He was so proud. That was almost two-hundred dollars that he still owed on it. I don't know where he got the money. Didn't ask him."

"We understand. . . ," Gar began.

"Figured if he wanted me to know, he'd tell me," she continued.

". . .We understand that Steve is deeply involved in murder, and there is evidence, from what Chief Sherman has just told you, that he may be using hard drugs. We don't know what his involvement is, but we want to talk to him and find out."

"I know what you're thinking," her words came out slowly, but easily. "You're thinking he's gone off the deep end with drugs, and took some money to help in that killing. But I just don't believe it.

"When Steve got messed up with drugs before, he was really messed up. He didn't act good one day and bad the next. He was always spouting off about how drugs were good for you, to expand your mind.."

"How did he get started on drugs?" Gar asked.

"Well, I don't know for sure. Drugs were around the school for a long time, but Steve was never interested. He went out more for sports. I think it was because of losing his Dad that he . . . sort of like . . . wanted to get drunk and escape." She took a long, slow drag on the cigarette, and continued. "When he was five his real Daddy was killed. He was real close to Steve. They were buddies. Steve's real Daddy was a truck driver. One morning he left out before daylight on a run to San Antonio." She looked down and lowered her voice. "It was real foggy, and he ran his semi into the side of another semi that was jack-knifed in the middle of the wet highway. Then another semi ran into his." She raised her head and looked into the distance for a moment. "Something happened to Steve then. He wouldn't play for a while, and was just withdrawn. But he got over it.

"Two years later, I married Steve's step-daddy. They just hit it off great. He was a fireman. When Steve was sixteen, his step-daddy was killed in a fire. Steve was so broke up that he just quit everything. He started hanging out more with boys that drank and smoked dope. He just withdrew. Even quit school.

"I was pretty broken up myself, and felt like I should be able to lean on Steve some, but it didn't work out that way. Well, anyway . . ." Her face saddened. "Anyway Steve and these other boys went in together and bought a kilo of grass. It was in Steve's car. He was speeding and got stopped. They found the kilo, and charged Steve with possession with intent to sell, which I understand they can do when they catch you with so much.

"I had to put up our home to get him out on bond. Then he and the same buddies who had been with him in the car got stoned and held up a grocery store. They were all pretty stupid. Didn't get three blocks.

"Things were tough, paying for lawyers and all. I ended up having to sell the house. Things just got worse." She paused a moment, then her face brightened. "But things got better. Once Steve got off the grass in prison and got his head straight, he began to realize what had happened to him. You ought to see some of the letters he wrote me from prison. After he was in for about a year, he wrote and told me that he had become a Christian, and that his life was completely changed. Now, I don't go for that 'born again' stuff myself, but it seemed to really do something for Steve. He got on a drug education program with some other prisoners, and was allowed to go out with a prison officer and make talks in schools and churches.

"When he got out, he went to church every Sunday, and continued to speak out against drugs." She shook her head. "I just don't think he changed back again. He's his old self again, the way he was before his step-daddy died." She paused and took another drag on the cigarette. "He even tried to get me to quit smoking. Said it was a drug, and that I was addicted. He tried to get me to quit drinking, said it was as bad as marijuana." She put her feet to the floor, and sat up straight in the recliner. "Don't misunderstand. I'm not a problem drinker, just occasionally when I go out," she explained. "But anyway Steve's a reformer. He's like a reformed drunk." The smile returned. "He wants to reform everyone else."

The Chihuahuas scratched louder. Mrs. Pierce eased to her feet. "Guess I'll have to let those babies in."

"We'll be going, Mrs. Pierce," Gar stood. "Thank you very much. If you hear from Steve, tell him to please contact me. If he's innocent, and frankly it does look bad for him, we'll do everything we can for him."

Chapter 18

The Eyebrow

Gar walked up the hill through long shadows of black oak trees to the sky ride terminal. Although it had been searched before, he methodically searched every square foot of the floor of the building, occasionally picking up a leaf or other piece of trash for close examination. Dusk overcame the daylight. Gar wriggled under the heavy steel framework. He took a small pen light from his shirt pocket and swept its beam in the dark shadows of the steel frame. The light stopped on a hairy object about an inch long with black hair on one side, and an adhesive strip on the other side. He dropped the hairy object into a small plastic envelope, and resumed his search.

Back in his room at the Inn, Gar took a shower, and lay across the bed, naked as a shelled pea. On his stomach with his chin resting on the edge of the bed, he checked over the thick stack of pink, carbon copies of investigators' reports. They had been pounded out by officers on manual typewriters. The "xx'ed" out mistakes added to smeared carbon on the pink paper. Then, using a magnifying glass, he peered at the hairy object he had found that evening.

The black and shiny hairs stuck to a sticky fabric backing. He studied the sticky side of the fabric, and saw a single, white hair, curved like a scimitar.

Meanwhile Wednesday Evening, Day One

Bearl Blitzboggen's office at Dallas Security Adjustments faced west into the setting sun on Greenville Avenue, a busy North Dallas street known for its night clubs and restaurants.

Blitzboggen had come in early that Wednesday morning. He chatted with his supervisor about reports in *The Dallas Morning News* and on television about the murders in San Marcos.

"The name *Clara Masters* rang a bell," Blitzboggen told his supervisor. "I checked. She's an *insured* of one of our clients."

"I guess we'll have some work to do on that one," the Supervisor said.

"I'd like to be assigned to that case."

"It'll be tough. Why don't you let one of the younger guys do it?"

"I hate to say so," Blitzboggen said, "but I'm in deep trouble with my wife. If I can do something commendable, maybe she'll think more of me." Blitzboggen quickly added, "That's just between you and me, okay?"

"Okay. I know what it's like to lose face in front of your wife. Three divorces will attest to that. Since I'll have to go to San Marcos anyway, I'll just check some of the other companies and see if they have any insured clients involved," he remarked half to himself.

"You need some help?" a secretary asked dutifully.

"No. I'll handle it." Blitzboggen called insurance company clients to learn if the sky ride tragedy had injured or killed any of their *insureds*. He toiled all day on the telephone.

Late in the day, from low in the west the hot sun

shined brightly through plate glass windows on the west, front of the building. The receptionist, the only buffer between the twenty workers and the public, got up from her desk and lowered the window blinds. Heat radiated in from a small entry area with a wall of glass. The hot afternoon sun filled the tiny room.

At 4:30 the staff began leaving like rats off a sinking ship. Several remarked as they passed through, how hot the entry had become.

"I need this list typed, please," Blitzboggen addressed his secretary for the second time that day.

"It's four-thirty, Mr. Blitzboggen. I'll miss my ride," she protested.

"Okay. Go ahead. I'll do it."

He moved to her desk and laboriously began typing. He made a list of seven insurance companies that had a Clara Masters of San Marcos, Texas, insured. One was a major life insurance company that had had her insured for fifteen years for $20,000. Four companies specialized in accident insurance, sold through oil companies, travel clubs and credit unions. Each offered up to a million dollars coverage for accidental death. Clara Masters had the maximum coverage for each of three oil companies, a travel club, and a credit union.

The last of the staff to leave, the supervisor went out through the small, hot entry, and locked the door behind him.

Blitzboggen continued working. "That's five million, plus, so far," Blitzboggen said to himself, and continued typing data about Clara Masters' coverage. Another company had credit life insurance for Mr. Burke Masters or Mrs. Clara Masters that would pay off their

$200,000 home mortgage, a $150,000 note at the bank on an auto dealership, a $350,000 note on a ranch in South Texas, and $500,000 on his office building.

"That's over six million, total," he muttered to the typewriter.

He slowly typed a list of the companies, and the amounts of coverage, then added a note to his supervisor.

"Dave, this looks like a big deal. I don't think we'll need to pay on any of these accidental death policies because it was murder, and each has homicide exclusion. Still there will be big claims on the credit life policies. I'll go to San Marcos first thing in the morning. I'll call in."

He placed the note on his supervisor's desk. Carrying his keys in one hand, and a stuffed, leather briefcase in the other, he unlocked the first door. Blitzboggen stopped suddenly. "Rats," he said to the big empty room. He set his briefcase in the open door. The door closer pressed the door against the leather briefcase. He went to the copy machine, laid his keys on it, made a copy of the note, and hurried out and into the hot glass entry area, carrying the copy in his hand. When the door shut behind him, he looked down at the document in his hand and then through the glass door to his keys lying on the copy machine. He whirled in his tracks, dropping the copy and the briefcase, and lunged for the closing door.

"Click." The door shut and locked. He pushed on the door. It didn't budge. He pushed on the outer door. Locked tight. He peered through the door into the office at his keys on the copy machine as if he might levitate them through the glass and into his hand.

Perspiration beaded up on Blitzboggen's face. The blinding sun shined unmercifully straight through the big, plate glass window. Blitzboggen shaded his eyes with his hand and squinted in the blinding light. The heat settled in on his body; sweat soaked his clothes. Within fifteen minutes he had shed all his clothing except shorts and undershirt. He sat behind a little patch of shade made by his coat and shirt that hung from the long push-bar of the outside door. He tried to work with the papers from his open briefcase. Sweat dropped from the end of his nose onto the papers.

Inside the office the phone rang.

After the sun went down, the heat began to diminish. After darkness settled in he put his pants back on. The phone in the office rang intermittently all night.

Many night club patrons used Blitzboggen's company's parking lot. Near midnight, Blitzboggen awoke. Flat faces of two couples pressed against the glass, staring at him. They removed their faces from the glass, smiled, and waved to Blitzboggen. They looked at each other and laughed. They waved at him again. He turned his face to the wall and went back to sleep.

Chapter 19

Sniper

In the Clearwater Inn Gar drifted off to sleep. An officer's report fell from his hand to the floor. The telephone rang like a loud alarm. Gar jumped up and grabbed the receiver.

"Garcia."

"Ranger Garcia, this is the dispatcher at police headquarters. We have a report of a gunshot through the window of a Laurence Wilkins. He said the bullet came through a window narrowly missing his son Larry the main witness in the sky ride killings."

"Are any officers on the scene?" Gar asked into the phone.

"Yes, sir. They have the perimeter covered."

"I'm on my way," Gar said.

Remembering the route to the Wilkins home, Gar drove slowly, looking in every direction. An officer moved one of two patrol cars that blocked the street. As Gar passed, he thought, *The shooter probably had a car nearby. If he didn't get out before the perimeter was sealed, he may still be with his car.* Those thoughts had barely passed through when Gar spotted a late model Cadillac, clean and shiny except that mud covered the license tag. He turned his spotlight beam into the Cadillac's rear window, and walked carefully around to the driver's door. Suddenly a dark figure raised up from the front seat and started the motor.

"Stop. Police," Gar shouted and drew his right hand .44.

The Cadillac's rear tires left a black track as the car bolted forward. By the time Gar got into his car the Cadillac had gone a block ahead. Gar turned on his red lights and siren and gave chase.

The officer who had recently moved his car, got out and stood in the open door. "Maybe someone spotted the shooter." Just then the clean Cadillac with muddy plates roared through the opening, followed closely by Gar's screaming Dodge.

One patrol car stayed with the roadblock while the other fell in behind Gar and added volume to the screaming sirens and yelpers and lighted the area with flashing red white and blue lights. Gar spoke into the microphone, "Dispatch, this is Texas Ranger Garcia."

"Yes our patrol car is behind you and gave the suspect car's position."

"Get word to Chief of Detectives Arnold. Although I could only see a silhouette, the guy driving the Cadillac is very tall."

Gar continued to gain on the Cadillac, which sped on out of the residential area and on to Highway 80 on the outskirts of town. A slow freight train approached. *That ought to stop him.* The Cadillac bounced over the railroad tracks ahead of the train. Gar continued full speed ahead. He could imagine the train hitting the rear of his car as he almost made it across. He did make it however and continued to gain on the Cadillac.

The Cadillac swerved around a slow eighteen-wheeler. Oncoming traffic went off the road. The truck driver made a panic stop. Gar stomped his brakes as the eighteen-wheeler jack knifed and blocked the road. The following police car skidded to a stop just short of Gar's rear bumper.

Oncoming traffic got out of the way of the bright lighted Dodge as it raised a cloud of dust on the shoulder and sped around the truck. Gar could see a clear road ahead, no cars at all. A mile down Highway 80, he turned off the emergency lights and siren and drove more slowly. The patrol car followed suit.

"Okay San Marcos Police, you can take it from here. I'm going back to bed," Gar said into the microphone. An auto repair shop with a large gravel circle drive made a good place to turn around. A faded sign read, "Mueller's Auto Repair."

Thursday, Day Two

Thursday morning illuminated the now quiet night clubs, still as death and deserted and as quiet as falling dew. The morning sun came up behind the Dallas Security Adjustments' building. The building shaded the glass entry from the morning sun. One solitary car occupied a spot in its center. Blitzboggen's supervisor arrived early. Blitzboggen stood in the entry, fully dressed in rumpled clothes and holding his briefcase. The supervisor unlocked the outside door. "Did you work all night?" He closed the outside door behind him.

"Yes," Blitzboggen answered, and pushed the door open. He walked out to his car and found it locked. He set his briefcase by the car door and walked back into the office.

"Forget something?" the supervisor asked with puzzlement. He looked up from papers in his hand to Blitzboggen's unshaven face.

"Yes," Blitzboggen answered. He grabbed the keys from the copy machine, and left without another word.

The supervisor looked at the copy machine, then at Blitzboggen going out the door carrying his keys, and shook his head.

Chapter 20

Meanwhile Thursday, Day two

More Witnesses

In San Marcos that Thursday morning Chief of Detectives Roy Sherman parked his black car in a *No Parking* zone at the emergency room of the sprawling San Marcos General Hospital. The midmorning sun got hotter as it reflected off the black asphalt parking lot. Both front doors of the car swung open. Gar gave his rested body a satisfying stretch as he stepped out. "I wish you'd do something about the way this car smells," he said across the car's roof to Sherman.

"I am," Sherman answered. "I used to couldn't smell it. But since I quit smoking it smells bad to me too."

A few quick steps brought them to double glass doors with round, bright red stickers at eye level. Gar stepped on a rubber mat and the automatic doors slid open. Cool air felt good on Gar's face as he stepped inside. The doors slid back together, shutting out the noise of traffic and tree leaves rustling in the breeze.

"My division's getting two new cars today. I'll get one of them."

"Good."

A white-clad nurse looked up from her work behind a desk. Seeing Sherman, she smiled in recognition. She fixed her eyes on Gar, looking him up and down: the big hat, the round *Texas Rangers* badge on his chest, the big, shiny pistols on each hip, and the well-polished boots. Gar removed his hat and nodded to her. She nodded back and smiled.

The men followed a trail of red, yellow, and blue tiles in the hall floor. At a hall intersection, the yellow tiles turned to the right, and Gar and Sherman followed them.

"First there's Reverend Paul Albert," Sherman said, removing a dog-eared notebook from his pocket. "He and his wife were in one of the sky ride cars that fell. He suffered a concussion and cuts and bruises. She's in intensive care with head injuries, fractured skull. Hadn't regained consciousness, last I heard," Sherman continued.

In Rev. Albert's room they found him wide awake with his bed raised to an almost sitting position. The gray-haired minister peered through brown plastic-rimmed half glasses at a thick copy of *The Reader's Digest.*

After introductions, Gar asked Rev. Albert to recount what he had seen and heard when the cable car fell.

Rev. Albert removed the reading glasses, and described the sudden jerk backward and the fall. As he spoke of his wife's injury, he choked up with emotion.

"Tell me about *before* you went on the sky ride. Did you see four men, all dressed in dark suits, and with heavy black hair and mustaches?"

"No." Rev. Albert thought a moment, sat straight up in the bed, and tapped the reading glasses on his sheet-covered knee. "I did see one man like that come into the restaurant," he said reflectively.

"Would you describe him?" Gar asked.

"He walked right by my wife and me while we were having lunch." The white-haired minister had a far-away look on his face. "He was a giant," he continued, "at least six and a half feet tall, and must have weighed over two-fifty. He had thick black hair, in bangs down to his eyes. He had a *Fu Manchu* mustache, only thicker, and I noticed too that he had several flesh-colored bandages on his face."

Gar and Sherman sat erect in their chairs. "Where?" they asked in unison.

"Well, he had one here, on his chin," Rev. Albert touched a finger to the tip of his chin. "One here." The finger went to his right cheek. "And another one . . . about here," he said, touching his left cheek with the other finger.

"Did he have anything in his hands?" Gar asked.

"Yes. He carried a walking stick, and a black attaché case. He sat at a table with three other men. I got a good look at only one. He was a Mexican-American, and seemed somehow familiar to me. Then I saw his picture in the paper. I realized he was Reynaldo Diaz, the head of *La Gente Unida*." Rev. Albert paused, then smiled, "You know I voted for him when he ran for Governor."

"Are you *La Gente*?" Gar asked.

"Oh, no. I'm a life-long Democrat. I was just . . . well, at the time, I was just sore at both major parties, and it was either vote for Diaz or not vote. And besides, I like to help the underdog when I can."

"Reverend Albert, had you ever seen the big man before?" Sherman asked.

"Oh, no."

"Do you have any enemies that might want to do away with you?" Gar asked.

"Oh, no."

"How about your wife; does she have any enemies?" Sherman asked.

"Absolutely not," Albert said emphatically. "Now let me ask you something. Are you making any progress?

Do you have any idea who could have done this thing?"

"We have some leads," Gar said. "The big man is our main lead. We're also looking for a young man who worked on the sky ride named Steve Pierce. He left with the killers. Apparently he was their inside man."

"Well, what caused the cable to break?" Rev. Albert asked.

"It didn't break. It was cut with an axe," Gar said.

"I may be telling you something you already know, Ranger Garcia, but let me share something with you. I haven't always been a preacher. When I was a young man I knocked around the country quite a bit, and one of the things I did was to roughneck on an oil drilling rig. I remember those many years ago that when we had to cut a cable, we did it with an axe."

"Hey," Sherman said, looking from Rev. Albert to Gar.

Rev. Albert continued. "I also saw the picture of the Police Chief holding the cable end and the knot used to tie the nylon rope to the cable. That's just the way an oil field roughneck would have done it, wrapped six times and tied behind the wraps. The pull on the rope just tightens the wraps and they won't slip."

"Thank you, Reverend Albert. That bit of information is a great help. We've been looking for someone with a Navy or sailing background, but it could be an oil field man," Gar said. He stood to his feet.

Sherman stood. "Is there anything else you can think of?" he asked.

"It probably doesn't mean anything," Rev. Albert said, "but this tall man was really perspiring. I noticed him blotting his eyes and face with a handkerchief. Sweat was literally rolling off his face."

"It was hot," Sherman commented.

"He had been inside the air conditioned restaurant for some time. None of the rest of us was sweating," Rev. Albert said.

"It means something," Gar said.

"What?" Sherman asked. "Suppose he was sick?"

"Don't know," Gar replied. "Maybe we'll find out."

The two men stood to leave.

"Wait a minute. That's not all," Rev. Albert said.

The two lawmen stopped in their tracks and turned.

"Have you prayed about this?" the preacher asked.

Gar looked at Sherman. Sherman looked at Gar. Neither spoke.

"Well, wait a minute. Let's pray together and ask God to help." The preacher wrapped his arms around his sheet-covered legs, bowed his head, and spoke softly, "Dear God, in Heaven . . ." Gar and Sherman bowed their heads. ". . . Please help these men to do their jobs. Give them wisdom to find the killers before they can harm more innocent people. And, Oh God, I pray, please help the people who were hurt, and comfort the families that lost loved ones. Especially, I ask for my dear wife. In Jesus' Name, Amen."

"Amen," both lawmen said with gusto. They shook hands with Rev. Albert and left.

"Wow," Gar said, "I've always believed in looking under every rock and behind every bush. I'm sure glad we shook that bush, aren't you?"

Sherman smiled in agreement, and once again consulted his notebook. "The next one is Bob and Shirley Patterson, newlyweds. They're in the same room together."

Further down the yellow tile trail, in another room, Gar could see a young woman in bed weeping. Mussed covers on the other bed suggested someone had lain on it recently. A motherly nurse stood over the young woman, patting her hand. "There, there, Shirley. He's in good hands. Dr. Southman is one of the best neurosurgeons in the business."

"I love him so much," the girl sobbed. "I'll just die if he doesn't get all right. You know we were just married the night before it happened."

Gar and Sherman entered the room and introduced themselves. Seeing the empty bed, Gar asked, "Where's Bob Patterson?"

"He's gone to surgery," the nurse replied, looking up, but still patting the young woman's hand.

"I'm sorry to disturb you, Mrs. Patterson," Gar began. "But we need to ask you a few questions."

The nurse patted Shirley's hand again. "I'll go on now, Shirley, and check back with you later." The nurse turned and left.

"I'm so worried about Bob," the girl said. "He has no feeling from the waist down, and the doctors said he had only a fifty-fifty chance of regaining feeling in the lower part of his body."

"I'm sorry to trouble you at a time like this, but you might be able to help us to find the people who caused all this," Gar said. "I just want you to tell me about what you were doing before the sky ride fell. Were you in the restaurant?"

"Yes." She touched a tissue to her eyes, and pulled the sheet tight up under her chin.

"Did you see some men who were dressed in dark

suits?"

"Oh, I don't know. I wasn't really paying much attention."

"Did you notice men with long hair over their foreheads and black mustaches?" Gar asked.

"Yes . . . yes, and I believe they were wearing dark suits too." She thought a moment, and continued. "We were already seated, and waiting for the waitress to come and take our order when they came in. There were three of them."

"Did you see a fourth man join them?" Gar asked.

"Yes, now that you mention it . . . a big man, carrying a suitcase and an umbrella. He came and sat down with them."

"Did you notice anything about his face?"

"No. Just the mustache. He was big all over," she said.

"Do you, or your husband, have any enemies that might want to harm you?" Gar asked.

"Oh, no. Bob has no enemies that I know of. And I don't for sure," she said. Then relaxing her hold on the sheet at her chin, added, "He, the big man, was sweating a lot. It was nice and cool in the restaurant, but he sweated, and wiped his face with a handkerchief."

Glass walled patient rooms circled the nerve center of the Intensive Care Unit. Elizabeth Albert lay on a hospital bed that had been raised to its limit. Electronic instruments surrounded the head of the bed. A cathode ray tube with a spot of green light bounced along a horizontal line, showed an electronic picture of her heartbeat.

The preacher's wife's gray tongue protruded from

her mouth, held there by a strap attached to the tip of her tongue. Her eyes hid behind slits in her swollen face. A white bandage covered the top of her head. Her breathing came in short gasps.

"My wife's name is Elizabeth," Gar said softly, emotion filling his voice.

Tears filled the eyes of the tough Chief of Detectives beside Gar. "You okay?" Gar asked, laying a hand on Sherman's shoulder.

"Yes." Sherman cleared his throat. "My wife looked just like this two years ago. A drunk ran a stop sign. She hit him broadside." Sherman paused, and shook his head slowly. His voice filled with emotion. "She lay like that for twenty days. She never regained consciousness."

In the next room they visited Bernice Masters. "She has never regained consciousness," the nurse said. "But she's doing well, considering that she was under water for fifteen minutes." The nurse patted Bernice's hand, and turned to leave. "Call if you need me," she said, and left the room.

"I used to know her," Sherman said.

"Oh?"

"She was a freshman in high school the year I graduated. Cute as she could be. She was a cheerleader. I played football. One Friday night I got my bell rung and was out of it. When I came to, I looked up and saw her. She was holding my head and dabbing a wet cloth on my forehead. I thought I had died and gone to heaven," Sherman said. He looked long at her face. The bouncing green spots on the heart monitor showed her heartbeat to be steady. "It's too bad she was under water so long," Sherman said. "Her breathing seems normal. Suppose she'll ever wake up?"

"According to Jim Bradshaw, there's hope for her," Gar said.

"How so?"

"I don't know how much of an expert Bradshaw is, but he insists that since the water was so cold that she can recover with all her mental faculties," Gar said.

"Wouldn't that be great. I'd hate to see her just be a vegetable . . . if she lives," Sherman said. "Hope Bradshaw knows what he's talking about."

Chapter 21

Internal Affairs

At police headquarters, Gar relaxed in a small private office. Dapper Detective Sam Arnold, dressed in a light blue seersucker suit with dark blue tie and a white carnation in his lapel, came into the office carrying several sheets of paper and photographs.

"We've got some reports here from San Antonio that you might want to see," Arnold said in his disarming, high pitched voice.

"Tell me about it," Gar yawned, leaning back in his chair.

Sam Arnold sat down, but before he could speak the chief's secretary, a stern matron, stood in the little office's door. "Ranger Garcia, the Chief asked for you to come into his office. There are a couple of DPS people there to see you."

"Stand by," Gar said to Sam Arnold, and followed the Chief's secretary.

As Gar entered the Chief's office, three men stood. The Chief remained seated. "These men wanted to talk to you, Ranger Garcia. I thought it would be better in here."

Gar had heard of Lieutenant G. W. Posey. Only two years from mandatory retirement, he had asked for and received an assignment to Internal Affairs. He hated dirty cops and wanted to finish up his career as a clean-up man.

Holding his I.D. and badge in one hand, he extended the other to Gar. "G. W. Posey, Internal Affairs," then introduced his partner, Detective Jay Lewis. On the other end of the retirement scale, Jay Lewis but had already established a reputation. He disliked sloppy cops. Five years working with the Austin DA, he had learned to be a stickler for details, little nit-picking things that kept cases from being lost or dismissed.

Posey introduced the third visitor, Assistant District Attorney Harlan Bright from Marshall County, Oklahoma. *A kid lawyer, apparently on his first job.*

"We're following up on a complaint by a Ms. Maria Diaz, widow of Ben Diaz, who drowned Tuesday in Lake Texoma. The complainant alleges that you and DPS Officer Phil Parks, with the assistance of two Coast Guard Auxiliary volunteers, took her husband from a boat, put him on a helicopter, tied a rifle to his arm to weight him down, and dropped him from a thousand feet into eighty feet deep water."

Gar laughed.

"Is that funny, Ranger Garcia?" Posey asked.

"Yes. It's a funny story," Gar said, "because it's so fantastic."

Harlan Bright interrupted: "Marshall County Sheriff divers recovered the body today. The deceased's right arm was twisted in a rifle sling."

"The complainant says her brother-in-law, Johnny, was an eye-witness, however, we have not been able to locate him," Posey said. "Tell us what happened on Lake Texoma Tuesday."

Gar related everything that took place on the island in Lake Texoma except that his face had turned orange.

"We'll be in touch," Posey said at the close of the interview.

Back in Gar's office, Sam Arnold, laid the papers and photos on the desk, and began. "A white male thrown from a moving car and killed by an eighteen-wheeler Tuesday night has been identified."

"What's the connection?" Gar asked.

"It happened in front of the San Antonio Rose Motel, where the suspect, Steve Pierce's fingerprints were found."

"Okay. Go ahead," Gar said.

"This subject, the one who was killed by the eighteen-wheeler, was identified as Alfred James Giovan. He used several aliases, including John Grimes. He had served time in New York for killing his wife." Arnold tossed a photograph across the desk. "Here's his mug shot. Notice anything about his nose?"

"He sure fits the description of Hawk Nose," Gar replied, picking up the photo.

"On the list of known associates is a white male Donald Thomas Harmon, who has used the alias Don Thomas. This subject had been charged with impersonating a police officer. Thomas' New York record includes a murder, second degree, conviction. His height and weight indicate he may be the Thomas we're looking for," Arnold said.

"Reckon this could be our phony FBI man?" Gar picked up another photo. "Let's get an artist."

Arnold returned in a few minutes with a police artist, a tanned, skinny woman in her thirties with nervous, jerky movements. The artist laid sheets of clear acetate over the mug shots and drew thick, black hair down over the foreheads, long, black sideburns, and thick, black, drooping mustaches.

Sherman came in to see Gar, Arnold, and the woman bent over the desk. Sherman put on a pair of black, plastic-rimmed reading glasses, and peered through to the artwork. "Hey. I believe that's them."

"Could be them," the artist said.

"A car was wrecked in San Antonio Tuesday night. It hit the concrete railing of a San Antonio River bridge," Arnold continued. "It's probably the same car Hawk Nose flew out of. Anyway, the car had Steve Pierce's finger prints in it."

"Were any other prints found in the motel room?"

"Yes, as a matter of fact there were," Arnold's voice rose in excitement. "Prints of both these subjects, Thomas, and Giovan, were in the motel room."

"The same room where Steve Pierce's prints were found?"

"The same."

"That puts them all together for sure," Gar said. "But no other prints of a fourth man?"

"Not that San Antonio P.D. found but here's some more stuff. The wood block we found at the scene was identified as ironwood."

"Do you need me anymore?" the artist asked Gar.

"Get us some copies of those doctored mug shots, will you?"

"Yes, sir." The artist picked up her material and left the office.

"What's ironwood?" Arnold asked to no one in particular.

"Maybe it rusts," Sherman answered with a chuckle.

"It's a super hard wood," Gar answered. "Grows in

South Texas and Mexico. It has sharp thorns, and delicate fern-like leaves, kind of like Mesquite, except a lot tougher."

"Well, the lab says," Arnold continued, "that the block of ironwood was cut with a chainsaw and shaped with a router and wood chisels of various shapes. They found traces of chainsaw oil that they identified as a brand marketed by the Sharpest company. The pattern of the teeth cut also matched the Sharpest chainsaw." Arnold looked up from the report sheet. "And, by the way," he said, "Sharpest just recently entered the chain saw market, so that might help narrow our search." He looked back to the paper and resumed. "Samples of the ironwood block were sent to the U.S. Department of Agriculture Forest Service, Forest Products Laboratory in Madison, Wisconsin, for further study."

"Don't guess they had time to get anything back from the Navy or Coast Guard," Gar speculated.

"It'll probably take a while," Arnold said.

Knuckles tapped on the frosted glass window of the office door.

"Yes," Gar answered.

A uniformed officer opened the door. "Ranger Garcia, there's a guy here from Dallas, an insurance adjuster. Says he has some information that might be helpful."

"Send him on in."

The officer closed the door. Gar leaned back. A rusty spring in the base of the old wooden swivel chair squeaked. Gar put his hands behind his head and stretched.

The office door swung open, and Bearl Blitzboggen

entered. "Ranger Garcia?" He set his stuffed, leather briefcase on the floor.

Gar stood and extended his hand. "Yes," I'm Ranger Garcia."

Blitzboggen stepped forward and shook hands with Gar.

"This is Chief of Detectives Roy Sherman, and Detective Sam Arnold, Mister. . ."

"Blitzboggen," Blitzboggen said, shaking hands with the other two. "Bearl Blitzboggen. I'm an insurance adjuster with Dallas Security Adjustments." He laid a business card on the desk.

"What can you tell us, Mr. Blitzboggen?" Gar asked.

"My company does adjustments on a contract basis for many different insurance companies. We, you might say, are specialists. We don't sell insurance, or do actuarial work, we just do adjustments."

"Okay," Gar encouraged him on.

"I have found more than five million dollars' worth of accident insurance and over a million dollars' worth of credit life insurance on a Clara Masters, Mrs. Burke Masters, the woman who drowned."

"Accident insurance. This was murder."

"I know," Blitzboggen said. "So it won't pay because of the homicide exclusion. She also had twenty thousand dollars' worth of whole life."

"Who's the beneficiary?"

"Her husband, Burke Masters. In all cases, her husband."

"Suppose she was the real target of the murder, and the rest was just a smoke screen?" Gar asked, looking at

Sherman and then Arnold.

"I don't think so," Sherman said. "Her husband would have to be the perpetrator, and he would have to be stupid, not to know that accidental death insurance won't pay off for a murder victim."

"And Burke Masters is not stupid," Arnold piped in.

"Are you sure it won't pay?" Gar asked Blitzboggen.

"I'm positive it won't pay, especially if the murderer stands to profit from the murder," Blitzboggen said. "I'm also a lawyer," he added, almost apologetically.

"Suppose," Gar said, "suppose this victim died only as a result of the murder, that she was not the intended victim, and her beneficiary was not the perpetrator. Might her death be considered, technically, an accident, since she was not the intended victim?"

"I don't think so," Blitzboggen said. "I'll check it out."

"Please do, and let me know as soon as you find out something. Okay?"

Blitzboggen picked up his heavy briefcase. "Yes. I'll be glad to."

"If you can't reach me here, call me at the Clearwater Inn."

"Nice to have met you gentlemen," Blitzboggen said, shaking hands all around.

The door closed behind Blitzboggen. Gar's chair squeaked. "Tell me about Burke Masters."

Sherman and Arnold looked at each other. "Go ahead," Sherman said.

"Well," Arnold began, "he's about the biggest wheel in San Marcos. He owns a big new car dealership.

He owns a large downtown office building, and a big ranch in South Texas."

"He's got a lot of oil production in West Texas, too," Sherman added.

"What does he look like? Is he tall, big?" Gar asked.

"Oh, yes," Sherman answered. "He's tall, but he's skinny. I bet he won't weigh over a hundred and sixty, and he's about six four or maybe six six."

"Let's go see him," Gar said

Chapter 22

Fresh Cut Flowers

Gar picked up his hat from a square, walnut-stained coat tree and headed out of the Police Headquarters subdued light.

"The new cars came in," Arnold said, as the three walked toward the outside door.

"Yes, I heard," Sherman said. "I think mine's ready."

The three men stepped out into bright sunlight that reflected off the new, white Ford at the curb. Unmarked except for a spotlight, and two antennas that sprouted up from the rear, the new car hid its red lights inside the front grille. "This one's mine," Sherman said.

"I was supposed to get a new one today too," Arnold said.

"You get my old one, which will still be new to you," Sherman said, pointing to the black car.

"Thanks a lot, Chief," Arnold said with mock enthusiasm.

Gar and Sherman got into the new, white Ford. "This one smells better," Gar said, as he slid into the soft, cloth-covered seat.

Sherman drove down a quiet street with apartment buildings and office buildings on the left and an eight-foot chain link fence on the right. Beyond the fence a thick stand of black oak trees stood like sentinels.

"This is the back of Clearwater Springs Park," Sherman said, jerking a thumb toward the right. "Through those woods, and down the hill is where it all happened."

A heavy padlocked chain secured a large double gate in the chain link. As the car came abreast of the gate, Sherman turned left to a drive and into an underground parking garage. An empty parking spot nearest the elevator announced with yellow letters, "Reserved For Burke Masters."

"Looks like he's not here, but we can check." Sherman stopped the car near the elevator in an area striped with yellow paint and labeled, "No Parking." Thuds of car doors slamming shut echoed off the concrete walls of the parking garage. Hot air carried a strong smell of exhaust fumes. Through a glass door they stepped into a small foyer with two elevators. A glass-encased, black felt directory board announced in large, white letters: "MASTERS BUILDING." Smaller white letters listed names of occupants including "Masters Oil Company, 4th Floor."

In the elevator Gar pushed the *four* button. It filled with yellow light. The door closed. The elevator rose.

"You know, Bernice Masters is his sister," Sherman commented.

"The one who was under water for fifteen minutes."

The elevator doors slid open silently to a room covered thick green carpet. To the left a receptionist who might have come straight from a modeling agency sat behind a small desk decorated with a vase of cut flowers. A green telephone console with square, transparent buttons covered a fourth of the desk top.

The perfectly-groomed receptionist looked up to the visitors. Her perfectly-painted lips smiled, exposing perfect white teeth. "Good afternoon. May I help you?"

Gar removed his hat. The delicate smell of fresh

flowers took his mind back to his wedding day. The receptionist looked up expectantly and brought Gar back to the present. "We'd like to see Burke Masters, please. I'm Texas Ranger Gar Garcia, and this is Chief of Detectives Roy Sherman of the San Marcos Police Department.

"I'll see if he's in." She smiled, and pushed a transparent, plastic button. It lit up. She pushed the Number 1 button.

"Yes. This is Julie," she said into the telephone. "Is Mr. Masters in?" She listened a moment, and said, "Thank you," and hung up. "I'm sorry. He's not in. Could anyone else help you?"

"This is official business, and we need to talk to him personally," Gar said. "Do you know where he can be reached?"

"Just a moment." She smiled, picked up the receiver, and went back to the buttons. "Yes. This is Julie again. There are two gentlemen here . . . ah, from the police. And they would like to know where they can reach Mr. Masters." She listened a moment, and said, "Yes. All right. Thank you," and hung up again.

A door opened to their right revealing an array of desks, people, papers, and fluorescent lights over a busy office. The noise of typewriters and voices poured out into the quiet reception room. A young man in a short-sleeved shirt with loose dark necktie stepped through the door. The door closed and turned off the noise. The young man crossed the room and pushed the elevator button but never took his eyes off the receptionist.

Pointing to another door to their left, the receptionist said, "Mr. Masters' secretary will see you. She's the only one who might know where he is. Go right through that door, and all the way to the end of the hall."

"Won't you sit down, Gentlemen?" Burke Masters' private secretary said. Her baby face, indicated early thirties. Red lipstick accentuated perfect white teeth. Her large black curls contrasted with her creamy white complexion. Large eye glasses with gold frames made her small, slightly upturned nose look even smaller. Fancy gold initials, "JR" adorned the lower left lens.

"I'm Joann Rainey, Mr. Masters' secretary," she said in a high, nasal monotone.

Gar introduced himself and Sherman. They sat in gold-colored fabric chairs with wooden arms and legs. The chairs sat on ball rollers half buried in the thick carpet. A tall vase of fresh cut flowers stood between the secretary and the visitors. She moved the vase slightly to the left, and said, "How can I help you?"

This guy sure likes fresh flowers. I'll bet on the receptionist as his baby doll, Gar thought. "We're looking for Mr. Masters," Gar said. "We want to ask him a few questions. I understand his wife was killed and his sister was severely injured." *This one's pretty, maybe she's his baby doll.*

"Yes, he's quite broken up about them," she said, with a hint of relief in her voice. "So many people want to see Mr. Masters that we don't give out this information. Here is his home address." She wrote an address in flowing script on a white scratch pad.

Gar stood watching her write. The delicate smell of cut flowers again flavored the air. *Maybe both of them? I need to get my mind back on business.* On the desk he saw four file folders lying opposite the flower vase. One label said, "B.M. Accident Insurance," another said, "B.M. Personal, Insurance," the third, "B.M. Personal, Credit Life, and the fourth, "MYT vs TRFI." Gar accepted the paper with the address and thanked her.

    Gar and Sherman stepped out of the basement foyer into the hot air of the parking garage. As soon as the car doors closed, Sherman asked, "Did you detect some fear, or panic in her voice?" He started the engine, and a blast of hot air from the air conditioning vents, heavy with new car smell, hit them in the face. "There was emotion in her voice all right," Gar said. "She might be just upset about the death of the boss' wife, and then too, maybe she knows something we don't," Gar said. The car climbed out of the drive and into the street. The blowing air turned cool.

    As Sherman drove across town the homes became progressively larger. He turned on a tree-lined, asphalt-covered lane with neatly mowed grass in shallow ditches. He lifted the note paper with Masters' address, and peered over his amber framed reading glasses at a large, dark green mailbox with only a white number, "4139."

    High, evergreen shrubbery stood on each side of the drive to guard the privacy of expensive real estate owners. Like a big-eyed robot, a convex mirror on a post, enabled drivers from either direction to see around the corner. Sherman turned into the drive and drove a quarter of a mile through thick woods. Suddenly the woods thinned to reveal a picture-perfect lawn spread out in front of a long, rambling, light brown brick ranch-style home. Sherman drove into a driveway that circled a flower garden with a white statue of Cupid spouting water from his mouth into the air. As the water fell, a south breeze blew it back into Cupid's face.

As Gar exited the car, he surveyed the long, rambling house and four-car garage with freshly-painted white doors. Delicate, green leaves of royal palm trees waved lazily in the breeze against the bright, blue sky.

As Gar reached for the doorbell, the heavy door swung open before him.

"Hello, Mr. Garcia, Mr. Sherman. I've been expecting you."

Chapter 23

Trophies

Burke Masters stood almost as tall as the door opening. Gar surveyed Masters' narrow waist, and wide, bony shoulders, ruddy complexion, small blue eyes, and white eyebrows. His blond mixed with white hair had been cut close to the sides of his head. Deep dimples marked the center of his chin and each cheek. He reached out a hand so big that could have held both Gar's and Sherman's at the same time, and shook hands with each. "Please come in, gentlemen."

This guy's tall enough, Gar thought, *but he's skinny, and plainly Anglo.* Masters ushered them into a sunken living room covered with white, plush carpet, and twenty feet of white, sectional sofa. "Would you like something to drink?"

"I wouldn't mind," Sherman said.

"It is pretty hot out there," Masters said. "Would you like something too, Mr. Garcia?"

"Well, yes. Thank you," Gar said.

Masters stepped back up from the living room, and motioned to a wide door toward the interior of the house. "Why don't we just go into the den? It'll be handier. Maria, my housekeeper, just fixed up a big pitcher of iced tea. Hard to beat on a day like this."

The three men stepped through a wide doorway into an expansive den. Gar, by habit, took an inventory: Various liquors and shiny glasses stocked his bar. Beyond the bar, sounds of tinkling ice in glasses came from a kitchen.

Visible through a floor- to-ceiling glass wall, sparkling sunlight reflected off a large swimming pool. A green lawn dotted with palm trees edged the pool. Mounted hunting trophies, including heads of a jaguar, lion, deer, and a cape buffalo, covered one wall of the den.

Ice cubes cracked as Masters poured the amber liquid. "How can I help?" Masters smiled, set the clear glass pitcher on the white marble top of the coffee table, and sat back in a low, plush overstuffed leather chair. Gar and Sherman sat on a matching sofa with their backs to the hunting trophies.

"Mr. Masters, do you know of anyone who would want to harm your wife?" Gar asked.

"No. I can't imagine such a thing," Masters answered quickly. "Surely you don't think she was the target of the murderer."

"We're just exploring all possibilities. It's probably just as it appears, that someone wanted to kill Reynaldo Diaz in a spectacular way, the kind of thing a drug syndicate might do as a lesson to others," Gar said, and added, "And the other victims just happened to be in the way." Gar watched Masters over the top of the tea glass and took a long drink. "But in any case, we have to check everything, and we have to question everyone who is even remotely connected with the case."

"My wife had no enemies," Masters said. "I haven't been around my sister a great deal for the past several years, but as far as I know, she has, uh, had, no enemies, at least none that would want to kill her."

"Did your . . . I mean, does your sister live here in San Marcos?" Gar asked.

"Yes. But you see, I've been gone a lot of the time.

I've been back here for the past two years, but before that, for the better part of five years, I was in South America. We have quite a bit of production in Peru."

"Was your wife with you in South America?"

"No. We had two teen-age boys in school and she stayed here to take care of them." Masters abruptly changed the subject. "Have you heard any more about my sister's condition?"

"We were at the hospital this morning. She hadn't regained consciousness."

"It's too bad for Bernice. If she does live, she'll just be a vegetable, not knowing anything." Masters shook his head.

"Not necessarily," Gar said. "Jim Bradshaw, the manager of Clearwater Springs, told me he's convinced that she can live and that she can have all her mental faculties."

"Really?"

"Your wife and sister fell into unusually cold water, sixty-eight degrees. As soon as they were brought up, Bradshaw and his boys began immediate resuscitation. Your sister began breathing on her own, and her pulse returned. Unfortunately, your wife didn't respond."

"I never heard of such a thing. They were under water for a long time."

"Fifteen minutes. Bradshaw was convinced that because of the cold water, and the immediate resuscitation, they could live. Come to think of it too, your sister had no water in her lungs."

"How could that be?"

"Many people drown without ever getting any water into their lungs. Probably ten to fifteen per cent of drownings are called 'dry' drownings. It's because the shock of the cold water causes a spasm of the larynx, which protects the lungs from taking in water. But of course the person may become asphyxiated. In your sister's case, she has the 'diving reflex' Bradshaw talked about and the lack of water in her lungs, both in her favor," Gar said. "So there's a possibility she'll recover."

"I hope he's right. I hope she will recover," Masters said, and put the glass to his lips.

"Have you been in the oil business long?" Gar asked.

"All my life."

"How does a man such as yourself, obviously quite successful, make it big in the oil business. How did you start?"

"I bet it wasn't as a policeman," Sherman said.

"I'm a geologist. I worked hard, and got lucky, and then worked harder."

Gar finished his iced tea, picked up his hat, and stood. "Thank you, Mr. Masters. We appreciate your cooperation. And the tea. It hit the spot.'"

Sherman stood and said, "Yes, thank you."

Gar turned to leave, faced the wall covered with hunting trophies, and asked, "Are you a hunter, Mr. Masters?"

"Oh, yes. I've hunted all over the world." Warming to the subject, he motioned toward the mounted head of a large spotted cat with wide head and muscular jaws. "This is a jaguar I shot in Peru. He almost got me first. It's not like hunting lions in Africa, out in the open. The jaguars live in the jungle. They are literally kings of the jungle in South America. They fear neither man nor beast. I had been hunting this one for hours. He turned the tables on me, and started hunting me. He lunged on me from a high tree branch. I shot him in mid-air, killing him instantly. He landed right on top of me. Knocked me unconscious. Can you imagine what it feels like to wake up in the middle of a jungle to find yourself covered with a giant cat?" A smile covered Masters' face and he spoke in a more relaxed voice.

Masters stepped to the left, and motioned to the black head of a cape buffalo with a shiny black nose and heavy black horns. "Now this one I shot in Africa. I was on my way home from Saudi Arabia in Fifty-Eight, and stopped off for a hunt. The cape buffalo is the meanest critter in Africa. A lion won't tackle a healthy one, and an elephant will treat them with respect."

Several deer heads flanked the cape buffalo. To the left of them a single-shot, twelve-gage shotgun rested on two brass wire coat hooks attached to the wall. Gar looked at the shotgun, then to a fine walnut gun case across the room filled with well-polished rifles and shotguns. "Does this mean something special?"

"Is this what killed the jaguar?" Sherman asked.

"No. This one killed a man. When I was just getting started with my own drilling rig, people were stealing me blind. Money was so close, I was about to go under. We kept our fuel and heavy equipment in a yard in McAllen in the Rio Grande Valley, and every day we found that gasoline, or something, had been stolen the night before. I kept watch out there several nights. One night I caught three wetbacks in the act, trying to haul off an electrical power plant. I ordered them to halt. Two did, and one didn't. He ran, so I shot him. I figured that old shotgun saved my business, because it stopped the thievery. If it happened today, I probably would have been charged with a crime, but things were different in the Fifties."

Next to the shotgun a gray shaft of rock, three inches in diameter, and two feet long, lay on two brass wire coat hooks. Masters rubbed the rough surface as if fondly caressing a pet. "This is the first core that showed signs of oil out of my first well. From the moment I saw this core, and got a good whiff of oil, I knew my wildcatting would pay off." Gray powder came off on his fingers, and he rubbed his hands together.

Sherman pointed to another set of brass coat hangers holding a gray steel mechanism with an eighteen-inch long handle. "What's this?"

"It's a brake," Masters answered. "It fits on a cable that runs from the top of an oil derrick to a tree or post on the ground. The cable fits through here." He demonstrated use of the brake. "It's for a derrick man to use to escape in case a well blows out or catches on fire. You can't just grab hold of a cable and slide down. It would cut your hands, and you'd have no way of slowing down.

"I was a roughneck during the summer while I was in college at the University of Texas in Austin. I worked the derrick. Do you know what a derrick man does?" Masters asked.

"Vaguely," Sherman said.

Masters looked questioningly at Gar.

"Only vaguely," Gar answered.

"Well, the derrick man stands on a small platform near the top, called a 'monkey board.' When a ninety-foot length of drill pipe, called a 'stand,' is pulled up and the floor hands disconnect it from the rest of the drill pipe in the hole, the derrick man disconnects the pipe from the elevators, and stacks the top end of the pipe against the side of the derrick. When the drill pipe is going back into the hole, he does just the opposite.

"I stood on the monkey board, with a safety strap around my waist, so I could lean out and work the pipe. We were coming out of the hole. The floor men had disconnected the stand of pipe, and I had leaned the top end against the derrick, when the well blew out. Mud and oil shot straight up ninety feet to my monkey board; nearly knocked me off it; and clear out the top of the derrick. I was afraid that oil would catch on fire, so I disconnected by safety belt and reached this brake," Masters said, rubbing a hand along the handle. "It was hanging on the escape cable right behind me. I looped this over my shoulders, and I jumped. As soon as I did, the blowout caught fire. It singed my hair. I was sliding fast enough that I cleared the heat. This thing saved my life. Everybody else on that rig was killed. Later I went back and got this, to keep as a souvenir. . . Me and this thing were all of that rig that weren't burned." Then he added thoughtfully, "All the other roughnecks and the driller were incinerated."

Masters followed Gar and Sherman out the front door and stood on the small concrete porch as they drove away.

"What do you think? Sherman asked, as he wheeled the car around the circular drive.

"I think we've got us a suspect."

"He's tall enough, but not heavy enough," Sherman said. Overhanging tree branches formed a canopy through which patches of sunlight streaked over the moving car.

"I'll bet he doesn't weigh over a hundred and seventy. He's downright thin."

"That's a problem, along with the motive. If he did it, why?"

"Maybe he's stupid, and doesn't know about the insurance policies' homicide exclusions."

"I don't think he's stupid," Gar said, "but he might not be as smart as he thinks he is."

Chapter 24

Almost Made It

"Get some men on Masters," Gar said as they drove out of Masters' lane. "I'd like to find out everything about him, his holdings, his debt, any criminal record or history of mental illness. Dig out everything you can. He may be a dead end, but he's the only suspect we've got right now."

As evening rush hour traffic moved through the downtown streets, bright, yellow sunlight accentuated otherwise drab colors. Sherman parked his new white Ford in front of the old red brick police headquarters building.

As the two men entered the building, an officer behind a glass window called to Gar, "Ranger Garcia, the Chief wants to see you right away."

"Okay. Thanks," Gar said, and turned into the Chief's office. Sherman continued on down the hall.

"Oh, Mr. Garcia. The Chief wants to see you," the secretary announced as Gar stepped into the office. She pressed an intercom switch. "Ranger Garcia is here, sir."

A deep voice squawked back, "Send him in."

"Go on in," she said, motioning to a door on her left with a window of snowflake pattern frosted glass.

Chief Bryan stood behind a cluttered desk. On the wall behind him an array of certificates, plaques and photographs attested to his interesting life. They showed Chief Bryan during varying ages of his life posing with well-known figures, including Lyndon B. Johnson. The Chief leaned forward and rested part of his weight on his knuckles like an ape.

"I just wanted to know if you deliberately made a fool out of me?" the Chief asked in his low, rolling voice.

"I'm afraid I don't follow."

"Look here." The chief picked up a newspaper with his picture on the front page. In the picture the Chief held a length of cable with a rope knotted around it. "Here's the evening paper." He threw it on the desk.

Gar picked up the paper. Beside the picture an article quoted the Chief asking the public's help in identifying the knot and locating a giant of a man who might have tied it. "What's wrong with that?" Gar asked, puzzled.

"This paper has been out for just a few hours. It hasn't even been delivered to most of the homes yet. But already our switchboard looks like a tangle of Christmas lights. It seems that lots of people knew this was a knot commonly used in the oil field. That is, everybody but me. Then to top it off, a kid invited me to his Boy Scout meeting to learn how to tie knots."

Gar took a seat in a heavy, wooden chair. He removed his hat, and smiled.

"I don't see anything funny about it," the Chief said, picking up the paper and then tossing it back down.

"Do you think I deliberately embarrassed you?" Gar's continence changed from smile to grim.

"Did you?"

"No."

The Chief sat down. The heavy wooden swivel chair squeaked. He rolled a cigarette between his palms several times until loose tobacco protruded from the ends, put the cigarette too far into his mouth and lit the cigarette. Smoke obscured his face.

Gar straightened in his chair. "We ran the picture to get some help from the public. I thought the publicity would help you, so I suggested you be in the picture. The public responded. So the effort succeeded." Gar sat silently a moment. "Too bad you got your feelings hurt."

The Chief leaned back in the squeaky chair, pulled the wet-ended cigarette from his mouth and exhaled smoke.

Gar stood to his feet. An intentional *don't mess with me* look covered his face. "Anything else, Chief?"

The Chief stuck the wet end of the cigarette back in his mouth, whirled around in the swivel chair and grunted, "No. Thank you for coming in, Ranger Garcia."

In the Detective Division Gar found Sherman issuing rapid fire orders to three detectives.

Two of the detectives wore crumpled short sleeve shirts and slacks. Sam Arnold looked like a bridegroom, nattily dressed in a gray vested pinstripe suit, white shirt with maroon silk tie with a delicate gray pattern, and black patent leather shoes.

He raised a gold pen over a black leather-bound notebook, as if to call for the group's attention.

"Five years ago," Arnold began in his high-pitched voice. "Masters could have fit the description of our mysterious tall man, Peters. He weighed over three-hundred pounds most of his adult life, but it was all muscle."

"We found out he used to roughneck," Sherman said. "He was a derrick hand in college."

"Do you suppose he learned things like knots and cables?" another detective asked.

"Oh, yes," Arnold came back. "To be a derrick hand, you have to be experienced working on the floor first.

Really, if there were a 'rank,' the derrick man would be next to the driller, who is 'lord over all.'"

"If you know so much about oil field drilling, why didn't you tell us about that knot?" Gar asked.

"I only roughnecked for a short time, not long enough to learn 'knots and cables.'" Arnold folded his notebook and put it in his pocket.

"Did you get anything on the little black fuzzy thing I found on the floor of the sky ride terminal?" Gar asked Arnold.

"Oh, yes," Arnold replied. "It's definitely a false eyebrow. They're sold lots of places, along with wigs and mustaches."

"What about the little white hair stuck to it?"

"Definitely a natural hair," Arnold replied. Probably an eyebrow hair from its shape. "Lab said it still had its root."

"Masters had white eyebrows," Gar said.

"Lab said this was natural blond," Arnold said.

"Natural blond or gray," Gar said. "Masters has both kinds."

"Not many natural blond eyebrows around," Sherman commented.

Gar went back to his temporary office at Police Headquarters, picked up the phone, and called his room at the Inn. The phone didn't ring a full ring before Liz answered in her excited, feminine voice.

Gar talked through a big smile. "Hello, Beautiful. I'm glad you're there. I'll be there in ten minutes."

"Well, I don't know if I want you to come or not."

"Why not?" The big smile left.

"Well, just who are you?"

The smile returned. "I'm your ever-loving husband. You know who I am. And in nine minutes, you'll see who I am."

"Hurry," she sang.

"Bye," he sang back, and hung up the phone. Gar stepped out, then back into the office. An anticipatory growl came from deep in his chest as he reached for his hat.

"Do you want to take me to the Inn?" Gar called to Sherman across the room.

"Sure," Sherman replied, and continued talking to the detectives.

Gar stood on one foot and then the other. He tossed his hat into the air. The spinning hat came down. Gar caught it. "You about ready?"

"Yes, just about."

"I can make other arrangements."

"You must be in a hurry."

"I am," Gar said. The big smile covered his face.

"*Vamonos*," Sherman said, and rushed out in front of Gar.

Sherman unlocked the right door, got in and scooted across the seat. Gar bent over, and lowered himself into the car seat when a uniformed officer ran out and grabbed the door.

"Important call for you Ranger Garcia," the officer said.

Gar backed out of the open door. The smile vanished. He followed the officer back into the building and walked briskly to the reception window. Through the semicircular opening in the glass front, an officer handed out a black telephone receiver.

"Hello," Gar spoke into the phone.

"Gar?" A familiar voice came over the phone.

"Yes."

"This is Captain Summers. Listen, Gar, we just got a tip; it may be just what we've been waiting for to get the rest of Diaz's organization. San Antonio P.D. has a reliable source that tells them a DC-Three full of grass is coming in from Mexico tonight. We got another tip from your two eye-witnesses who helped nail Reynaldo Diaz. They told us about the plane too, and get this: They said Diaz isn't dead. The subject killed on the sky ride was someone else."

"His family identified the body," Gar said.

Chapter 25

Imposter

"Reynaldo Diaz's family identified the body," Gar said into the phone.

Captain Summers continued, "Ask San Marcos P.D. to double check positive ID. Anyway, I want you to get down to Pearsall and lead the interception. Your two eye-witnesses say it's Reynaldo Diaz who's working this operation and is supposed to meet the plane."

In silent protest, Gar slapped his hat against his knee. "What time are they expecting the plane?"

"We don't know. 'Sometime tonight,' is as close as we can get. You can be there by dark. I'm sending a helicopter for you."

"Okay. I got it, Captain. Anything else?"

"That's it, Gar. Hope you nail them. Good luck."

"Thanks."

"Good-bye."

"Good-bye." Gar bowed his head, tossed the telephone receiver into his left hand, and reached his right hand through the hole in the glass. With head still bowed, he located the phone, pushed down the hang-up button, and then felt for the dial buttons. By touch he punched out the phone number of the Inn.

"One Twenty-Four, please."

"Hello," Liz's voice came back quickly.

"Hi, Honey," Gar said in a downcast voice. "Emergency. I've got to go. It'll probably be the wee hours of the morning before I get back at the earliest."

"Oh, do you have to?"

"I'm thinking about killing myself instead," he said, and let out a lung-full of air.

"Don't do that, Lover. Tomorrow's another day."

"I'm beginning to wonder," he said dejectedly. "But I won't kill myself if you don't want me to. Expect me when you see me coming. I love you."

"I love you," she said longingly.

Gar reached through the hole in the glass and hung up the receiver. He walked slowly out to the car, and fell through the open door into the seat. Like Gar's countenance, the car sank with his weight.

Aboard the airborne helicopter Gar relaxed his body and enjoyed the rapid ascent. As the chattering craft gained altitude, Gar looked in every direction at the horizon. The big evening sun slowly sank out of sight leaving the western sky a brilliant orange. As the ground got darker, lights became more visible. *It's like being at sea with the circle of horizon visible all the way around.*

Gar raised his voice over the noise of the motor and whirling blades. "Hope you don't mind. . ." He struggled over the seat belt and within the confined space to remove a boot; ". . . but I've had these on all day, and it looks like I'll have them on all night." He strained to get the second boot off.

The pilot looked at Gar, then at his boots. He reached an air vent and opened it. A stream of fresh air flowed through the cabin.

Relived that the orange had worn off his face enough that the pilot didn't mention it, Gar sat back, relaxed, and enjoyed the view. Soon the helicopter flew over San Antonio, a living mass of glittering and moving lights that thinned toward the edges of the city. As the helicopter left the city behind, the white numbers of the helicopter's black, liquid-filled compass read 135 degrees.

Now, he saw lights below only occasionally. Powerful mercury vapor yard lights showed up as tiny white specks in a black sea.

After several minutes, the pilot spoke, "That'll be Lytle over there," he said, motioning to the right toward a thin smattering of lights. "And that's Devine," he said, pointing forward to a slightly larger group of lights several miles distant, sharp little white points twinkling in the blackness.

The helicopter lost altitude as it passed over the small town of Devine. Then it descended onto a field near a two-lane, state highway. The headlights of a blue, unmarked, Chevrolet Impala lit up the field. The helicopter settled down gently on the grass. Gar hurriedly put his boots back on and jumped out. The helicopter rose quickly and vanished into the night.

A uniformed man walked in front of the car's bright headlights. He wore a western hat and khaki uniform with an American flag sewn on one shoulder, and a "Frio County, Texas, Sheriff" patch on the other. A gold and silver-colored badge reflected the bright lights of the car. "Ranger Garcia?" he asked.

"Yes." Gar offered a hand.

"I'm Deputy Ray Montgomery." The men shook hands. "The Sheriff asked me to take you to the rendezvous point." The sound of the helicopter faded in distant blackness of the night sky.

After a short distance down the two-lane, asphalt,

state highway, they turned right onto Interstate Highway 35 in light traffic. In a few minutes they turned off the highway, and onto an unpaved road that ran behind the airport.

A line of low brush and gnarled mesquite trees, with their delicate leaves waving in the soft breeze, concealed police vehicles from view of a rural airport. Gar noted three unmarked DPS cars, and the Sheriff's car, an unmarked, white, Chevrolet. Six DPS officers, armed with twelve-gage, pump-action shotguns gathered in the darkness around the Sheriff's car. Gar got out of Montgomery' car and joined them.

Montgomery introduced Gar. He shook hands all around, then leaned on a car, and joined the rest of the lawmen talking shop.

"We're maintaining radio silence until the operation is well under way," The Sheriff began. "Captain Summers advised that these subjects had scanners and might get alarmed at any radio traffic. We've got to know when they've been spotted and on the way, so we've set up a code system, using the C.B. channel twenty-two."

The grandfatherly Sheriff laid a hand-drawn diagram of the airport in the seat of his car and turned on the bare-bulb dome light. "Here's the runway, hangar buildings and offices." He pointed to the diagram. "A man lives on the premises, but he doesn't turn on the landing lights unless he's expecting a plane."

Gar went over the plans with the Sheriff, then climbed to a high spot of ground near the brush, stood on his toes and peered through the mesquite trees toward the airport. An orange wind sock with its mouth open to the south drooped a limp tail.

Headlights appeared from the east. "Here come the deputies now," the Sheriff said. Yellow clearance lights became visible above the approaching headlights, bouncing over the rough road.

A small cloud of brown dust moved ahead of the bus and danced in the bright glare of headlights as the bus stopped behind the cars. On the bus' side a sign proclaimed, "First Baptist Church, Pearsall, Texas." The door unfolded, and twenty uniformed deputies filed out. As quickly as the last man stepped out, the door folded shut, the motor grew louder, and the bus moved away. As the whine of gears changed pitch, the five red lights on the bus' rear grew smaller in the distant darkness.

The deputies, half carrying rifles, and half carrying shotguns, and all with side arms, stood at ease, facing the Sheriff like a platoon of soldiers before a drill sergeant.

The C.B. radio in the Sheriff's car squawked to life. "Break twenty-two for the Purple People Eater. How about it, Purple People Eater?"

The Sheriff stood and addressed the deputies. "Okay, men, we just got word that the trucks are coming in to the airport. . ."

"One more time for the Purple People Eater," the radio squawked again.

". . . This is Ranger Garcia, who will be coordinating this operation," the Sheriff said, projecting his voice. Then he lowered his voice and spoke to Gar. "You want to speak to these men?"

Gar stood straight and looked over the group. "I guess you men are about ready to learn why you're here. If word of this operation gets out, you can be assured nobody will blame you.

"We're expecting a DC-Three to set down here tonight and we have reliable information that it will be full of contraband. We've learned that trucks have entered the airport, probably to load the grass when the plane lands.

"We want to confiscate the airplane, the trucks, and the grass, and to arrest all the people involved. We don't want to hurt anybody if we can help it, so please, don't anybody fire a weapon unless it is absolutely necessary. We especially don't want you shooting each other, or the Sheriff, here," Gar continued.

Some of the deputies chuckled under their breath. "Aw shucks," one said.

"Seriously, we don't want anybody to get hurt, so follow proper procedure," Gar said, and explained the plan of action.

The deputies moved to a rusty barbed wire fence and began crawling through. Mumbles of conversation filtered back. The Sheriff put his hands to his mouth and called under his voice, "Keep it down."

"Break twenty-two for Sweet Sue. How 'bout it Sweet Sue," the radio squawked.

The Sheriff reached for a note pad on the dash of his car. "What's Sweet Sue?" He asked nobody in particular. He turned on the dome light and held the paper toward it, then announced, "Sweet Sue. The plane has been spotted over Laredo. It'll be here in twenty minutes or less."

Montgomery handed Gar a leather-covered, walkie-talkie radio. Gar, the DPS officers, and the Sheriff spread out and made their way quietly toward the main hangar. Gar and the Sheriff stationed themselves around the corner of the building and out of sight.

Four yellow trucks, with the names of different truck rental companies on their sides, gathered under the glow of a pole light like overgrown chicks in an incubator. The dark figures of two men stood at the far edge of the circle of light, peering into the south sky.

Suddenly one of the dark figures ran across the circle of light to the office in one corner of the corrugated iron hangar building. He jerked the door open, and called in Spanish.

On each side of the north-south runway, a row of orange lights came to life. The sound of airplane engines droned away the night's silence.

"It's a shame that a plane with such a history has come down to hauling dope," the Sheriff said under his breath.

"They've been working a long time, haven't they?"

"Since Nineteen Thirty-seven," the Sheriff's voice sounded far away. "I flew one in World War Two. DC-Threes were in action all over the world, Africa, Asia, Europe, and the Pacific Theater. Now, after forty-one years of being useful, it's hauling dope."

"Maybe we can confiscate this one and reform it."

Gar watched from the dark corner of the hangar building as a single landing light shone brightly from one wing of the approaching plane.

A deputy on the far end of the runway froze in his high grass nest as the bright light came in from the north. Two fat black tires hanging low on ladder-like landing gear barely cleared the mesquite trees on the end of the runway. The wheels of the plane touched down on the grassy runway and the plane bounced up and down as it rolled over the uneven surface. The slowed engines rattled hollowly. The tail dropped to the runway and rode on a small wheel. The plane waddled down the wavy, grass-covered runway. Then the pilot revved the engines, and with a roar and taxied toward the spot of light and yellow trucks.

When the plane stopped, a side door opened, and a man stuck his head out, waved, and yelled in Spanish. Four men ran toward him. A yellow truck's engine roared alive, and its driver backed it to the door of the plane

The deputies lay still, watched and listened to the conversation of the smugglers over the low-pitched coughing of the DC-Three's idling engines. For thirty minutes the men hefted bales of marijuana and loaded them into the truck.

Gar extended the antenna on his walkie-talkie, and with his mouth close to the microphone, said, "Stand by Fifty-two."

The truck moved away from the plane. A dark-complexioned man with an automatic pistol stuck in his belt, jumped down from the plane door and closed the truck's tall yellow doors. The truck's engine revved and the truck headed for the airport exit.

Gar spoke into the radio again, "Fifty-Two, execute. Do it now." He hooked the radio onto his belt and leaped forward, drawing a forty-four from his right holster as he ran.

"Police. Stop where you are, and raise your hands. *Alto. Manos arriba*," he shouted. The six patrolmen fanned out on each side of him, their shotguns at the ready. Deputies from each side converged on the plane and trucks.

The man who had just closed the truck's doors

stood still in shock. His jaw dropped. A line of deputies with raised shotguns advanced. An officer shouted, "Police. You're under arrest. Raise your hands. *Esta arrestándola. Manos arriba.*"

The door of the plane slammed shut and the motors roared. The truck went faster. The plane moved forward. A staccato of shots rang out from both sides of the runway. The plane's left wing lurched downward as the left tire went flat. The plane continued to move, turning left. More shots. The right tire went flat, and the right wing vibrated as it went down level with the other.

The pilot looked through the window into the barrel of a shotgun and turned off the engines. They coughed and quit. Officers continued to shout orders to the smugglers. The hollow hum of the truck's engine faded in the distance.

"Open the door," deputies at the door of the plane demanded. The door opened a crack and a voice shouted from inside, "Hey, man. Don't shoot. We ain't got no guns in here."

Meanwhile, northbound on Interstate 35, a flat-nosed, blue and white semi-tractor trailer rig's tires hummed in loud monotony. Its C.B. radio interrupted the steady stream of mechanical noises. "How about it, Bedbug? You still up there?"

The driver snatched the microphone from its hangar. "Ole Daddy Bedbug is still up here, just passed that Pearsall town."

Suddenly a highway patrol car sped past him.

"There's a Smokey coming up behind you with the hammer down, Bedbug," the C.B. spoke back.

"Man, he just passed me like I was backing up," the

driver said.

The patrol car's rear turned bright red as the brake lights came on, and the car slowed, then turned left, bouncing across the grassy median, across the southbound lane, and bounced over a shallow grass-lined ditch and onto the service road. The patrol car sped over the service road and into the drive leading to the Frio County Airport. All four wheels locked as the car skidded to a stop, blocking the gate.

"You wouldn't believe what that Smokey just did. . ." The semi-truck driver said into the C.B. microphone. The big truck continued northward, its tires and motor noises reflecting off the hard concrete highway into the distance.

The yellow rental truck that had so hastily left the plane sped down the narrow road. Two men armed with M-16 rifles ran down the dark road toward the airport. They jumped out of the way of the oncoming truck. The truck sped by them. "Hey, man, what's happening?" the older one shouted after the truck. Faintly visible through the trees, red lights flashed like far away Christmas trees. "Cops," he shouted.

"I'm not shooting it out with any cops," the younger man exclaimed. "I came to guard against hijackers. . ."

"You'll do what you're told."

"I'm leaving," the youth offered his rifle to the other man.

"Shut up. You're not leaving."

The youth calmly took out his handkerchief, wiped the rifle clean, and dropped it at the other man's feet. Before it hit the ground the other man hit the youth with the rifle butt, opening a gash on his chin. The young man turned and ran into the brush. The other man flicked off the safety and aimed at the fleeing youth, took a deep breath, exhaled, and then lowered the rifle.

The younger man faded into the darkness and disappeared among the mesquite trees.

The older man looked toward the flashing red and blue lights of the DPS car in the distance. He hastily wiped the rifle on his pants and threw both rifles into the weeds beside the road. He ran into the brush.

The yellow truck skidded to a stop just short of the patrol car blocking the road. Four patrolmen jumped out. The driver of the truck bowed his head and let his chin rest on his hands clamped on the steering wheel. Excitement gave way to resignation. Easy money turned into a trip to jail.

An officer jerked the door open. "Out," the officer shouted.

Meanwhile in the airport building, a slight man with dark complexion, straight black hair, and brown eyes so dark they seemed black, sat on the edge of a desk. Beside him small red lights danced on two radio scanners. The loud reports of shots fired outside aroused him. He sat upright and vaulted off the desk. He grabbed for an M-16 rifle on the table, but stopped short.

A twelve-gage shotgun barrel burst through a window pane, sending glass flying before it. "Police. Stand where you are. Raise your hands." The voice came from behind the shotgun. The door burst open. Gar rushed in with a cocked forty-four Colt in his hand. "Against the wall. Quick." Gar grabbed the young man's arm and pushed the suspect toward a wall. "I want to see this guy who claims he's Reynaldo Diaz."

Chapter 26

The Raid

A patrolman burst into the airport building behind Gar, and the shotgun barrel disappeared from the broken window.

The suspect leaned with the flat of his hands against the wall. The patrolman tossed his shotgun from right hand to left, and kicked the suspect's feet back and farther apart. Gar eased the hammer forward on his forty-four, and holstered it. He frisked the suspect and fished a switch-blade knife out of his pocket. Gar jerked the man around to face him.

"Johnny Diaz," Gar exclaimed.

Gar pressed the button on Johnny's knife and a six-inch blade flashed out and locked. For an inch back from the point, the blade showed both edges had been sharpened. Gar used the knife to cut the cords that bound the old caretaker of the airport.

"Boy am I glad y'all are here," the man said, and sighed with relief. He reached to his eyes and pulled off the tape. "I couldn't imagine what was going on. What's happening?"

"They just landed a DC-Three full of marijuana, and were loading it into trucks," Gar said.

"Oh. I couldn't figure it out. These guys came in with knives and guns and tied me up, and put that tape over my eyes. Then I just heard calls on the police radio for a while, and these guys speaking in Spanish. It just didn't add up," he shook his head. "But now it does. I'm glad you're here."

The patrolman read the suspect his rights and sat him down on the chair that had previously held his own prisoner.

"What's your name?" Gar asked.

No answer. The suspect stared into space.

"What's your name?"

Still no answer.

"I'll tell you your name and I'll tell you where you're going to spend the next ten or fifteen years," Gar said.

"We was ratted on by a traitor, and now we're being busted by another traitor," Johnny spit out the words.

Gar reacted as if Johnny had released a coiled spring. "You are a disgrace." Gar jabbed an index finger toward the suspect's nose. "You're a disgrace to America, where you hold citizenship. You're a disgrace to the Mexican-American people you claim to be loyal to. You're a greedy criminal who hides behind a political cause. And you've fooled a lot of people. But you haven't fooled me." Gar's pointed finger punctuated each accusation.

"Now I don't want any song and dance with you, Diaz, I just want some answers," Gar said with contempt. "I'm not even going to ask you about this contraband haul; we've got you cold, we've got your people, your plane, and we've got your stuff. You've had it.

"I want to know about your brother, Reynaldo. Who killed him? And why?" Gar asked, as he grabbed another chair, swung it around and sat down face to face with the suspect.

"You killed him," the suspect blurted.

"Listen, Johnny," Gar's voice softened. "You're facing a long time in the pen. We might be able to put in a good word with the judge if you'd come up with some good solid evidence to help us find out who pulled your brother's head off," Gar said.

"Drop dead and rot," Johnny snarled like a cornered animal.

The door swung open and the Sheriff stepped in. "We've got everything secured out there." He looked at the suspect. "Are you Johnny Diaz?"

The suspect sat silently.

"That's him," Gar affirmed. Then to the patrolman, "Put the cuffs on him and bring him on."

The patrolman none too gently turned the suspect around and handcuffed his hands behind his back.

The Sheriff stepped outside, followed by Gar, the handcuffed Johnny Diaz and the patrolman. The large, yellow bus whined in a low gear up the drive and stopped in front of the office. The door unfolded and deputies ushered their prisoners into the bus.

The bus driver shouted through his open window as the Sheriff approached. "Looks like you made a good haul, Sheriff."

"Think so," the Sheriff said, and stopped. "Gar, this is our Chaplain, Brother Buford Post."

"Howdy." The driver waved a hand.

"Howdy, Brother Post," Gar said. He and the Sheriff walked around the bus. "Is he a reserve deputy?" Gar asked.

"Yes. All these deputies here tonight except Montgomery are reserves."

"You've got an army here, Sheriff," Gar said.

"Sometimes you need one," the Sheriff said, leaning back with one foot against the bus bumper.

"They seem to be well-trained," Gar said.

"They are. They're trained, sworn, and bonded. The only difference between them and my full time deputies is that these guys don't get paid. When not on duty, they're ordinary citizens."

"I think you've got a good thing going here," Gar commented.

"We've got another crop coming up too," the Sheriff said. "The Explorer Scouts have thirty boys in our law enforcement program. They manned a string of C.B. radios and a phone network from here to Laredo tonight, and reported the plane's position."

"I'd say you have a well-organized posse," Gar said.

"I think so. It's citizen involvement, the Sheriff said. "It's fashionable to be straight in Frio County."

Johnny, with his hands cuffed behind him, stepped into the bus.

"Do you think Johnny Diaz had anything to do with his brother's murder?" the Sheriff asked.

"Not really," Gar said. But we've got to check every possibility."

At the county jail, Gar had two of the arrested men brought into an interrogation room. "You guys still smell like grass," Gar said to two men lounging on chairs at the table.

"It was your idea, man," the speaker stroked a short, black goatee. "Ain't that right, Santiago?"

"Sure, *hombre*, we just done like you told us."

"Pedro, what's this business about Diaz not being dead?"

"Course he's not dead. You just arrested him,"

Santiago, the beardless one answered.

"That was Johnny Diaz, not Reynaldo," Gar exclaimed.

"He told us he was Reynaldo. He looked just like Reynaldo's picture in the paper. We thought he was the big shot," Santiago said.

"Johnny Diaz told you he was Reynaldo?"

"Yes. How was we to know? We don't know no big shots in the *La Gente Unida*," Pedro again stroked his goatee. "Man, you ought to be grateful. We risked our lives to get information to you."

"You swore in an affidavit that Reynaldo Diaz organized and ran this grass smuggling operation," Gar's voice got louder.

"He told us he was Reynaldo," both Pedro and Santiago echoed each other.

"How'd we know he was just playing big shot?" Santiago said.

"What did you call him?" Gar asked.

"He liked to be called Mr. Diaz," Pedro answered. "We usually just called him *El Patron* or Mr. Diaz."

"You guys have sure put me in a spot. I arrested Reynaldo Diaz for something he didn't do. Now he's dead."

"We didn't do it. Johnny did it. He claimed he was Reynaldo. How was we to know? They look so much alike?" Pedro whined.

Friday, Day Three

It took until three in the morning to book the prisoners into the County Jail. Gar spent another hour writing reports, the part of police work he disliked most. At four a. m. Gar rented a room from the sleepy owner of a small motel in Pearsall.

He fell asleep leaning against the ceramic tile wall in the hot shower, then popped awake. He lay in bed wide awake for a half an hour. He again felt the same unease he had experienced on the island on Lake Texoma. *Maybe it's the loose ends.* Maybe his subconscious had been trying to tell him something about Johnny Diaz all along. *I'll tie up those loose ends tomorrow,* he thought, too tired tonight. He chuckled inwardly, thinking of Scarlet O'Hara in *Gone With The Wind,* saying, "I'll think about that tomorrow."

He fell into a deep sleep.

Saturday, Day Four

The phone's loud rude ringing startled Gar awake. Morning light flooded in the motel room through thin red curtains. He reached for the phone.

A bored voice came over the phone. "It's eight o'clock, sir."

"Okay. Thank you," Gar said, barely over a whisper.

Two doors from the motel, a white frame residence had been converted into a café, and added on several times. A sign advertised home-made bread, steaks, chicken, fresh farm-raised catfish, and breakfast served all hours. Men dressed in work clothes and cowboy boots drank coffee and talked about cows.

Gar chose a booth in the corner. He sat in a deep indentation in the plastic-covered seat. He didn't fit the hole, so he slid over next to the wall.

"Would you like to see a menu, sir?" a fortyish woman with half gray hair, offered a small dog-eared menu.

"No thanks. I know what I want."

She readied her order pad.

"Three eggs, over easy. . ."

"Coffee?"

"Yes. . . hash browns. . ."

"Cream?"

"Yes, and ham. . ."

"Thank you," she said, and started to leave.

"And a stack of hotcakes," Gar said.

The waitress stopped, turned to face Gar again, and poised her pencil over the pad. "Three eggs, over easy, hash brown potatoes, ham, and pancakes. Anything else?"

"Plenty of butter and syrup."

"All right. Anything else?" she said, as if ready to stay as long as necessary to get the whole order.

"That's all. I forgot to eat supper last night," he explained.

After breakfast, Deputy Montgomery drove Gar to San Antonio where Gar picked up his DPS car, a white, unmarked Dodge.

At 11:30 Gar arrived at Johnny Diaz's home, a typical, old frame house to which rooms had been added as the family grew into three generations. The house spread out across a wide lot, shaded by great pecan trees.

Three preschool children played in bare dirt in front of the porch. Unpainted boards of the front porch rattled as Gar walked on them, as did the door when he knocked.

A middle-aged woman answered the door. A younger woman, holding a baby, peered at Gar from behind her. Gar removed his hat and introduced himself.

"I guess you heard about Johnny being arrested, Mrs. Diaz."

"I heard. His lawyer called me," she spoke with a combination Mexican and Southern accent.

The children ran noisily upon the porch, stood back and looked at Gar.

"Mrs. Diaz does Johnny, or your husband have a shop?" Gar asked.

"Yes."

"I would like to check some things in it."

A higher-pitched female voice came from behind the older woman, "You got a search warrant?"

"This is Johnny's wife, Debbie," Mrs. Diaz said.

"No, I don't. I don't want to search the house, just the shop. But I can get a search warrant if necessary."

"I'll have to call my lawyer first," Mrs. Diaz said.

"Okay. I'll wait."

The porch squeaked as Gar shifted his weight from one foot to the other. The children stood a few feet away, pointing toward his shiny guns, whispering and giggling.

In a few minutes, the older woman returned and gave permission to check the shop. She led Gar to a freestanding, wooden building in the back with a sagging door. He found several woodworking machines: a wood lathe, a table saw, various sanders, drills, and saws, but no router or chain saw. He picked up shavings and sawdust from different parts of the shop and dropped them into small plastic bags.

Chapter 27

San Antonio Rose

In far north San Antonio, the owner of the San Antonio Rose Motel sat in the sales manager's office of a Cadillac dealership. The showroom smelled of new rubber and new cars. Rose smelled of a double dose of expensive perfume.

"Okay," the sales manager began, pointing to written figures on a printed form. "We're allowing a thousand dollars for your trade-in. That makes a difference price of twenty-five thousand dollars. We'll have to have at least another fifteen-hundred down. . ."

"I'll pay cash," she said in a throaty voice. Her perfectly coiffed hair matched heavy make-up and tight red dress that showed generous curves.

"Cash?"

"Yes."

"Okay. Then there's a thousand and forty dollars sales tax. We'll pay for the title and license, and a full tank of gas. So we'll need twenty-six thousand, forty dollars, and the title to your trade-in," the sales manager said.

The woman squared her tightly-swathed bottom in the chair and set her alligator purse on the desk. She withdrew the cash from brown envelopes. "That ought to do it."

"Yes," the sales manager said with astonishment. "That will do very well."

The woman pulled a beat-up, white, square envelope from her purse and withdrew a pink-tinted document. "Here's the title."

"Business must have been good lately."

"Extra good," she said. "Trash these, will you?" she asked, handing him the three empty brown envelopes. "I've been saving up, too."

Meanwhile in another San Antonio motel Thomas nursed his wounded arm and cursed Steve Pierce. He opened his wallet and counted forty dollars. He cursed Steve Pierce again.

"Yea. Deluxe Motel on Alamo Street," he said into the phone. "To the airport. Make it snappy, will you. I've got a plane to catch."

"Any luggage?" the cab driver asked.

"No luggage," Thomas answered and sank into the back seat of the yellow taxi.

An hour later the taxi entered the airport. "Over to short term parking," Thomas said.

The driver drove slowly through the parking area. "There it is the blue van. See it?"

The driver turned off his meter, and turned to face Thomas. "That'll be forty dollars."

"Forty dollars," Thomas exclaimed. "That can't be right."

"That's it, buddy. I drove you clear across town in heavy traffic. Now pay up."

Thomas drew his .38.

"Now just a minute..."

Thomas shot the man in the face. He slumped down in the seat. Thomas took a wad of bills out of the driver's pockets and tried to get the coins out of a dispenser on his belt. Unable to get the coins out except one at a time, he cut the man's belt. Thomas wiped clean everything he had touched in the taxi, took the coin dispenser with him, and drove away in the blue van.

    Another yellow taxi stopped in front of the Diaz home. Johnny bounded noisily across the front porch and pulled on the door. He banged the door with a fist. "It's me. Let me in."
    "Oh Johnny, I'm so glad you're out." Mrs. Diaz said as she opened the door.
    His wife ran to the door, handed her baby to Mrs. Diaz and embraced her husband.
    "You made bail awful quick," his mother said.
    "I gotta go," Johnny said, prying away his wife's arms. He ran inside.
    "You just got here," his wife pleaded.
    "Gotta go," Johnny called behind as he grabbed a garment bag, a rifle, and box of shells from a closet. His wife cried. His mother cried. Johnny ran to an old, black pickup truck parked in the yard, and drove away

Chapter 28

Homicide Exclusion

In the Masters Building in San Marcos, Blitzboggen stood, holding his overstuffed briefcase, and beheld the Masters Oil Company's model receptionist. "You can go in now, Mr. Blitzboggen. Just go down that hall," she said, motioning toward Masters' office.

Joann Rainey, Masters' secretary, looked at the approaching Blitzboggen through her large, monogrammed glasses, greeted him in her nasal monotone voice, and ushered him into her boss' office.

Masters' big hand enveloped Blitzboggen's. "How do you do, Mr. Blitzboggen? Won't you have a seat?" Masters smiled, accentuating his three dimples. A white, short-sleeved, Christian Dior shirt, blue silk, striped tie, and blue slacks set off his tanned face. Masters' short hair stood at attention, but short blond and gray hair over his ears also accentuated his golf course tan.

Blitzboggen sat down and reached for papers in his overstuffed briefcase. The secretary handed Masters several file folders.

"I have some good news and some bad news about your wife's insurance," Blitzboggen began, and laid several sheets of paper on the desk. "Her whole life policy will pay. It has a homicide exclusion, but only for the perpetrator of the homicide. However, the accident policies and credit life policies won't. They have homicide exclusions. They won't pay if the insured was a victim of homicide."

"Her death is a great loss to our company," Masters said sadly. "I had hoped at least the credit life policies and the 'key man' policy would pay."

"I'm sorry." Blitzboggen pushed a form toward Masters. "I have a check here for the regular life policy, paying in full. Please sign this."

"What's this?" Masters asked, and laid the file folders on the desk. He picked up the form.

"It's a release for the companies we represent," Blitzboggen answered.

"I won't sign it," Masters said firmly. Then added with a smile, "You never know what might happen. They might change their minds."

"Not a chance," Blitzboggen said with finality.

"Thank you for coming in, Mr. Blitzboggen," Masters said, and stood.

Blitzboggen stood and laid the check on a file folder marked "MYT vs TRFI."

Masters swooped up the check and handed it back. "No hurry," he said. "I don't want to close any doors in case there is a change. You see, our company will suffer greatly from the loss of my wife's talents. We really should be able to collect on the insurance."

"The homicide exclusion has always been there," Blitzboggen said, accepting the check. "Any time you're ready, you can have this back."

"I'll let you know," Masters said.

After Gar's last stop questioning leaders in the *La Raza Unida* party in northwest San Antonio, he found himself close to his parent's home at six o'clock. Gar quickly drove to the home where he had grown up. Like the

Diaz home, it had been added on as the family grew, and the two-car garage had been remodeled into a large den. The entire wood frame structure had been covered with gray composition siding that was supposed to look like stone.

Gar drove down the street to an intersection, made a U-turn and parked on the opposite side of the street from the house and seven other cars parked at the curb and in the drive.

Without knocking, he walked into the living room. The aroma of roast beef enriched the air.

"Hey, Uncle Enrique." A slender twelve-year-old girl, with long black hair ran to him and hugged his neck. Gar's mother came from the kitchen, wiping her hands on a paper towel. A typical Mexican-American grandmother: slightly overweight, busty, black hair streaked with gray, gave Gar a big smile and motherly hug.

"We've been trying to get ahold of you. We're getting ready to have Junior's birthday dinner, and wanted you and Liz to come. Where is Liz?"

"Liz is in San Marcos. I'm on my way there now," he said, giving his mother a squeeze. "Good to see you, Mama."

Sisters and sisters-in-law came from the kitchen carrying bowls of food to the den. Each in turn smiled and spoke.

"Hey, Enrique. You made it after all," Gar's father entered from the den. He grabbed Gar's hand, shook it vigorously, and patted his son roughly on the shoulder. At five-ten, George Garcia was an inch shorter than Gar, and carried a slight paunch. Under a Roman nose and close-trimmed gray mustache, Mr. Garcia smiled easily and often. His full head of gray hair fell over the ears and combed straight back. "Where's Liz?" he asked.

Gar's descended from Spanish settlers who had moved to San Antonio in 1765. His great, great, grandfather had fought at the Alamo for Texas independence. Gar's maternal grandmother, however, had crossed the Rio Grande illegally and had been considered a "wetback."

Gar's family had been well-assimilated into mainstream Texas society, with the exception of his younger brother, Joe, who had become involved in a "Chicano Consciousness" movement, and alienated from the mainstream.

Eight-year-old Enrique charged into the room, "Hi, Dad." Gar bent over and hugged him. "Where's Mom?"

"She's in San Marcos. I'm on my way there now. Just finished a case in Frio County."

Gar's older brother, George Junior, threaded his way through the welcoming committee. "You're going to stay here for my birthday dinner aren't you?" he asked, extending a hand to Gar. Junior was a younger carbon copy of his father. His hair and mustache showed only a few gray hairs among the black.

"Hi, George. Sure I'll stay. As a matter of fact, I'm starving."

Chapter 29

The Stalker

Johnny's old black pickup slowed as it approached the Garcia home. Johnny drove past Gar's car parked on the curb, and turned left at the next corner. He turned into an alley and drove slowly through the alley until Gar's car and Gar's parents' home came into view. Johnny turned off the motor and silence enveloped the alley. He raised the rifle, pointing it through the pickup's window, and found the Garcia's front door in his telescopic sight. He lowered the rifle, and waited.

At the dinner table in the Garcia home, Gar's younger brother, Joe raised his voice.

"I don't even like the term, Mexican-American," Joe said. "It's like a guinea pig. It's not a guinea, and it's not a pig. We're Chicanos," he said proudly.

George, Jr., sitting next to his father, beckoned with a hand. "May I say something?"

Joe ignored him and continued. "Here's a good example of how our people were ashamed of their heritage," he said gesturing with a bowl of candied yams that had been passed to him. "Grandpa named Dad 'George' instead of *Jorge*.'"

"Hey. Just a minute," George, Jr., raised his voice. "Let someone else say something, Joe. This is my birthday; besides, I'm bigger and older," he said with a smile.

"How old, Uncle George?" a cute niece demanded.

"Forty. Life begins at forty, sweetheart," he

answered. Then his smile left. "Listen. Things are a lot different now than they used to be. When I was a kid, I went to South Texas to get rich working in the oil field. You know why I couldn't get a job?" He didn't wait for an answer. "Because I was a 'Mexican.' They didn't ask me if my great great, I forget how many greats, great-grandfather came to San Antonio in Seventeen Sixty-five. I just couldn't get a job in the oil field, where the real money was, because I was a 'Mexican.'" His father handed him a large platter of sliced roast beef, which momentarily diverted George's attention.

"Things are far from all right now," George, Jr., continued. But they're a lot better than they used to be." He stabbed a large slice of roast, and passed the platter. "A lot of Spanish people quit acting like a nation within a nation. And some Anglos developed a more sensitive conscience. Then there were new laws. Laws don't make people take a liking to other people, but they did make some people stop and think that these 'different' people were people too."

In the alley, fatigue overtook Johnny. He had been up all night. He relaxed in the pickup seat, and laid his head back, still keeping the target door in view. He dozed off and slept like a cold snake on a warm rock.

An old man, dirty in rags patrolled the alley looking in trash cans and gathering aluminum cans in a black plastic bag. He peered through the open truck window at Johnny sound asleep. The old man gently set his bag of cans on the ground and reached in through the window to Johnny's rifle. The old man gently pulled the rifle off Johnny's lap. He grunted and shifted his weight, but didn't wake. The old man left the bag of cans beside the pickup and hurried away carrying the rifle.

At the Senior Garcia's dinner table, Joe raised his hand and opened his mouth to speak.

"How'd you get that cut on your chin?" George, Jr., asked.

"I ran into a door," Joe said instantly.

George, Jr., poked a finger in Joe's direction. "I'm not through. Another thing that had a bearing on it is what the Blacks have done. I know. When we were kids I called them 'niggers,' and so did nearly everybody else. The worst insult you could give a Mexican kid was to call him a nigger. See, I've changed too," the smile came back. "I think Alex Haley's book, *Roots*, did more to help race relations than Martin Luther King, John Kennedy, Lyndon Johnson, and Joe Garcia, and all the *La Gente Unida* put together. It made people stop to think, me included, that other people have feelings too, they love their kids, and hope for better things for them."

Joe quickly swallowed a mouthful of wine and said, "Blacks don't have anything to do with this. *La Gente Unida*...," he began.

Mr. Garcia, who had been standing, busily carving the roast through all the oratory, terminated the rhetoric.

"Listen to me," he said. Mr. Garcia's family treated him with great respect. "Things happen slowly," he said. "There will always be different races of people living together: the Spanish, the Indians, the Anglos, the Germans, the Czechs, and now lately the Vietnamese. We're all here in this country, thank God, because it is the best place to be. Don't ever forget that," he punctuated the remark with a jab in the air with the knife.

Emotion filled the older man's voice. "Love your

family. That's what's important, now and for the future." He straightened, stabbed the fork and knife into the roast, and smiled. "Now sing 'Happy Birthday' to George."

In the alley, voices stirred Johnny awake.

"I don't know whose it is. It's been parked there for quite a while," a woman's voice came from behind a shrub-covered fence.

"Somebody's sitting in it," a man's voice said.

Johnny sat bolt upright. He looked around startled. He quickly started the motor and drove away. The alley opened to a cross street.

Meanwhile Gar fully satiated with home cooking, left his parents' home and drove away.

The old man, carrying the rifle, walked briskly, crossing the street. "*Ladrón cabrón* you stole my gun," Johnny shouted and floor boarded the pickup. The front bumper of the pickup hit the old man solidly. The rifle flew from his grasp. Johnny stopped the truck, got out, stepped over the old man's broken body and picked up the rifle just as Gar's white Dodge entered the cross street.

Seeing the crumpled old man on the pavement and Johnny Diaz with the rifle, Gar pushed down hard on the accelerator. Tires squealed as the Dodge lurched forward. Johnny got back in his pickup and drove away. Gar stopped to render aid to the old man. Blood flowed from his mouth, nose and ears. *He's still breathing.* He snatched the microphone of his car radio from its holder and called for an ambulance.

"Hang in there buddy. Ambulance is on its way."

Another car stopped, and a woman got out and rushed to the side of the old man. "I'm a nurse," she said. "Maybe I can help."

"Take care of him as best you can until the ambulance gets here. I need to report the hit and run."

Again the heavy Dodge lurched forward as Gar chased after Johnny Diaz. On his car radio, Gar gave a description of the black pickup. "I recognized the driver. Johnny Diaz. He was released on bail just today."

The black pickup had vanished out of sight. Gar continued straight ahead, looking carefully down each cross street. He glimpsed a black pickup on one of the side streets two blocks away. It turned the corner and again disappeared out of sight. Gar gunned the Dodge's Hemi V8 engine, turned on flashing red lights and hurried to the corner. As he rounded the corner, the black pickup again came into view. Gar's car rapidly gained on the old truck. When he got to within 100 feet of the black pickup Gar turned on the loud siren and yelper.

Johnny abruptly turned into an alleyway, too fast for a 90 degree turn. The pickup rolled over and came to rest upside down against a utility pole. Johnny scrambled out through a window as Gar drove up. Johnny vaulted over a board fence into the back yard of a modest frame home. Gar climbed over the fence to see Johnny disappear over the front side.

Gar rushed to the other side. A woman ran out the back door screaming, "What are you doing here. Get out."

"Police," Gar said and climbed up the fence.

"Hold it right there, or you'll get a back full of buckshot." A man with a 12 gauge double-barrel shotgun rushed toward Gar.

Chapter 30

Setback

With an excited man holding a shotgun at his back Gar released his hold on the fence, slid to his feet, and put up his hands. *This guy is nervous enough to pull both triggers.* "I'm a Texas Ranger, chasing a murder suspect."

"Maybe you are," the man said viewing Gar's badge. The man lowered the shotgun. "You can't blame us for being alarmed."

"No, I can't," Gar said. "The suspect is probably long gone."

Gar methodically made the rounds of Johnny's known associates. Except for Gar's two informants, Pedro and Santiago, the smugglers continued to refer to Johnny as "Patron," still thinking he was his brother Reynaldo. Authorized by a warrant, they allowed Gar to enter their homes and look.

Back in his car, Gar's beeper sounded. The number matched that of Pedro, one of his informants followed by "9-11." Silently but with red lights flashing Gar broke traffic rules all the way to Pedro's house. Rather than knocking, he shouldered the front door and burst inside. Pedro's body sprawled on the kitchen floor, his life's blood having drained through a deep cut on his throat.

The sound of a garage door motor whirred. Gar found the back door leading to the garage in time to see Pedro's car backing up at full speed. Johnny Diaz backed the car into the middle of the street and left a smell of burning rubber as he accelerated away.

By the time Gar got to his car Johnny Diaz was out of sight. Gar drove around for an hour trying to get a glimpse of the car. Johnny Diaz had slipped away. Since he had been to all the other smugglers' homes, he decided to go to Santiago's.

"Come in," Santiago said trembling. "Johnny killed Pedro, said he had ratted him out." Santiago sank down in a chair. "He bragged about cutting Pedro's throat." Santiago nervously lit a cigarette. "It won't be long before Johnny figures me out too."

"Johnny's going away for a long prison sentence or he'll get a hot shot. In either case, you won't have to be afraid of him."

"He thought I was still loyal. That's why he came here. He figured the cops would be looking for Pedro's car, so he took mine."

Cries of a child came from behind a closed door.

"My wife and kids are scared to death," Santiago continued. "Have you picked him up yet?"

"No, not yet. But there's an all-points bulletin out for him. Hundreds of officers in San Antonio and surrounding area are looking for him. He's wanted for a hit and run; ran over an old derelict. He's wanted for attempted murder because he and his brother Ben tried to kill me. Now he's wanted for Pedro's killing." Gar got a description of Santiago's car and license number and phoned the information to San Antonio P.D.

"I've got to go hide, and I'm afraid for my wife and kids. I don't want to take Pedro's car because I'd be stopped by the cops."

"Do you have a place to hide?" Gar asked.

"My wife's sister lives in Fredericksburg. She said

we could come there until they get Johnny. But I only have one car, and Johnny took it."

Gar got on the phone again and had a long conversation with his younger brother, Joe.

"Joe didn't have anything else to do. He's coming to take you and your family to Fredericksburg. I'll see that the State pays for the gas."

Chapter 31

Day Four, Trauma

In the Intensive Care Unit of San Marcos hospital, Rev. Albert bent over his wife's bed, holding her hand in both of his. "Oh, thank God," he said. "Do you know me, Sweets?" She now breathed without aid of the respirator. The tether that had held her tongue outside her mouth had been removed. The swelling in her head had gone down. Her eyes and face had black marks as if from a severe beating. Her eyes struggled to half open.

"Of course, I know you, Doctor," she mumbled slowly, her eyes a little more open.

"Doctor? It's me, your husband," he said, perplexed.

"You've got a doctor's degree, haven't you, husband?" she slurred accusingly.

"Well, yes."

She closed her eyes. He slapped her hand. "Wake up."

"I'm sleepy," she said slowly.

"Open your eyes, and talk to me," he said sharply.

"Okay, husband." Again she managed to get her eyes half open. "My tongue's so sore."

"Oh, but you can use it again, Sweets. And you're getting some color back into your face," he said, with elation. "And the doctor says we can expect full recovery." He bent his face to her hand and kissed it. "Thank God," he said. His eyes filled with tears. "Thank God."

At seven o'clock Gar phoned Liz from San Antonio. "I'm on my way."

Just short of the main part of San Marcos, he turned right under a white sign arching over the park road. He drove down a tree-lined lane to the long, white building of the inn lying next to the glittering water of the San Marcos River.

Over the San Marcos Police frequency, the female dispatcher called for all officers in the area to respond to a manhunt at the railroad switching yards. Steve Pierce had been spotted there.

Gar made a U-turn, drove back under the arching sign, and switched on two bright, red lights flashing through the car's radiator grille. He sped toward the railroad yards. Ten minutes later the car bounced over several railroad tracks, and came to a stop between Sherman's new Ford and a black and white police car.

"I hear you made a good bust at Pearsall," Sherman said, extending his hand to Gar.

"We got a plane load of grass, and both ends of the smuggling gang," Gar said. "Did you double-check the ID on Diaz?"

"Yes. It was him all right. Family, identifying marks. He'd never been arrested, so there were no print records. Dental records checked out. It was Reynaldo Diaz okay."

"Well, I just found out something that knocked me over," Gar said with embarrassment.

"What's that?"

"My two plants in the Diaz smuggling operation said Johnny was playing big shot and told them *he* was Reynaldo. So they swore that Reynaldo ran the contraband operation."

"So you don't have a case against Reynaldo Diaz," Sherman said.

"That's it. And the poor guy's dead. Man. I feel responsible." Gar shook his head and removed his hat. "Now Johnny Diaz has killed two more men, a poor bum and one of my informants." He paused downcast and then perked up. "What's this situation?" he asked, as he wiped his forehead. "A railroad detective spotted Pierce in an empty boxcar on the other end of the yard. We've got the yard surrounded. Some men are making a sweep now. We're hoping to flush him out on this end," Sherman said, motioning toward the tracks Gar had just crossed.

"Chief." Sam Arnold stood in the open door of the white car, and held a microphone on a black, spring cord toward Sherman. Sherman hurried with long strides and took the mike.

"I hardly recognized you, Arnold," Gar said. Arnold wore a gray jump suit, spotted with drips of white paint. His badge hung from a cord around his neck. A shoulder holster and automatic pistol under his left arm looked out of place tightly strapped around the loose jump suit. "The sweep team has just spotted him, and he's running this way," Arnold said.

Sherman motioned to three officers crouched behind parked cars on the opposite side of the acre of railroad tracks. "Keep sharp. He's coming this way," he shouted.

They waited.

Several minutes later, a ragged line of uniformed policemen emerged from the railroad yard, but no Steve Pierce. They swept back the other direction, searching every empty car, and every dark corner. They then fanned out to the alleys and streets in the area. Still they saw no sign of the suspect.

Meanwhile, an officer peered into a darkened boxcar. A pile of loose wheat lay in one corner. The officer shined his light on the wheat briefly, then left. Had he left the light on longer he would have seen the wheat breathe. Steve lay still with only his nose sticking out of the loose grain.

The officers made a final sweep of the yard and reported "saw nothing" to Sherman.

"How do you like our fashion model now?" Sherman asked, surveying Arnold's paint-speckled jump suit.

"I won't ask what you've been doing, Sam," Gar said.

"Frankly, I'd rather be home painting my den," Arnold said. "My wife and son accused me of arranging this emergency so they'd have to finish it."

"Got anybody watching the Pierce apartment?" Gar asked.

"Yes," Sherman answered. "We've got two men there, front and back."

"I'll go over there on my way back and have a look," Gar said.

"I think this is about over," Sherman said. "Sam lives close to there; would you mind dropping him off, so he can finish his den?"

"Glad to," Gar replied.

"I'll stay here and phase out this search," Sherman said.

Sam Arnold got into Gar's car. "They're probably

finished by now, but I might get home in time to move the furniture back and re-hang the pictures."

As Gar's car approached Pierce's apartment building, he saw a black and white patrol car parked across the street and a half block away. Gar stopped behind the car and got out. Arnold hit his knuckles on top of the police car as he walked around the other side. Leaning down to the open window, he spoke to the officer inside. "Hi. Seen anything?"

"Hi, Arnold," the officer said. He looked up from binoculars aimed at the Pierce apartment door. "Haven't seen a thing of Pierce. Some other people came and went, but there's been no sign of Pierce or his mother." The officer looked at Arnold's attire. "Never saw you dressed like that before."

Arnold introduced them. Gar reached a hand through the window to shake hands with the officer, then turned to Arnold. "Don't you want me to take you on home now?"

"No. I'll check it out with you. The den will wait another five minutes," Arnold said.

"Where's your partner?" Gar asked the officer.

"He's around back. There's a good spot there where he can watch, concealed in some bushes. He can see both the back door to the building, and the Pierce apartment's private back door," the officer said.

"We'll take a look," Gar said. "Then I'll take you home, Sam. It's midnight already." Gar and Sam Arnold walked toward the apartment building. "Then I'm going to take myself home shortly too. My wife's waiting for me at the Inn."

Chapter 32

The Fugitive

In the Pierce kitchen, two tiny brown Chihuahua dogs jumped up and down around Steve's legs as he pulled up a chair and sat at the breakfast table. The dogs' eager claws raked grains of wheat out of Steve's pants cuffs and onto the floor.

"Oh, Steve, Baby, I'm so afraid some cop will shoot you." Mrs. Pierce, dressed in a long silken robe, straightened his hair.

"I'm afraid I'll starve to death before that," Steve said weakly.

"Have you not had anything to eat?" Mrs. Pierce asked, moving toward the refrigerator.

"I haven't had anything since lunch Tuesday. I'm so weak, I can't hardly walk." Steve still wore the uniform that had been clean and starched on Tuesday, now wrinkled and dirty. Dried blood stained a long tear in the right pants leg.

"I'll fix you something," his mother said.

"No. Just give me a glass of milk, and maybe some bread. Right now milk and bread sound better than anything to me," he said.

Mrs. Pierce set a half-gallon carton of milk and a glass on the table. While she went back to the refrigerator, Steve poured the glass full and put it to his lips. He swallowed down half of the glass of milk before putting it down. "Oh, that's good," he said.

Mrs. Pierce set a bowl of cold fried chicken before

him, and a loaf of bread. He ate a piece of bread and drank the rest of the glass of milk. Steve picked up a chicken leg and took a bite, chewing it slowly.

"Did you see the police car out front?" she asked.

"Yes. I came in the back."

"Wasn't there no cop out there?" she asked.

"No. Nobody out back," Steve answered, pouring another glass of milk.

"Eat some more chicken, Honey."

"I'm full."

"How can you be full on one glass of milk, one slice of bread, and one chicken leg? You ate more than that when you were two."

"Guess my stomach shrunk, Mom."

Another person entered the main back door of the apartment building, a man with graying brown hair, and wearing a brown plaid sports jacket. The dim light dulled his facial features so Gar didn't recognize him in the distance. The obscure man examined each door as he walked from the back door down the hall.

Gar looked down the long hall and watched the figure as he knocked on the Pierce door.

Hearing the knock, Steve sat upright in alarm. Mrs. Pierce opened the door. "Yes," she said.

"Mrs. Pierce?" the man asked.

"Yes."

"I'm Don Thomas, with the FBI"

"Steve jumped straight up. The chair he had been sitting in fell over backward. The dogs scattered, yelping excitedly.

Gar hurried down the hall.

Meanwhile Arnold stood in the alley behind the building's rear door looking around for the officer on duty.

Thomas spoke through the partially opened door to Mrs. Pierce. "I'd like to speak to you a moment," Thomas said.

"No." Mrs. Pierce tried to close the door.

Thomas put his weight behind his shoulder and hit the door, sending Mrs. Pierce flying into the room. She fell over a coffee table. He ran past her.

Gar ran down the hall toward the Pierce apartment.

Steve ran out the apartment's private back door.

Seeing Steve run out, Arnold ran to meet him. Arnold opened his arms and grabbed the running youth. Steve stopped, and offered no resistance.

"Police. You're under arrest," Arnold said, and held Steve, who swayed, almost falling. Arnold held the young man, more to keep him from falling than to restrain him.

Thomas bounded down the board steps of the private rear entrance, gun in hand. Seeing Thomas coming, Arnold held Steve's wrist with his left hand and reached for his holstered weapon. "Police," he shouted.

"FBI," Thomas shouted, and continued to run toward the detective and his prisoner.

Sam Arnold hesitated.

No more than three feet away, Thomas shot Arnold squarely in the center of the chest.

Arnold fell to the ground. Steve reached with both hands and grabbed Thomas' gun hand. The panicky youth pulled the phony FBI man's hand to his mouth. Steve stuck his thumb under the sharp pointed firing pin on the .38's hammer. Steve bit down on Thomas' hand.

Thomas yelled and pulled the trigger on the .38. The firing pin punctured the web of Steve's thumb but did not connect to the cartridge. Blood ran over Steve's hand. He held the gun tight, and bit down harder on Thomas' hand.

Sound of the shot echoed through the apartment. The dogs barked. Gar ran through the apartment, past Mrs. Pierce struggling to her feet.

Gar reached the back door to see Arnold down and bleeding, and Thomas, cursing, kicking and punching Steve. Steve bit harder and hung on like a pit bull dog. Thomas pulled the trigger again, but again the firing pin hit Steve's flesh instead of the cartridge. Blood now covered the blue steel gun.

Gar cocked the forty-four and leveled it at Thomas' temple. "Drop it."

Thomas released his hold on the .38 and it fell from his hand. Steve released his bite on Thomas' hand. Steve pulled the hammer back on the .38, released his bloody thumb, gently let the hammer go back into safe position, and allowed the bloody pistol to fall to the ground.

Gar shoved Thomas to the ground. "Spread eagle. Quick," Gar ordered, then Gar shoved Steve to the ground beside him. "Lie down. Spread your arms and legs."

Both men quickly complied.

Still pointing his cocked forty-four in their general direction, Gar reached down to the bloody form of the man who had earlier been at home with his wife and son painting his den. Gar felt for the carotid artery. *No pulse.*

Thomas, without moving anything but his lips, said, "Listen, I'm with the FBI, let me up and I'll . . ."

"Shut up," Gar ordered. Then with emotion in his voice, said, "You twitch one muscle, and I'll consider it an attempt to escape."

The officer, who had been watching the front, ran around the apartment building with drawn service revolver.

"Oh, no. Arnold," he exclaimed. "Is he dead?"

"Yes, I'm afraid so," Gar said. "Get back to your radio and get some help out here . . . Cuff this one first," He said motioning Thomas. The officer handcuffed Thomas' hands behind his back. He started to roll over.

"Back on your face," Gar ordered. Thomas rolled back to his stomach, and again laid his cheek in the dirt.

Suddenly another uniformed officer came crashing through the bushes behind them, holding a walkie-talkie in one hand and a revolver in the other. "What's going on?" he asked breathlessly.

"You're late," Gar said. "Where've you been?"

"I had to go. Went to the little café," he said, motioning with his revolver back through the bushes. "You know how it is: when you got to go," he said plaintively.

Chapter 33

The Bust

Meanwhile Joe Garcia took the State Highway 16 exit off I-10. "There's a highway cop right on my bumper," he exclaimed. Red lights flashed. Joe stopped.

"May I see your driver's license please?" the Patrolman asked.

"Listen, I'm on an errand of mercy. My brother, Texas Ranger Gar Garcia sent me to take this family to safety..."

"Driver's license, please."

"Okay." Johnny fished his wallet out of his pocket and handed the driver's license to the Patrolman. "These people were afraid for their lives..."

"Who's van is this?"

"My father's."

"You were speeding, sixty-seven in a fifty-five mile an hour zone. I'll have to give you a citation."

"That's a crazy law, making people drive fifty-five. Everybody knows seventy is plenty safe on these interstate highways."

"I don't make the laws." The Patrolman continued to write on his pad of tickets.

"Well, you don't have to be so unreasonable in enforcing it."

"Here, Mr. Garcia," The Patrolman said, handing Joe the ticket.

"Thanks for nothing, pig," Joe retorted and turned the key to start the ignition.

"Just a minute." The officer reached past Joe and pulled out the key.

"What are you doing. You have no right."

"Get out of the vehicle."

Joe sat still stone-faced.

"Get out of the vehicle."

Joe sat still. The patrolman opened the door, grabbed Joe by the collar and pulled him out. The kids cried. Santiago's wife protested.

"Lean against the van. Spread'em." Joe leaned against the van with the palms of his hands. "I said spread'em." The Patrolman kicked Joe's legs farther apart, then searched his pockets. "Turn around."

Joe protested. The Patrolman expertly cuffed Joe's hands behind his back, shoved him into the caged back seat of the patrol car and locked him in.

"Do I have permission to search your van?"

"No."

"Either I'll search your van now, or I'll put you in jail and tow your car into the pound. Then I can get a warrant and search it there."

Santiago's wife screamed. "Please don't do that. My husband's best friend was just murdered, and they're after my husband. Please let us go."

Joe cursed the Patrolman, who went quickly to the van and opened both rear doors.

"Did he give you permission to search?" she asked.

"No, but if I find no contraband, I'll let you go." He searched the vehicle starting in the back and ending under the driver's seat. There he found a plastic baggie full of marijuana.

Chapter 34

Day Five, Evidence

At 1:30 a.m., Gar sat in his small office at San Marcos Police Headquarters. He braced his fatigued body with an elbow on the desk and rested his head on the telephone receiver.

"Sorry to wake you, Baby," he said softly into the phone, exhaustion apparent in his voice.

"You didn't wake me. Where are you?" Liz asked.

"I'm at the station. We just arrested the subject who had claimed to be an FBI agent, and Steve Pierce, the inside man. Detective Sam Arnold was killed."

"Oh. I'm sorry. I didn't know him," Liz said.

"He was a great guy, and a good officer. He had been painting his den with his wife and son. . . ." Gar's voice choked with emotion. He cleared his voice. "There was a foul-up. A man wasn't at his post. A terrible loss, and unnecessary."

"I'm so sorry for his wife," Liz said.

"Well, anyway, I won't be in for a while. We got these subjects and now we need to question them while they're fresh," Gar said. He straightened and stretched his free arm.

"One of these nights I'm going to pitch a fit like the cops' wives do on TV."

"I hope not, Baby."

"Well, not tonight anyway," Liz said, I'm too tired. Then she interjected, "By the way. A Lieutenant Posey from Internal Affairs came to see me today. Wanted to know all about what happened on Lake Texoma. Of course, I didn't know anything happened."

"Don't worry about it. I don't know what happened except that Ben Diaz drowned out there two-hundred yards from our island. He had a rifle strap twisted around his arm. So what was he doing out there with a rifle with a telescopic sight?"

"After you left, Enrique noticed the boat out there going around in circles," Liz said.

"Well, it's strange, but nothing for us to worry about," Gar said.

Liz yawned, "I guess I'll go to bed. Wake me when you come in."

"Okay, Baby. See you later."

"Bye."

Gar hung up the phone, stood to his feet, and stretched his entire body.

Sherman knocked on Gar's open office door and stuck his head in. "They're booked in now. You ready to question them?"

"I'm ready," Gar said, and stepped out the door.

As the two walked down the hall toward the interrogation rooms, Sherman said, "San Antonio P.D. got a positive match on prints in the San Antonio Rose Motel room. They're Donald Thomas Harmon's, alias Don Thomas, the known associate of the Hawk Nose subject who was run over by an eighteen-wheeler in San Antonio."

"Did they get an analysis on the dope?"

"Yea. The heroin in the motel room was pure. Dopers around here aren't used to that. One packet would have been fatal," Sherman pointed to a door marked with an "A," guarded by a uniformed officer. "Thomas is in there."

The officer nodded to Gar who handed him his guns. Sherman handed the officer his revolver. The officer put the weapons in small lockers, handed Gar and Sherman locker keys, and unlocked the door to the interrogation room.

Gar and Sherman entered the room to find Thomas, sitting on a heavy wooden chair with his elbows resting on a dark, heavy wooden table with a black composition top inlaid in the wood. Red swelling surrounded the red teeth marks. A thick gauze bandage covered his left forearm.

"Have you been advised of your rights?" Gar asked.

No answer.

"You have the right to remain silent. . . ," Gar began.

"Okay. I've been advised," Thomas interrupted impatiently.

"Why were you at the Pierce apartment tonight?"

No answer.

"What is your name?"

No answer.

"Do you know this man?" Gar asked, and laid a mug shot of Hawk Nose Giovan, on the table.

Thomas remained silent.

"Look, we know you and your partner here, Hawk Nose Giovan, alias John Grimes, were with Steve Pierce in a motel room in San Antonio Tuesday night. You left the motel room in such a hurry you didn't have time to clean it up. You left your fingerprints all over the place. You even left a heroin outfit behind, with a half-fixed hot shot," Gar paused.

Thomas rested his chin in his left hand. His swollen

right hand lay on the table. He looked straight ahead and said nothing.

"There's an officer there who can probably identify you as the one who shot his partner between the eyes. If we check under that bandage. . ." Gar pointed to Thomas' swathed left forearm. ". . . I'll bet we'll find a bullet hole put there by the partner of the cop you killed. We've got you cold on murder of a police officer here tonight."

Gar walked around the table, bent over, and looked Thomas straight in the eye. "You've had it, Thomas. You've bought yourself a one way trip to Huntsville and a hot shot of your own. You might just as well come clean, and help us clear up the sky ride murder."

Thomas continued to rest his chin in his hand and said nothing.

"We want to know why Reynaldo Diaz was killed," Gar demanded.

Thomas stared straight ahead.

Gar turned the suspect over to Sherman and left the room.

"Where's Pierce?" Gar asked the officer outside the room.

"Next door," the officer said, pointing to a door marked "B."

Like the first interrogation room this one had only one entrance and no windows, and furnished only with three chairs and a heavy table. In this room, however, the suspect lay on the table, sound asleep.

"Get off the table, Pierce," Gar demanded, and shook Steve's shoulder. Steve sleepily surveyed his surroundings, and swung his feet over the edge. "Have a seat," Gar said, pulling out a chair.

Steve sat down, put his elbows on the table, and rested his chin.

Gar sat down opposite him. "Tired?" he asked.

"Yes."

"Hungry?"

"No."

"How about a cup of coffee?" Gar asked.

"Okay."

Gar tapped on the door and asked the officer outside to send for coffee.

"Steve, I want you to start at the beginning, and tell me exactly what happened," Gar said.

"You mean from the killing or before?"

"I mean from the very beginning," Gar said.

"Well, I guess the beginning was Sunday when Don Thomas, who said he was an FBI Agent, came to see me at Clearwater Springs."

Gar interjected, "We found out his name is Donald Thomas Harmon. He was no FBI agent."

Steve told in detail of Thomas' visit, and his gift of $200. "I thought I was helping the FBI," Steve said.

After Gar finished questioning Steve, Gar stepped outside and inhaled fresh air as the new day dawned, then went back into his office where he met Sherman.

"I don't think we've really got any reason to hold Pierce," Gar said.

"You believe him?" Sherman asked.

"Yes. San Antonio P.D. bears it out. Also, Thomas had only one reason to come back here, and that was to kill Pierce, the chief witness against him."

"Let's go back in and talk to him," Sherman said.

They entered the interrogation room to find Steve again on the table, sound asleep. Sherman shook him, and got him upright on a chair.

"We'd like to believe you," Sherman said to the groggy young man. And we'd like to let you go, Steve, but we've got to have some assurances from you first. Ranger Garcia here believes you're telling the truth. I'm not too sure," Sherman said.

Steve raised his head to face Sherman. "Listen. I've done drugs. I did a robbery. I was arrested, and went to prison. But I'm not a criminal. This may be hard for you to understand, but it's not in my character to be a criminal."

Sherman and Gar each pulled up a chair and sat down.

"This is interesting," Sherman said. You did drugs and a robbery but you're not a criminal."

"For six months, around the time of my seventeenth birthday, I got messed up on drugs, and stepped out of character. I did things I never would have done otherwise. In prison I got my head straight, and realized what I had done. Even though I knew I deserved to be there, I felt out of place locked up with a bunch of criminals."

"That's the worst part of being in jail," Gar said.

Steve continued. "While I was in there I began to think about people and what they did. I realized that people had to work to grow crops so other people could eat, and how other people had to make things and fix things, and haul things, and there had to be doctors, and other experts to keep people going. I figured out that these people were all working together, even though they might not realize it.

"Then I saw how people who did what I had done were like disease germs in the general body." He paused, looked Gar in the eye, and continued, "I wanted to be part of the body instead of part of the disease, and decided that was my true character.

"Guys would sit around and plan jobs to pull when they got out. Lots of times they would invite me to plan with them. I felt that I was different. I didn't try to explain that to them. Instead, I just said, 'I don't like it in here. I like it on the outside better, and when I get out, I plan to stay out.'"

"I had lots of time to read in Huntsville. I read about patterning and self-image. My self-image is not that of a criminal."

Steve's voice grew stronger. "I would have died before I would have thrown in with Thomas and the little guy.

"Something else happened to me in Huntsville. I put my faith and trust in Jesus Christ, and became a born-again Christian. Society might not forgive me, but I know God has," Steve said, now wide awake.

"Jailhouse religion," Sherman muttered.

"Steve," Gar spoke up. "You're a valuable witness in this case. We could drop the suspicion of murder charge against you and still keep you in jail as a material witness. If we release you, would you stay in town and be available?"

"All I ever wanted to do from the beginning was just go home," Steve answered.

"What do you think?" Gar asked Sherman.

Steve looked expectantly to Sherman.

"Okay. I'm convinced," he said to Gar, then turning to Steve, said, "But you stay within reach. We'll need you to help identify the tall man, I hope," Sherman added.

"Does that hurt?" Gar asked, motioning to the thumb web of Steve's left hand that was swelling around two round holes left there by the firing pin on Thomas' revolver.

"Sure does."

"Since it was heroic action on Steve's part that he got that injury, don't you think the City can fix him up?" Gar asked.

"He's still a prisoner, and will be till I can get hold of the District Attorney to drop the charges. Let's take him to the hospital, and get him fixed up," Sherman said.

"*Vamos*," Gar said.

In the sterile Emergency Room, men and women worked quickly and efficiently. White uniforms made their flesh seem darker.

A matronly woman nurse, softly plump, with a kind voice, insisted that Steve lie on an examining table.

"I feel like a hog in the nursery," Steve said as he lay back on the table. His blond hair fell in dirty strings on the white sheet. A four-day growth of blond whiskers, and bags under his bloodshot eyes, made him look older than his twenty-one years. Plunging through a window glass and sleeping on damp dirt and in railroad boxcars had transformed the beige cotton uniform into a dirty rag.

A young doctor entered the treatment room. A nurse took shiny L-shaped scissors with blunt ends and began cutting through the black, blood-encrusted fabric of Steve's right pants leg. She pulled back the fabric to reveal a jagged twelve-inch cut, with dark red scab and spots of light yellow showing through thin skin, surrounded by red flesh.

"This is pretty badly infected," the doctor said.

Then looking up from the wound to the patient's face, he added, "We're going to have to do some work on this."

Steve held up his hand to show the holes in his swollen thumb web. "This is what hurts."

"We'll get to that later," the doctor said.

"I've got to go make some telephone calls," Sherman said.

"I've got to go visit some people," Gar said. "We'll be back."

Outside the treatment room door, Sherman spoke quietly. "I've seen a lot of gore, but I don't care about watching this. I'm going to call Steve's mother, so she can get him some clean clothes down here and take him home. I'll clear with the DA first."

"I'm going to Intensive Care to see how the Preacher's wife and Bernice Masters are doing. See you later," Gar said.

At the Intensive Care Unit, Gar pushed the doors. They opened to activity more like that of a stock exchange. A heated discussion of doctors and nurses around an instrument-crammed, central nurses' station gradually got louder.

"I'm sorry sir, you can't come in here," a woman nurse stepped briskly to meet Gar. Then noticing his badge, she asked, "Are you here on official business?"

"Yes, I am. What's the trouble?" Gar asked.

"We've just discovered that the electrical power to one of the patient's breathing machine has been disconnected," the nurse said.

A young orderly on the periphery of the group spoke up, "Somebody pulled the plug."

"Who was the patient?" Gar asked.

"Bernice Masters," the doctor answered.

"Don't let anybody leave," Gar ordered. "Is she all right?"

"Oh, yes. She's fine. She's been in a coma since Tuesday, but she's been breathing on her own all the time. The equipment that was disconnected was just standby equipment that would come on automatically if she stopped breathing. Fortunately she didn't," the doctor said.

"When did it happen?" Gar asked.

"Nobody knows. The cleanup orderly just discovered it a while ago, but since the machine was just for standby, and hasn't been in actual operation, it could have happened any time," the doctor said.

The doctor and nurses questioned the shaken young orderly.

Gar took a turn. "When did you clean previously?"

"Yesterday."

"Did you notice then if the machine was plugged in?"

"Oh, yes. It was plugged in then," he said.

"Did she have any visitors this morning?" Gar asked the group generally.

"Yes," a tall nurse spoke up. "We only allow visiting for five minutes on the hour, and she had several visitors this morning."

"Who were they?" Gar asked.

"I don't know. We don't ask."

"Could you describe them?"

"There was a man who came in early, right about the time I came on duty at seven. He was just in there a minute, then there were two older ladies." The nurse thought a moment. "At eight, there was a younger woman."

"What did she look like," Gar asked.

"About five-five, with black hair and big glasses."

"Little turned up nose?" Gar asked.

"Yes."

"Initials in the corner of the glasses?"

"Yes."

"What did the guy look like who visited early?"

The nurse looked puzzled. "Just a man." She thought a moment. "Just average, I guess. Didn't notice anything peculiar about him."

"How was he dressed?"

"Well, he had on a jacket. A light-colored sports jacket, open shirt collar, and darker trousers."

"Was he fresh looking, I mean clean. And did his pants have a crease?"

"No. As a matter of fact he looked like he had slept in his clothes, and his pants bowed out at the knees. He looked like he was getting ready to jump over a fence."

"Okay. Who visited at nine?"

"Well, now I remember. I knew him. It was her brother, Burke Masters. He's on the board of the hospital here. But I know he didn't do anything. I was in there with him all the time," she said.

Two detectives came through the swinging doors. Gar briefed them on what he knew, and went to the bedside of Bernice Masters. She remained asleep. He spoke to her, but she did not respond.

In Mrs. Albert's room, Gar found her awake. Black, blue and red splotches covered her swollen face.

"Hello," she said, in a soft voice.

"Hello, Mrs. Albert. I'm Texas Ranger Garcia. I'm so glad to see you awake. How are you doing?"

"Well, under the circumstances, I suppose," she said in a high-pitched, soft, and feminine voice. "My husband, Reverend Albert, sweet man, told me about the terrible murder."

"Can you remember anything about three men in dark suits with long sideburns and mustaches?" Gar asked.

"I noticed them, yes. My husband and I discussed it yesterday. I remember the tall man, how he perspired so profusely. And he had three bandages on his face." In a weak voice she went on to tell Gar everything she could remember about events leading up to the murder.

"I won't bother you any more, Mrs. Albert. Thank you," Gar said.

In Bob and Shirley Patterson's room, Gar found Bob and two men carrying on a heated discussion. Shirley's bed had apparently been freshly made. The two men stood by the new bridegroom's bed, both talking at once.

"Hello, Bob. I don't want to interrupt anything," Gar said.

"Oh you're not. It's all done," Bob said. He motioned toward a fiftyish man dressed in a gray business suit. "This is my father-in-law, and that's his lawyer."

Bob lifted a document; several legal-sized sheets of paper stapled to a blue document cover, and waved it toward Gar. "They want me to sign away my marriage," his voice grew louder. "My operation wasn't a success. I'm numb from the waist down, and will be the rest of my life, so they want me to annul my marriage," his voice choked with rage.

"We thought since the marriage was never consummated, and never could be, that Shirley should be free to marry again. You see the church. . . ," his father-in-law began, but Bob interrupted.

Bob's voice exploded with emotion, "Never consummated. It was too consummated. You want me to sign a lie. We were legally married and the marriage was consummated. There is absolutely no grounds for annulment." Then he relaxed, and his voice tone lowered. "I love Shirley, and she loves me."

"It's just a technicality. We have to have grounds for an annulment. She could never get a divorce," his father-in-law explained.

"You just talked to Shirley on the phone. This is what she wants," the lawyer interjected.

"I'm afraid this is none of my business," Gar said. "I'll talk to you later, Bob." Gar walked to the door. "Excuse me," he said, and left. Down the hall, Gar could still hear angry voices from the room.

"Here, give me a pen," Bob said angrily. "I'll sign it. Now get out of here you hypocrites," Bob screamed. Gar paused on his journey down the hall, and looked back to see the two men leave the room. He walked back toward the room and heard Bob sobbing. Gar paused outside the door, then went back into the room.

Gar told the distraught man to take his time regaining his composure, then patiently asked questions. Gar wanted to know what Bob had seen in the restaurant before the murder. Bob too had noticed how the tall man sweated so profusely in the cool air conditioned restaurant. "Those guys seemed to be making a tacky fashion statement. They acted secretive, but yet they had to want to attract attention." Bob thought a moment. "Suppose they were trying to divert attention from something else?"

"That's a good thought, Bob. A distinct possibility,"

Gar said.

Chapter 35

Recovery

In the Emergency Room Steve, dressed in clean, faded blue jeans and a white t-shirt, sat on a wheelchair by the checkout desk. His mother stood beside him.

"I can walk," he said.

"We'll take you out to your car," said a tiny young nurse, who looked admiringly at the patient through big, brown eyes.

"I can walk," Steve started to rise.

"Sorry, sir. It's the rules," the tiny nurse said with authority, and pushed him back into the seat. As she pushed the wheelchair, she smiled.

Sherman walked with Mrs. Pierce behind the nurse and the wheelchair.

"I'm certain we'll get the charges dropped, Mrs. Pierce. Right now, the only thing I can do is to release him on his own recognizance. I couldn't get hold of the District Attorney, but the Judge told me to go ahead and release him. And we'll talk to the DA tomorrow about dropping the charges."

The front wheels of the wheelchair bumped over an aluminum strip threshold onto a rubber mat. Two glass doors slid open.

Gar stepped off the elevator just in time to see Sherman go through the Emergency Room doors. He followed, and caught up with Sherman, who helped Steve into his mother's car.

"Let's go see Joann Rainey, Masters' secretary,"

Gar said quietly to Sherman.

Sherman turned to see Gar go by, and followed.

They got into Gar's car. "What's up?" Sherman asked.

Gar put the car in gear and accelerated. "Somebody's pulled the plug on Bernice Masters."

A startled look covered Sherman's whiskered face.

"She's okay," Gar said. "Most laymen wouldn't have known it, maybe, but the breathing machine in her room was just there for standby. That's what they unplugged. But it looks like somebody intended to kill her."

"You think Joann Rainey did it?" Sherman hit the foot-feed and the Ford accelerated into the busy street.

"She was there this morning, according to the nurse's description. . . black hair, short, turned up nose, big, monogrammed glasses," Gar said. "Of course there was another person there too, who could fit the description of Thomas, just medium in every way, and dressed like he was when he killed Arnold. If it was Thomas, and the nurse can identify him that will be a tie between Thomas and Masters."

The two lawmen stepped off the elevator on the fourth floor of the Masters Building. The large reception area had no flowers, no beautiful receptionist, and no people. They walked straight to the left door toward the hall that led to Joann Rainey's office.

"Wonder where everybody is," Sherman wondered.

"This is Saturday," Gar said.

"I've about lost all track of time," Sherman said.

"I needed a vacation before all this started," Gar

said.

At the end of the hall they found the second receptionist's desk as empty as the first. Without pausing or knocking Gar and Sherman rushed into Joann Rainey's office.

Mascara dissolved by tears left dark streaks down her baby face under the curly black hair. Joann Rainey held her glasses in one hand and a wad of tissue in the other.

"We'd like to ask you some questions, Miss Rainey," Gar announced.

"Ask," she said defiantly.

"Did you visit Bernice Masters in the hospital this morning?"

"Yes."

"Did you pull the plug on her respirator?"

Joann Rainey sagged to her chair. Tears filled her eyes and ran down her round cheeks. She quickly removed the glasses and applied the tissue. "Oh, no," she cried.

"Did you?" Gar asked.

"Oh, no. No. Is she dead?" She didn't look at Gar.

"No, she's not dead."

"Oh, thank God." She wept softly.

Gar and Sherman sat and waited.

Within a few minutes Joann Rainey dried her eyes and faced them. "I wouldn't pull the plug on Bernice. She's my dear friend. They told me this morning that she seemed to be doing better."

"You were crying when we came in just now," Gar said. "Why?"

"That's a private matter."

Sherman spoke up. "We have sufficient cause to take you to police headquarters for questioning, Miss

Rainey, and if you don't cooperate fully, that's the least that will happen. Now we want some answers," he demanded.

She wept again. The men waited.

"Why were you crying?" Gar asked again.

"It has nothing to do with you or your investigation."

"Let us be the judge of that," Gar said.

She dabbed her eyes, looked up, and said, "I'm a woman scorned," she said with a shaky voice and forced a shaky smile.

"Who scorned you?" Gar asked.

"I've been scorned, dumped, put aside, discarded."

"By whom?" Gar insisted.

"Burke Masters. I thought he loved me, but I was just a warm body. That's what he told me: *a warm body*. He has been telling me for the past two years that if he weren't inextricably married to Clara, that he would marry me. Well, fate took care of his marriage, and when I pressed this morning for a decision, I learned of my true status. Not even a person, let alone a person loved, just a warm body."

"Where is Mr. Masters now?" Gar asked.

"I suppose he's at home. He took his mother and aunt to the airport this morning, and then stopped here long enough for a short fight. I'm sure he went home," she said.

Gar stood to leave. "One more thing, Miss Rainey. Were you here Tuesday?"

"Yes."

"All day?"

"Yes, except for lunch. I was gone from twelve to one."

"Was Mr. Masters here all day?" Gar asked.

"Yes. We had lunch together. He spent the rest of the afternoon alone in his office. . ." She suddenly stopped speaking, caught her breath, and put a hand to her mouth.

"What is it?" Gar asked.

"Oh," she said, as if in pain.

Gar sat back down and waited, looking at her expectantly. Tears again filled her eyes. She removed her glasses and buried her head in her arms.

Gar looked at Sherman. Sherman looked at Gar, and shrugged his shoulders. They waited.

In a few minutes the sobbing stopped. She raised her head, daubed her eyes, and put her glasses back on.

"Well?" Gar asked.

"I just remembered. . . ," she cried again, but recovered more quickly this time. "I just remembered that about an hour after we returned from lunch, the day of the terrible murders, I forgot. . . I forgot that he had told me to hold all his calls, and that he was not to be disturbed under any circumstances. I went into his office. I had to use my key. It was unusual that he had locked the door. I went in and was surprised to see that he was gone. I even looked in his private rest room. But apparently he had quietly gone out the back and down the stairs."

Gar and Sherman stood quickly. They hurried toward the door. "Don't leave town. We'll want to talk to you again," Sherman said as they left.

Back in the car, Gar said, "This Masters smells worse all the time. We've been so busy; I haven't had a chance to ask. What did your boys find out about him?"

"Nothing really that seems to incriminate him.

"He's a real big shot about town, owns the office building, has a lot of stock in the Farmer's and Stockman's Bank, owns a bunch of oil leases in South Texas and New Mexico, and has an interest in some oil production in Peru. His wife was vice president of the corporation, although she didn't take an active part in management," he paused. "Oh, yes, and he's got a big ranch in South Texas, the 'MYT.'"

"Where in South Texas?"

"In Hidalgo County, near Edinburg."

"Ironwood," Gar exclaimed. "Ironwood is native to South Texas and Mexico, remember? Have you ever been hunting in native brush in that area?" Gar asked.

"No. What would you hunt there, anyway?"

"Oh, javelinas, for one thing, wild hogs. They thrive in that brush, in with the cactus, mesquite trees, and ironwood trees," Gar said with excitement. "Did you find out anything about Masters' debts, gambling habits, or anything like that?"

"He seemed to be clean, no gambling or heavy drinking. He's active in several civic clubs, and a strong anti-drug abuse group," Sherman said.

"Which drug abuse group?"

"Citizens Against Drug Abuse. He lost a couple of boys to substance abuse. One committed suicide and the other pickled his brain with solvent inhalation. Suppose that makes him a candidate to knock off Diaz?"

"Don't know. Could be."

"Lots of people are involved in that group, including our own chief of police. He does owe a lot of money," Sherman said.

"The chief of police?" Gar stepped into the elevator

and pushed the "B" for the parking garage.

"No. Masters," Sherman said. "Just a week ago, he sold his year-old Cadillac, bought a brand new one and then a matching pair of Mercedes Benz sports cars, at twenty-five thousand apiece, and he just made minimum down payments, and financed the rest," Sherman said. "Guess you can do that when you're a big stockholder in the bank."

"He owes two hundred thousand on his home. Just re-financed it three months ago; it was almost clear then. He owes a half million on the office building, but it's worth a lot more. As best we can tell, he has borrowed about a million dollars within the past six months, but it's all well-secured, and he doesn't seem to be in any bind," Sherman said.

"I wonder what he's doing with all that borrowed money. You sure he's not gambling?"

"Can't be sure, but as best we can tell he's reinvesting it in real estate and stocks."

"Any kind of criminal record or arrests?" Gar stepped aside and waved Sherman first out of the elevator.

"No. The only thing we could find from anybody was a Coast Guard investigation five years ago into a crew boat accident in the Gulf. Masters, with four technicians, were returning from a rig about twenty miles off Galveston. The boat's motor quit, and the radio went out. A storm blew up, and blew the boat another fifty miles out to sea. The search pattern didn't go that far, so the boat drifted for three days before it was sighted by a freighter. Masters was the only survivor. The four technicians and two crewmen were lost.

"Two of the bodies were recovered, and they both

had fractured skulls. Masters told the Coast Guard that the boat was tossed about so much that he was knocked unconscious, and when he came to, all the rest of the men were gone."

The car turned into the long, tree-lined drive leading to Masters' home. "If he's our man, this could fit the personality," Gar said. "Our killer would sacrifice six men just to stretch out emergency rations of water and food for himself."

"It still leaves motive for the Diaz killing." Sherman raked his hand over red whisker stubble.

"Yes. The target was his wife, and Diaz was just a diversion. How about insurance on his wife?"

"Blitzboggen says only a small, twenty-thousand-dollar policy. We haven't been able to uncover any others," Sherman said.

"There are all those credit life and accident policies that add up to over six million. But they have homicide exclusions, according to Blitzboggen."

"Suppose Masters was just stupid. Took out six million dollars' worth of insurance on his wife that wouldn't pay?"

"He's not stupid. He's got an angle, if he's our man."

"By the way," Sherman interjected, "Blitzboggen called for you today. Said he visited Masters."

"Oh?"

"Yea, he visited Masters and offered him the payoff on his wife's insurance. Masters refused to accept it, and acted like he didn't much care that the six million dollars' worth of other policies had homicide exclusions that wouldn't pay," Sherman said.

"He's got an angle," Gar said. He stopped the car in the circular drive of the Masters home. The Cupid fountain gurgled water that made music for tired minds.

No one responded to the doorbell or loud knocking. "If he's in there, he's not admitting it."

Sherman waited at the front while Gar walked toward the four-car garage.

"Anybody home?" Gar shouted in the direction of the garage.

"In here," came a voice from within. Gar motioned for Sherman and walked around the corner to find a door opening into the side of the garage.

"Hello, Mr. Garcia. What can I do for you?" Masters wore a yellow baseball cap with a blue, jumping swordfish emblem, a white canvas carpenter's apron over a blue knit sport shirt and faded blue jeans. He held an unfinished, walnut gun stock.

Gar surveyed the shop and noted various power tools, a table saw, scroll saw, wood lathe, bench sander, drill press, and a radial arm saw. Well-organized tools hung neatly over their painted shadows impressed Gar. The shop smelled of freshly cut wood.

A Sharpest chainsaw, hung on the wall, and a router lay on the long workbench. *Not only is Masters' work clothing color-coordinated, but his workshop is neat to the extreme,* Gar thought.

"We'd like to ask you a few more questions," Gar said.

Masters picked up a piece of sandpaper. "Sure. Go ahead."

"Where were you Tuesday?" Gar asked, looking up to the tall, thin, man.

"I recall that on Tuesday, I spent the entire day in my office," he answered confidently, lightly rubbing fine sandpaper on the gunstock.

"Have you ever cut any ironwood?" Gar asked, looking at the chainsaw hanging on the wall.

"Sure. I've cut a lot of ironwood," Masters answered. "Why do you ask?"

"The block used to cut the cable on the sky ride was ironwood."

"Are you accusing me?" Masters asked matter-of-factly, continuing to sand the gun stock.

"We just want some answers, Mr. Masters."

"I suppose you have evidence that the ironwood was cut with a chainsaw?"

"That's right," Gar said.

Masters walked to a long workbench. He laid the gun stock on the bench, and reached for the chainsaw. "You're welcome to check this one." He handed it to Sherman. Sherman examined the cutting chain.

Gar watched Masters. Then an item on the wall behind Masters seemed incongruous with the array of neatly displayed tools. A two-foot length of oak rod, round, about two inches thick, apparently old, smooth with use, and splintered on one end with a heavy brass hook on the other. The rod laid on two brass coat hooks like the trophies.

Sherman handed the chainsaw back to Masters. "This has just recently been sharpened. Has it been used since?"

"No, it hasn't."

"Mr. Masters, we enjoyed looking at your trophies in your den," Gar said, motioning to the broken boat hook.

"Is that a trophy?"

"Oh, no, just a piece of junk, really," Masters said, leaning back against the edge of the workbench. "I found it on a beach a long time ago, and thought I might put a new shaft in it, but never got around to it."

"Did you ever use it on a man's head?" Sherman asked.

"Afraid I don't know what you're getting at," Masters said, removing his cap and slapping it against his hand, raising a faint cloud of wood dust.

"Maybe you used it on six men's heads, one at a time, and threw them overboard," Sherman said accusingly.

"Look, Chief Sherman," Masters slapped the cap back on his head and stood straight. "You men are here because I'm allowing it. You have no search warrant, and no arrest warrant. If you continue being abusive, you'll have to leave."

Gar more carefully looked over the tools on display. A double-bladed axe with a painted black handle occupied a prominent place among the assortment of hand tools. Instead of hanging at an angle like other tools, this axe hung level on two brass wire coat hooks like the trophies in Masters' den, and had no painted shadow.

Masters studied Gar's expression. Gar's jaw dropped, and his eyes widened.

"Get out," Masters shouted. "Get out of here, and get off my property," he waved toward the door. "You're trespassing." His ruddy complexion flushed deep red, and he stood looking down at Gar, face to face with a wild stare.

Gar didn't move.

"I said, get out. You're trespassing."

"You're under arrest," Gar said, looking up into the red face. "Turn around, and put your hands behind your back," Gar demanded.

"You're crazy. On what charge?" Masters yelled.

"Suspicion of murder. Now turn around."

Sherman grabbed Masters' hand and expertly slapped the wrist with a handcuff, which clicked tight.

"Okay. Okay," Masters said, turning. "I'm not resisting arrest." He offered the other hand behind his back. "But I'll promise you people something. You're going to be mighty sorry for this."

Within a few minutes of Sherman's radio call, a black and white patrol car with two uniformed officers arrived. Gar opened the back door of the patrol car, put a hand on the top of Masters' head, and pushed it down to clear the top of the door opening. As Masters sat down, Gar removed his hand, and in the process, pinched Masters' eyebrow and withdrew a few hairs.

While the officers took Masters to headquarters for booking, Gar and Sherman went back into the shop and began gathering evidence. Gar dropped the eyebrow hairs into a small plastic bag. The axe looked new, but it too had been recently sharpened. Both cutting edges had been ground deeply. The end of the oak handle, visible through the axe head, showed hammer marks, and the wedge driven into it to hold it tight, showed signs of having been pried out and replaced.

Two police lab men soon arrived. They photographed the displayed trophies in the den, and the displayed boat hook and axe in the shop, they took samples of wood shavings, and a dozen samples of router dust from various parts of the shop. The police lab technicians also took the chainsaw, router, axe, boat hook, and one of the brass wire coat hooks.

Left alone again, Gar and Sherman checked the shop's wet-dry vacuum cleaner. Still damp inside; it had apparently been recently washed clean. They walked a hundred yards behind the house and dug into the trash cans. "This is the part of detective work I enjoy most," Sherman said with mock enthusiasm. They found no shop debris, or anything else that might be evidence.

As the two men walked by the blue water of the swimming pool, Sherman reached down and felt the water. "Water's fine," he said. "Shall we just take a dip?"

"I wish," Gar lamented. "Let's go in the house and see if we can find something that'll explain how a man can look a hundred pounds heavier."

"I'm afraid of what a good defense lawyer can do with what we've got so far," Sherman said. He reached for the handle of the glass patio door. "It's locked."

They walked around the house toward the open shop door. "This doesn't open into the house. "We'll have to use the front door," Gar said.

As they stepped around the corner of the garage, a deep maroon Cadillac eased into the circular drive. The right door opened, and Masters stepped out. He held a rolled-up apron in one hand. His face flushed red. "Get off my property," as he yelled his jugular veins stuck out.

The driver's door opened and another man, middle-aged and dressed in a dark business suit, stepped out. "I'll handle this, Burke," the man said in a deep, but kind voice. He walked to meet Gar and Sherman.

Masters stood on the walk with his hands on his hips, still holding the apron, and watched as his companion faced the startled Gar and Sherman.

"I'm Allen Drake, Mr. Masters' attorney," he said, reaching to an inside coat pocket and withdrawing two documents. "Here is a writ of *habeas corpus*, signed by Judge Black, and here is a restraining order, restraining you from any further search of these premises."

"You work fast," Gar said, examining the documents, and handing them to Sherman.

"I had a good case," the lawyer said. The kindness went out of his voice. "And you had nothing."

Sherman handed the papers back to the lawyer.

"If you gentlemen return whatever has been taken, and cease in this harassment of my client, perhaps I can convince him to refrain from bringing a civil action against you personally," he said, slipping the documents back into his coat.

"We'll re-evaluate our evidence, and let you know," Gar said, and walked on past the lawyer. Masters glared as they walked past him, but said nothing.

Chapter 36

A Man with Connections

In Gar's car, moving through the long, shady lane, Sherman slapped the back of the car seat. "That shows what money can do. We don't even finish getting our evidence before he's out, and back with a restraining order." He reached to his chin and scraped his hand over his whiskers. "What do you mean, 'We'll re-evaluate our evidence?' Don't you think we've got a case?"

"It won't hurt us for him to think we're wavering," Gar said. "We need to get into that house before Masters has a chance to destroy evidence. He's been arrogant and self-confident to the point of carelessness in the past, but he'll get more careful now. Get some people out here to keep an eye on him and the place until we can get a search warrant."

Sherman picked up the microphone. "You on our channel?" Gar nodded. Sherman ordered men on stake-out duty. The dispatcher came back with a message that Chief Bryan wanted to see Sherman and Gar as soon as they returned.

"Want to guess what that's about?" Gar asked.

"Somebody heavy is leaning on the Chief, I'd say," Sherman answered.

"It's time for some good news, but I don't think that's it," Gar said.

Chief Bryan waited under the stone "City Hall" lintel over the entrance of Police Headquarters. Gar and Sherman walked up the steps. "You men come in here," he ordered, and led the way into his office. He breezed past his secretary without a word, entered his office, and stood holding the door until Gar and Sherman squeezed through the door. The Chief closed the door behind them.

"Sit down," Chief Bryan said, motioning to two heavy side chairs of dark wood. The chief walked around his cluttered desk and eased his body into a wood swivel chair. The chair uttered loud squeaks in protest. "I have just received a call from the mayor, wanting to know what we've got on Burke Masters. The Mayor had to wait for some time, because my line was busy. I was busy talking to three city councilmen. I even got a call from a member of the Dallas City Council. I have never been leaned on quite so hard from people who carry so much weight."

The Chief performed his usual cigarette mutilation. "I will not bow to political pressure if it costs me my job. I won't be pressured with threats because of my consideration for a much bigger job." He jabbed the air with the cigarette, pointing its wet end toward Gar and Sherman. His deep voice growled. "But you men had better have a case against Masters. If you've got some hard evidence, okay. Now I want to hear it." He stuck the limp cigarette in his mouth and lit it.

"Masters is close to the witnesses' description of the big man," Gar said. "His wife and sister were among the victims. He was having an affair with his secretary. He tried to establish an alibi by telling his secretary not to disturb him during the killings, but she went into his office and discovered that he had slipped out the back. So he was gone during the time of the murders.

"He has a peculiar way of displaying mementos of great events in his life. He hangs some reminder of the event, such as a shotgun he used to kill a thief, on brass wire coat hooks in his den among his trophies. Well, we found an axe in his workshop displayed the same way. It was a new axe, yet it had been sharpened and the handle had been removed and put back. The axe handle had been painted black, so it could have looked like a cane to the witnesses. The ironwood block that had been used as a backup to cut the cable against, was cut out with a Sharpest chainsaw, and shaped with a router. Masters had both of these tools in his shop. He is also apparently a skilled wood carver. We saw him finishing a gunstock.

"He has borrowed approximately a million dollars during the past year," Gar said, looking at Sherman, as if for backup.

Sherman spoke. "Guess that's as far as we've got . . . Oh, yes, Gar mentioned to Masters that there was a strong possibility that his sister, Bernice, who is in a coma, could recover completely, and then somebody pulled the plug on her," Sherman said, and looked back to Gar.

"That's it for the moment," Gar said, "except there's another six million dollars' worth of credit life and accident policies on Mrs. Masters, but they all have homicide exclusions."

"That's it. That's it?" the Chief demanded in his deep voice. He sat upright. The chair squeaked. "You don't have a case. Imagine what a defense attorney would do to you in court? Of course, the DA wouldn't take the case on such flimsy evidence anyway. But if he went nuts and took it, you wouldn't last as long as cotton candy in a rain storm. Why? Why did you arrest him?"

"When I saw his trophies in his shop, apparently of murders, I was convinced that he was our man, and Masters figured it out," Gar said. "If we had come back to get a search warrant, all the evidence would have been gone. We had to take him into custody then, in order to preserve the evidence."

"You call that stuff evidence. I don't blame Judge Black for issuing that writ and restraining order. You guys act like a couple of kids who just got your tin G-Man badges out of a box of Cracker Jacks." The chief stuck the wet end of the cigarette in his mouth, took a long drag, and spewed smoke over his desk while he shook his head. "You guys aren't good for each other." He paused and shook his head again.

Gar stood to his feet. "You have said enough."

"Ranger Garcia, please don't misunderstand. You will still have this department's cooperation. I'll assign Lieutenant Karn to be your liaison." The Chief stood. The chair gave a relieved squeak. The chief's voice calmed down. "Now, I'm not going to try to tell you how to handle your case, but I'll advise you to either make a solid case against Masters or get off him completely."

Chief Bryan then turned to his Chief of Detectives. "You'll get back to your regular duties immediately, Sherman. Take Ranger Garcia out and introduce him to Sylvester Karn. Then I'd advise both of you to go get some rest. And shave. You look terrible."

Both seething with anger, Gar and Sherman entered the Detective Division's large common office filled with cluttered desks, half of them occupied by busy men. Some talked on telephones, some typed reports. A thin, blue haze of cigarette smoke hung just below the ceiling. A short, wiry man jumped to his feet and came to meet them. His short bowed legs didn't seem to fit the average size trunk of his body, yet he took long steps like a taller man, which gave him the look of a little boy trying to walk like a man. His light brown crew cut hair and gray plastic eye glasses accentuated a narrow face.

"Syl, I think you've met Ranger Gar Garcia," Sherman said. "Gar, this is Lieutenant Sylvester Karn." A big smile suddenly transformed Karn's awkward appearance. He shook Gar's hand with a firm, confident grip.

"No. We've not met. I am disappointed, however. I was looking forward to meeting the orange ranger. Good to meet you, Gar." Karn's deep voice enunciated well with a Southern accent. But unlike some Southern accents, his words came out fast.

"I'm glad to say the orange finally wore off," Gar said. "Good to meet you. The chief says you're to be my liaison."

"Syl is a good officer and a good administrator," Sherman said. "He goes strictly by the book, and you can depend on him."

"Thanks, Chief," Syl said.

"You can also depend on him to report anything and everything directly to Chief Bryan," Sherman continued.

Gar's mind still boiled over the Chief's performance. *I've got to get back on track. I can't let this childish oaf affect me like this.*

"I just follow orders, Chief, you know that," Syl said without emotion.

"I know, Syl. I just want to make sure Gar understands, and that everything's out front," Sherman said.

"Suits me."

"Hey, you're not orange anymore," Sherman said. "It happened so gradually I hadn't noticed you fading. You wanted good news. That's good news."

The phone on Karn's desk rang insistently. "He's right here," Karn said into the phone. "Want to talk to him?" Then, handing the phone to Gar, "It's for you."

"Garcia," Gar said into the phone, and listened. "Yes, Lieutenant Posey." Gar listened, then replied, "Well, I could use some good news."

"I wanted you to know that we have concluded our investigation into allegations made by the Diaz family that you and Phil had dropped Ben Diaz from a helicopter into Lake Texoma. According to all the witnesses, Ben Garcia was not taken aboard a Coast Guard Auxiliary boat, nor was he forced into a helicopter."

"Glad to hear it," Gar said, grateful for something to divert his anger.

"Autopsy on Ben Diaz showed that he drowned. There were no signs of trauma such as would exist if he had been dropped from a thousand feet. He most likely would have been killed when he hit the water."

"So he just 'plain old' drowned?" Gar asked.

"That's it," Posey said. "The rifle sling was twisted around his arm. Apparently the more he had struggled in panic the tighter it held him. The rifle sank like an anchor and took Ben Diaz down with it."

Gar hung up the phone. "That was good news from Internal Affairs."

"How could you ever get good news from Internal Affairs?" Karn asked.

"When they tell you you're off the hook," Gar said.

"Amen," Sherman concluded.

Gar withdrew a small plastic bag and extended it to Syl. "Get this to Austin. See if it matches the hair I found on the false eyebrow at the scene." Gar then addressed Sherman. "Well the Chief was sure right about one thing. You look awful," Gar said with a chuckle.

"So do you," Sherman said.

"I think I'll go to the room and shave and shower, and maybe get a little nap," Gar said, looking at his watch. "It's one o'clock now. If nothing earth-shaking happens, I'll just stay gone until Monday morning. If something breaks, call me at the Clearwater Inn, Room One Twenty-Four."

"There are several reports on your desk now," Syl said.

"I'm so tired now, I can hardly see. I'll check them Monday." Gar turned and walked away.

Chapter 37

Frustration

In the plush carpeted lobby of the Clearwater Inn, Gar walked briskly past the desk.

"Ranger Garcia," the desk clerk called out. "I have a message for Garcia." The clerk, a neatly groomed young man in his early twenties, grinned.

Somebody else is interested in the Spanish American war, Gar thought.

The clerk answered a phone. He held up a finger to Gar, and mouthed, "Just a minute." Then into the phone, "Yes, sir. I'll notify maintenance that the water is too hot." He paused. "Okay. I'll tell maintenance the water is *scalding* hot. We'll get it taken care of as soon as possible. In the meantime, please be careful."

The clerk turned to a wall of dark, square boxes, reached into a box labeled, "124" and took out a note. "Your wife said to give you this message if you called or came in."

As he walked toward his room, Gar read the note: "Dear Gar, I've gone to New Braunfels to visit Mom and Dad. I'll be back in time for dinner. Don't eat without me. Love, Liz."

Gar's left hand, holding the note, sagged to his side. Pent up libido and sexual frustration had him hanging low. And he needed some comfort after the unpleasantness of Chief Bryan. Gar walked slowly to his room with a lack of enthusiasm. The room was lifeless, and as empty as a drum. He hurried into the shower, shaved, and fell, still half wet, onto the king-size bed. Before his tired body dried, he went sound asleep.

The faint smell of spring flowers and a soft hand on his bare shoulder awakened Gar. "Hey, Honey, wake up," Liz's said in a gentle voice.

Gar turned toward the soft sensations and opened his eyes. He saw Liz sitting on the edge of the bed. Her hair had been cut and small curls covered her head, accentuating the natural blonde tones.

"How do you like it?" she asked.

"Oh, I like it."

"Mom and Dad bought it for me today."

"They did?"

"Didn't you notice my new dress?" She stood. She turned around quickly, sending the dress' full skirt floating on air. The deep rust color lightweight fabric dress came down to mid-calf, with a draw string around a large low cut neck. The dress bloused over her breasts and another drawstring at the waist complimented her curves.

"Oh, yeah." More awake now, Gar raised on an elbow. "I noticed the new hairdo too."

"Oh, that's old. It's just been a long time since you've seen me."

"I see you now." He looked her up and down. "Come here and see me."

"Let's eat dinner first." She took a backward step.

"Let's eat dinner second."

"It's six. Aren't you hungry?"

"Not so much for food."

"I'm hungry. Let's go eat, and then we'll have all evening, and all night. When I take off this dress and my make-up, I want to leave them off."

"I'm afraid something else will happen," Gar complained.

"Something else has been happening for two weeks. The odds are against it. Come on, and take me out to dinner." Liz twirled the skirt again.

Naked, Gar jumped out of bed, grabbed her, and kissed her hard and long.

She sagged a little, then regained her composure. She looked up at her husband, smiled, and tweaked his cheek. "Let's go eat."

Gar ran to the bathroom and began brushing his teeth. "Where do you want to eat?" he asked through the toothbrush and foam.

"Right here at the Inn," she said. "And I want you to wear a jacket. Okay?"

"Sure. Only I don't have one with me."

"I brought you one."

Seated at a table near the window overlooking the twinkling waters of the San Marcos River, Gar and Liz looked at each other like newlyweds. A candle in an amber globe gave a soft, golden light.

"I didn't realize how hungry, for food, that I was. We've been running all day. Never stopped to eat." Gar sliced into the pink center of a thick steak.

"Me too," Liz said. "I haven't had anything since lunch. How's the case coming?" She piled an open baked potato with butter, sour cream, bacon bits, and chives.

"Not so good. We've located our man. I'm sure of it, but we don't have much hard evidence, and so far, no motive."

"What *do* you have?"

"He fits the psychological pattern of our killer, and he fits the physical description."

"You mean he's six feet six and weighs three-hundred pounds?"

"No. He's six four, and weighs a hundred and sixty or seventy pounds. You know how inaccurate witnesses' descriptions usually are," Gar said between bites.

"I don't mean to discourage you, Love, but they don't usually miss by a hundred pounds," Liz said with a smile.

"Something else too," Gar began sadly. "It looks like Reynaldo Diaz was clean."

"What?"

"My two plants in the Diaz drug operation swore Reynaldo Diaz was our man, but now they say they thought Johnny was Reynaldo. Apparently Johnny was trading on Reynaldo's name and reputation. Even had members of the bunch calling him '*Patron*.'"

"They do look a lot alike."

"I really feel terrible about it. As far as I know the only charge ever lodged against him was the one I made. Reynaldo Diaz might not be dead if I hadn't arrested him." A sinking feeling deep inside took over momentarily. *It was my fault.*

"It's not your fault, honey." Liz patted her husband's hand.

Her reassurance helped assuage the guilt, but it still lingered.

After their leisurely dinner, Gar and Liz stopped at the hostess' station for mints. A tanned man in a white jacket stopped abruptly when he saw Gar. "Ranger

Garcia?" he asked.

"Yes."

"I hardly recognized you without your badge and guns. I'm Jim Bradshaw."

"Oh, yes, Mr. Bradshaw. I hardly recognized you without *your* badge," Gar said with a smile. "This is my wife, Elizabeth. Liz this is Jim Bradshaw, the manager of Clearwater Springs. His shirt usually makes the world a little brighter." Gar popped a mint into his mouth.

"Mr. Garcia, I had intended to call you. You know the man you arrested, who killed the detective? Well I saw his picture in the paper this evening. I think I've seen him before. As a matter of fact, I'm sure of it. The article mentioned that he had impersonated an FBI agent. Well, this man came to see me." Bradshaw paused, reflecting a moment.

"Go on," Gar urged.

"It was last Friday. It was the same day the gate key came up missing, and it wasn't until I saw his picture in the paper that I put the two together."

"What did he want?"

"He wanted to know who was in charge of the hillside terminal of the sky-ride. It was all very hush hush, he said. I told him about Steve Pierce. He also wanted to know about the operation of the sky-ride, the speed, length of cable, thickness of cable, and all. I didn't think there was any harm in giving the information to the FBI" Bradshaw paused, and added, "We also found a key missing."

"What key was missing?" Gar asked, and bit down on another soft mint.

"It was a key to the back gate. Up on top of the hill there's a chain link gate, on the street. We keep it chained and locked except when we want to bring a truck in the back way, which is not often. We hadn't had occasion to use the key until today. We were getting ready to break the lock, when we discovered that the key was in the lock. The man who last had the key swears he hung it on the board in my office. And I remember seeing it there before the phony FBI man was there."

"Can this wait?" Liz formed an unconvincing smile.

"Sure," Gar replied. Then to Bradshaw, "Did the guy give you a name?"

"Yes. Thomas. He was looking at a map of the park when I was called away for a few minutes. When I came back to the office, he was gone. And so was the key."

"Thanks very much, Mr. Bradshaw," Gar said. Liz tugged Gar's hand. He continued, "I'll have an officer come to see you for a formal statement." Gar and Liz walked briskly to the door.

"Why are you in such a hurry?" Liz asked.

"Guess," Gar said, as he led her down the hall toward their room.

While Gar put the stubborn key in the door lock, Liz raised his left hand to her mouth and playfully bit it. He growled.

Finally getting the door unlocked, he left the key in the lock, and swung the door open. He bowed low, and sweepingly motioned her inside.

Gar extricated the key from the lock, closed the door and leaned against it. "Oh, no," he said, as if in pain. A small red light on the telephone blinked. He took giant strides to the bedside table and snatched up the receiver. He dialed the desk, and holding the receiver to his ear, let out a deep sigh.

"This is Enrique Garcia in One-Twenty-Four. You have a message for me?"

"Yes, Mr. Garcia. Just a moment," the desk clerk said. In a moment he returned. "Yes, here it is. Lieutenant Karn wants you to call him at police headquarters. It's very important."

Gar punched the police department number and asked for the detective division. "Sylvester Karn is out, but Chief of Detectives Sherman wants to talk to you," the police dispatcher said.

"Gar. This is Sherman. Sorry to disturb your rest, but we got a call from the stakeout at Masters' house. As soon as it started getting dark they saw smoke coming from his fireplace chimney. Both men saw it and reported it."

"It's for sure he's not cold enough for a fire in August. What do you reckon he's burning?"

"I don't have any idea. But it must be important to him to get rid of it. Karn is trying to locate Judge Black now to get the restraining order lifted and obtain a search warrant. The judge wasn't home, so Karn is out at the Country Club now trying to find him."

"Isn't there another District Judge here?" Gar asked.

"Yes, Judge Albertson, but if we go around Black and get a conflicting order from Albertson, they'll both be sore. I really think it would be dangerous for any member of our department to do it."

"Do you have Judge Albertson's address?" Gar asked.

"Yes, just a minute." Sherman returned after a moment and gave Gar the Judge's home address. Gar hung up the phone and turned around to see Liz down to her bra and panties.

"This is more than any man should be asked to bear," he said, as if near tears. "But I've got to go."

He stepped quickly to her, embraced her and kissed her on the mouth, then on the cheek, and several times quickly on the neck.

"It happened. Something did happen," he mumbled painfully as he went out the door.

Chapter 38

Up in Smoke

With red lights flashing through his car's grille, Gar sped toward Judge Albertson's home. Arriving there, he shined a spotlight on the number of a long, rambling brick home with a lawn that reflected many hours of care. Mrs. Albertson, an elderly woman with wide body and smile, answered the door and ushered Gar into the den where the elderly judge sat on a recliner before a loud television set. A veined nose, wrinkles and sparse white hair attested to his age. His wife turned down the volume on the television and introduced Gar to the Judge.

"Sorry to disturb you, Judge," Gar apologized.

"That's all right Ranger. You don't look like any of the other Rangers I've seen. They usually wear big hats, and at least one big pistol. You look more like a gentleman out on the town," he said, looking at Gar's jacket and tie. "Please excuse me for not getting up. I've been ailing lately. Now what can I do for you?"

"Judge this is an emergency. We have a suspect in a capital murder case whom we believe is burning evidence in his home fireplace, and we need a search warrant," Gar hastily wrote Masters' name and address on a form as he spoke.

"Sounds like you have reasonable cause, young man; you don't really need a warrant."

"That's the problem, sir. Judge Black issued an order today restraining us from search, but we can't reach Judge Black. He's not at home, and we can't find him."

"Slow down," the Judge said. "You'd better sit down right here, and tell me about it."

Gar sat on a soft divan and sank low as if it were a padded tub. He slowly and deliberately related the chain of events that led to Masters' arrest.

Several minutes later, Judge Albertson rubbed the rough back of his hand, and cleared his throat. "I'm sorry, Ranger Garcia. I cannot find sufficient cause or emergency to issue the order you request. You'll have to see Judge Black."

"Sorry to trouble you, Judge," Gar said, rising and extending a hand.

Judge Albertson shook hands with a firm grip. "Good luck to you, young man. I don't blame you for taking this route, but I hope you understand why I must refuse."

"Yes, sir," Gar said, and hurried Code two to Police Headquarters.

He found Sherman sitting on the edge of a desk occupied by Syl.

"Did you find Judge Black?" Gar asked.

"Yes, I finally found him," Syl said. "He was mostly concerned that I had disturbed his evening at the club. His answer was quick and negative."

"I went to see Judge Albertson. He kindly listened, but he refused," Gar said.

"What now?" Syl asked.

"I'm going back to my room," Gar said, walking toward his office. He stopped and turned. "By the way, Sherman, Thomas visited Jim Bradshaw at Clearwater Springs, posing as an FBI agent, and got some information about the sky ride and the park. Bradshaw thinks Thomas stole a key to the back gate." Gar stepped into his office, and turned on the light.

Sherman slid off the desk. Syl stood, and they both went to Gar's office.

"That gate's right across the street from the back entrance of the Masters Building. Did you tell Judge Albertson about the key?" Sherman asked.

"Yes," Gar answered.

"It sure seems to be fitting into place," Syl said.

"Did you see this?" Gar asked, holding up a report.

"Which?" Sherman asked.

"This one from the hospital investigation. Burke Masters visited his sister the evening before they discovered that the plug had been pulled. And another subject visited her that morning. This one fits the description of Thomas. Could have been Thomas," Gar said.

"Either one could have pulled the plug," Sherman speculated.

"Syl," Gar said, "Call the ICU at the hospital. Tell them to notify us immediately if Bernice Masters regains consciousness. I think Masters is afraid of something she'll say."

"Why else would a man want to murder his sister?" Sherman asked.

"Maybe she's the principal target." Syl hurried back to his desk.

"Motive. If we just could give these judges a motive," Gar grumbled.

"If Clara Masters or Bernice Masters were the target, how would Masters know when they were coming across on the sky ride?" Sherman wondered.

"If they were set up . . . "Gar began. "If Masters set them up, he'd know when they were coming." He slapped the papers down. "I hope Jim Bradshaw is right about that cold water, and Bernice does regain consciousness, and still has all her marbles."

"We've still got to have a motive," Sherman said.

Syl appeared, and again leaned against the door jamb. "It's all set at the ICU," he said. "I notified the nurse in charge, and the officer on guard. She's shown no signs of coming around, but another woman involved, Mrs. Albert, the preacher's wife, has regained consciousness, and they believe she's going to be all right."

"Glad to hear it," Sherman said. "Brother Albert seemed to have a lot of sense, for a preacher."

"You know something is nagging at me, something we're missing," Gar said and sat in the squeaky wooden swivel chair.

"Did you see that report from Hidalgo County?" Sherman asked.

"No."

Sherman reached to the reports, pulled out a sheet, and handed it to Gar. "This might be a real break. The Sheriff down there located a small area of virgin flora on Masters' MYT Ranch."

A diagram on the sheet showed the location of two ironwood trees that had been cut recently.

"Cuts from both stumps have been sent to the DPS lab in Austin, and samples were sent by air to the Forest Service lab in Madison, Wisconsin," Sherman said.

"If the chainsaw marks on the stump match the chainsaw marks on the block, this could be what we're looking for," Gar said. "How about the sample of shavings and dust that we took?" he asked.

"They're on their way to both Austin and Madison," Sherman answered.

Gar leaned back in the chair, and put his feet on the desk. "Did you ever have something on the tip of your tongue, and couldn't say it?" He didn't wait for an answer. "There's something I ought to be considering, but can't bring it to mind, and it seems to have a connection with Joann Rainey."

"You suppose Masters got rid of his wife so he could marry Joann Rainey?" Syl speculated. "Weak, but it might be motive if he hated his wife enough," Syl added.

"No. He dumped Rainey," Sherman said.

Gar sat back, his eyes closed, and clasped hands to his mouth, bouncing knuckles from his teeth. "Insurance," he said under his breath. He swung his feet off the desk, and sat up straight. "Insurance. Do you remember seeing some file folders on Joann Rainey's desk the first time we were in there?"

"Yes, but I didn't get close enough to read them," Sherman said. "Didn't have my glasses on anyway."

"One said 'MYT versus TRFI.' One said something about 'private insurance,' another said something about 'accident insurance,' and another said something about. . ." Gar slapped his hands together. ". . . credit life insurance. Now according to Blitzboggen there's about six million dollars' worth of accident and credit life on Mrs. Masters. Since those file folders were on Joann Rainey's desk, she and Masters must have been talking about the insurance, or Masters was studying the insurance situation."

"I've got credit life on everything I owe," Syl said. "But it's just on me. If my wife dies, I'm still in debt."

"Don't forget that homicide exclusion, Gar," Sherman said.

"Let's go see Joann Rainey." Gar jumped to his feet and walked briskly out the front door followed step-for-step by Syl. Gar started the engine just as Syl slammed his door. The right rear door swung open, and Sherman fell into the back seat.

"Hey, you've been re-assigned," Gar said, looking back.

"I'm off duty." Sherman slammed his door.

Gar hurriedly drove across town, following Syl's directions.

"I haven't been alone with my wife for two weeks. I envy you being off duty," Gar said.

"I envy you having a wife," Sherman said with sadness.

Syl looked out the window, as if to divorce himself from the conversation.

"My wife died two years ago," Sherman said. "It's hard to take." He paused a moment, then added, "I still can't hardly believe it . . . just try to stay busy."

"You mentioned your wife, Syl. Got any kids?" Gar asked.

"Yes. We've got two sons, one eight and one ten."

"I've got a boy eight," Gar said. "He's staying with my folks a few days, so my wife and I can have a little time alone."

"Is your dad in law enforcement?" Syl asked.

"No, he's a dispatcher for Holly Freight Lines. Been with them thirty years," Gar answered.

"How did you get interested in police work?" Syl asked.

"Well, it's kind of hard to explain. But I think that kid, Steve Pierce, expressed something, when we were questioning him that might help explain my thoughts. He compared society in general with a body and the criminal element as disease germs. The kid said he decided when he was in prison that he wanted to be part of the body, not part of the disease.

"Well, when I was a kid, some of my friends went in the other direction, started stealing and doping. There was a lot of pressure to go along. I felt a lot like Steve Pierce did, although I didn't put it into words then. But using his example, I wanted to be as far from the disease as possible, so I decided not only to be part of the body, but also to be medicine to try to fight the disease."

Sherman leaned forward with his hands on the front seat. "Aren't you about the youngest Ranger? How old are you?"

"Thirty-two."

"Guess you are the youngest."

"I don't know. Could be," Gar said.

"I know men who have been on the waiting list for years, and never get close. How did you make it?" Sherman asked.

Oh, I didn't start out to be a Ranger. I just wanted to be a good officer. I hoped someday to make detective. I started at San Antonio P.D. Went from there to the Department of Public Safety. At the DPS I was a highway patrolman for two years, and then went into the Narcotics Division. Of course during all that, I went to San Antonio Junior College, and then to Baylor University. For several years there, I didn't get much sleep."

"How did you get into the Rangers?" Syl asked.

"My captain in the Narcotics Division insisted that I could make it. I thought it wouldn't hurt to try, so I made application," Gar said.

"You and six-hundred other guys," Syl interjected.

"About a year after I applied, there was a vacancy. A Ranger was killed. I took the written test, and scored pretty well. Then there was an oral interview test.

"There was a Ranger, a Senior Ranger Captain, two Ranger Field Captains, a Highway Patrol captain, and a guy from the DPS personnel department. Scary bunch of inquisitors. By the time they all got through asking questions, I wasn't hoping to be approved to become a Ranger; I was just hoping to keep the job I had. Well, miracles still happen. I was lucky, and got the appointment."

"Luck didn't have anything to do with it," Sherman said with finality, and sat back in the seat.

"Druther be lucky than good," Gar said with a smile.

"Druther be both," Syl added.

Chapter 39

A Woman Scorned

"Whoa. This is it," Syl said, motioning toward a high brick fence with the tops of lighted palm trees visible over it. The bright green palms stood out against the black night sky, looking like a life-size three-D slide show.

    Gar turned quickly into the drive, and stopped at a small brick guard house in the center of the wide drive entering the up-scale apartment complex. As Gar rolled down his car window, a uniformed guard, holding a clip board, bent low in the guardhouse window to look into the car.

    "Who do you wish to see?" he asked.

    "Joann Rainey," Gar said.

    The guard looked past Gar. "Hi, Lieutenant." Then looking behind Syl, "Oh, hi, Chief."

    "Retired police officer," Sherman said.

    The guard showed Gar a map attached to the clip board and directed him to Joann Rainey's apartment. He then telephoned her, and came back to the car. "She's in and will be expecting you."

    The trio walked up concrete steps flanked by lush flower beds and green shrubbery. Before they reached the door to Joann Rainey's apartment, the door opened. Light from the apartment flooded through her white filmy robe. Lace along the edge of her nightgown's low-cut neck showed off a respectable amount of cleavage.

    "Come in, gentlemen." Joann Rainey's big, initialed gold-rimmed glasses occupied their perch on her little nose.

She led the men past a small entry into a large living room where several vases of cut flowers made the white living room suite appear even more brilliant

Looks like Masters furnished this place. This is a love nest extraordinaire, Gar thought to himself. *Masters must spend a fortune on flowers.* A delicate fragrance filled the room. Soft, classical music floated in from another room.

"Won't you sit down." Joann Rainey waved them to a long sectional divan. She sat on the edge of a matching chair. "What can I do for you?"

"Miss Rainey, when we were in your office the first time," Gar began, "I couldn't help seeing some file folders on your desk that had reference to insurance."

"Yes."

"We would like to know something about Mr. Masters' insurance. Does he have credit life insurance on his wife to cover his indebtedness?"

"Really, that is confidential information, Mr. Garcia," she said icily.

"This is an investigation into murder, Miss Rainey, and we must look under every rock," Gar said, leaning forward.

"If you have sufficient cause, I'm sure you can secure a search warrant, and examine Mr. Masters' records," she said precisely. "Otherwise, I can't give you any of this confidential information."

"You seemed quite cooperative the last time we talked, Miss Rainey. Has something happened?" Gar asked.

"The last time we talked, I was upset. I'm afraid you may have gotten the wrong impression, because I was upset."

"You told us that Mr. Masters had slipped out the back at the approximate time the murders were taking place. Yes, you were quite upset, Miss Rainey. And I gathered that it was because you thought Mr. Masters might be connected with the murders," Gar said firmly.

"I was simply upset because Mr. Masters and I had had an argument earlier in the day. It was all a misunderstanding. I was mistaken about him going out the back that particular day. He was in all afternoon Tuesday. As a matter of fact, I talked to him often that afternoon. It was another day that he had asked not to be disturbed and went out for some exercise in the middle of the afternoon without saying anything to me," she said, looking at the three men, one at a time, then asked, "Is there anything else?"

"Yes, there is. Let me tell you something about the killer we're looking for: He is arrogant. He is ruthless. He is so self-confident that he insists on doing his own dirty work quite elaborately." Gar unbuttoned the jacket, and shifted his weight on the divan and continued.

"The circumstances of the murder indicate that Reynaldo Diaz was the primary target. If so, the murder killed Clara Masters, an innocent bystander, incidentally, just because she happened to be there. If one of the people on the sky ride was the primary target, then Reynaldo Diaz was killed just as a diversion. This murderer didn't care that there might be twenty-four other, innocent people aboard those cable cars. It was just fortunate that it was a slow day, and that only the three cars were occupied. But the killer didn't know that. He didn't care. Two people are still in critical condition, and might die yet," Gar said in measured tones.

Gar looked Joann Rainey straight in the eye. "Now let me tell you something about the physical make-up of this man. He is tall, very tall. He had three bandages on his face, perhaps to cover some identifying marks. Mr. Masters has three distinct dimples on his face, doesn't he?"

"Yes," she said with resignation in her voice.

"This murderer is quite strong. We know something about his background too. He tied a peculiar knot to join a hangman's rope to a cable that wouldn't slip, a knot that wouldn't be known by the average person. This is an indication that he was either experienced as a sailor or as an oil field worker. It is quite probable, that since the inch-and-a-half cable was cut in two with three strokes of an axe, that this large man also did that personally." He paused again. "Are you seeing something of a picture of this man? I hope so, Miss Rainey.

"Now, let me tell you something about Mr. Masters," Gar continued. "He not only fits some of the physical description, and has an oil field background, but he also has a life-long record of surviving while other people die. He shot and killed a thief, and he believes this saved his business. He escaped from the top of a derrick when a well blew out and caught fire. Everyone else was killed. He was in a crew boat in a storm in the Gulf. Six men died. Only Masters survived.

"Masters has a way of displaying mementos of these grisly experiences. He displays on brass coat hooks the shotgun that killed a thief, the cable brake that he used to escape from the well that blew out, and in his garage, on two brass coat hangers, we found a broken end of a boat hook. Now if Masters is our man, it is quite possible that he used that boat hook to crack the skulls of six men, one at a time, and then threw them overboard during the storm," Gar said.

"Something else we saw in that shop," Gar began again, carefully watching Joann Rainey's face. "We saw a double-bladed axe displayed on two brass coat hooks, just like his other trophies of survival."

Joann Rainey's expression softened. "That doesn't prove anything."

"Remember this killer's psychological make-up, Miss Rainey." Gar looked intently at her. "Remember that this person is willing to sacrifice any number of other people to achieve his own murderous aims. Miss Rainey, did Mr. Masters suggest that you visit his sister, Bernice, in Intensive Care?"

"Well, yes."

"Somebody pulled the plug on Bernice Masters' respirator. Was it you?"

"No," she said softly, her eyes filling with tears.

"Was it Bernice's mother?"

"No."

"Was it her aunt?"

"No, of course not."

"Then who?" Gar asked, leaning back in the soft sofa.

Joann Rainey didn't answer. She ran out of the room. In a moment she returned with a white tissue, daubing her eyes, and holding her glasses in her hand.

"Are you suggesting Burke Masters arranged it so I might take the blame for unplugging Bernice's respirator?" she asked calmly. She resumed her position in the soft white chair opposite the three lawmen.

"It would fit the pattern," Gar said.

"I just can't believe it," she said, shaking her head.

"I think you can. I think you know him better than we do. But don't you want to know for sure?" Gar asked, leaning forward again. "There may be no motive for Mr. Masters' killing his wife. We may be on the wrong trail. Is there a motive?"

Joann Rainey didn't answer, but looked at the floor.

"I know you have doubts in your mind about Mr. Masters," Gar began again. "I think you know if there was a motive. Did he stand to gain financially by his wife's death?"

"Yes," she said with resignation. She wept quietly for a moment, and continued. "He has credit life insurance on everything. He has been borrowing money like he was working against a deadline for the past year. Things that were paid for were mortgaged. Things that were almost paid for were refinanced. One of the officers at the bank where Mr. Masters is a major stockholder and member of the board is getting a bonus from the insurance company because he has written so much credit life. The credit life was on both Mr. and Mrs. Masters, so if either died the other would be completely out of debt."

She straightened, put her glasses back on, and continued. "His latest purchase was a pair of matching silver blue Mercedes sports cars. He had a new Cadillac, but he sold it for cash, and financed a new one along with the two Mercedes at the bank, with credit life, of course. He also had *key man* life insurance on himself and on his wife. They just had their physical exams last week. The corporation is beneficiary, but then he owns the corporation. Then he joined every auto club in business. Each one offers fifty-thousand to a million dollars' worth of accident insurance. He took out the maximum on both himself and his wife.

"Just today, an adjuster from Dallas was in my office, representing seven of those companies. They had six million in coverage," she continued.

"What about the homicide exclusions?" Sherman asked.

"The policies had homicide exclusions, and Burke knew about it from the beginning. That's why I didn't suspect him," she said, and choked up.

"Do you suspect him now?" Gar asked.

"Yes. Now I do." She wept softly, and held the tissue to her nose.

"What made you suspect him?" Gar asked gently.

"As long as he couldn't benefit from his wife's death because of the homicide exclusions, I thought there was no motive. But I discovered today that he has a plan to get around those exclusions. I didn't want to admit it to myself. I just buried the thoughts in my mind."

"What is his plan to get around the homicide exclusions?"

"The day of the murder, Burke asked me to bring him some files. I should have known about it then, but I didn't look in the files. Today he asked me to bring him those same files again. I looked in one. It was about a court decision years ago."

"Was it a lawsuit involving MYT?" Gar asked.

"Why yes. How did you know?" she asked, looking up.

"Tell me about it."

"It was a lawsuit Burke's MYT Ranch brought against TRFI, Texas Ranchers and Farmers Insurance. The insurance company had refused to pay a claim for *key man* insurance when the ranch manager was killed. It was because of homicide exclusion," she said.

"What happened?" Gar asked.

"Well, the ranch manager was killed. The insurance company said it was homicide. Burke's lawyers claimed it was an accident." Her voice strengthened. "I remember the murder. It was in the paper and on television, but the lawsuit afterward wasn't publicized. A man who worked on the ranch was running around on his wife. I remember his name because the paper's headline writers made a thing about him, Billy Flipper and his wife Florence Flipper. They called her Flo Flipper. According to the paper, Flo Flipper caught Billy and the ranch manager's wife together. Flo had a bad temper, volatile as gasoline. She went home and got a shotgun. Billy didn't know what else to do, so he went back to work. He was working in a wheat elevator on the ranch.

"Flo went back to the ranch manager's house where she had caught the two in the act, and killed the woman. Shot her in the face. Then she went to the wheat elevator where her husband was working. He was up in the elevator about forty feet, standing on a plank, trying to unplug a pipe that wheat flowed through. The ranch manager was standing directly below.

"Well, Flo Flipper apparently wasn't too good a shot at that distance. She shot at her husband, but she hit the plank he was standing on. The shotgun pellets weakened the plank enough that it broke under the man's weight. He fell, and landed on his stomach on top of the ranch manager's head. It killed them both instantly.

"According to the court decision, the ranch

manager's death was an accident, because he wasn't the target, and his death was just incidental to the death of the target," she said.

"I can see how this whole scheme was hatched," Sherman interjected. "But it was still homicide, in my opinion."

"The court said if the murderer had benefitted from the ranch manager's death, the homicide exclusion would have been in effect. But since there was no connection, the death was ruled technically an accident and TRFI had to pay double indemnity," Joann Rainey said.

"Did Masters hate his wife?" Gar asked.

"He learned to. While he was gone. . ." Suddenly she stopped speaking. "I can't believe I'm saying all this."

"You know he's a lost cause, Miss Rainey. You might as well tell us all of it," Gar said.

Joann Rainey continued, "While he was gone for several years in South America, his wife started hating him. When he came back for a visit, she punished him every moment. I don't think he ever hated her as much as she hated him. I think he just learned from her example to hate her. When he came back to stay two years ago, he treated her like dirt. Later on he started treating her better. I took credit for his change of attitude. I thought it was because he was happy with his relationship with me. And lately they seemed to be enjoying a truce."

"At the point when they hated each other most, do you think one of them could have killed the other?" Gar asked.

"I don't think Clara would ever have killed him. She enjoyed torturing him too much. You see, she was left here with two teen-age boys to raise. Burke could control them, but she couldn't. They ignored her. She couldn't do anything with them. One got on drugs. The younger one started sniffing glue, and went out of his mind. He's in Terrell State Hospital now, doesn't even know who he is. The older one killed himself. He lay down on his mother's bed, and cut his wrists and throat. She came in and found him that way."

"Thank you, Miss Rainey. You have been most helpful. You will need to come to police headquarters tomorrow and sign your statement," Sherman said.

Rising to leave, Gar added, "Miss Rainey, you have done the right thing. If Mr. Masters is innocent, he will be exonerated. If he's a killer, you will have been largely responsible for bringing him to justice and saving yourself a lifetime of pain."

The three lawmen quietly headed to the door, followed by Joann Rainey. A chime ended the silence.

"Excuse me, please. That's my phone," she said, and turned back to the divan. She picked up a white telephone receiver from the white end table.

"Good night," Syl said the last one out the door.

"Wait. It's for Lieutenant Karn," she called after them. Syl stepped quickly back inside and to the telephone. Gar and Sherman waited on the small porch. "We'll be right there," Syl said, and hung up the phone. Then calling to Gar and Sherman, he said, "Bernice Masters just regained consciousness."

"Oh, thank God." Joann Rainey watched from the door as they hurried down the steps and into the car. She continued to watch as the car sped away. Then it almost stopped to cross a speed bump across the drive, sped up for a hundred feet, and slowed to cross another speed bump.

The tail lights grew dim in the distance and the car merged into darkness.

Joann Rainey stepped back inside, and slowly closed the door. She started to weep again. "Just a warm body? I'm not even that to him anymore. Just a pawn, a stupid, gullible woman," she cried aloud.

She sank down on the divan and put her face in her hands. After a few minutes, she sat up straight and wiped her eyes. She energetically punched numbers on the phone. "Mom, I'm sorry to call so late," She said in a strong voice, without a trace of the weepiness of the previous hour. She paused and listened. "Mom, the old saying, 'Hell hath no fury like,' like what?" She paused again and listened. "Yes 'a woman scorned.' Mom, I have been worse than scorned, and I have been so hurt, but right now I'm just furious. And I doubt there is any fury in Hell to match it."

Chapter 40

Day Five, Awakening

Double doors of the Intensive Care Unit swung open. Gar, Sherman, and Syl quickly filed in heading toward the ICU.

Syl asked, "You don't really think Masters was trying to set up Joann Rainey, do you?"

Sherman answered for Gar. "It didn't hurt for her to think so."

"Yes. It is possible, the way our killer thinks," Gar said.

They passed the central nurses' station with its electronic accouterments, and entered Bernice Masters' glass-fronted room. Two white-clad figures bent over the bed, and on the other side stood a uniformed police officer.

Bernice Masters looked at the doctor and nurse to her right, then to her left to the uniformed officer, who held a microphone tethered to a cassette tape recorder slung over his shoulder. The three new arrivals gathered at the foot of her bed.

"I know you're all wondering why I called this meeting," she said. Then looking to the doctor, "Old joke. Sorry." She paused and swallowed hard. "I really would like to know what's going on."

"You're in San Marcos General Hospital, Miss Masters. You were in an accident," the doctor replied.

"Must have been. I'm sore all over. Did I break anything?"

"No. You have no broken bones," the doctor replied, smiling big.

"What's the matter?" she asked.

"Nothing's the matter, Miss Masters. I'm just so happy that you're awake, and lucid." By now all six smiled big.

"Lucid? Did I have a head injury?"

"No. You were under water for fifteen minutes."

"Fifteen minutes? I'm supposed to be dead."

"I know, but you're not," the doctor said proudly. "Mind if I ask you a few questions?"

"Shoot."

"What is your name?"

"Bernice Evelyn Masters."

"When were you born?"

"August twenty-first, Nineteen Thirty-Seven."

"Are you married?"

"No. Used to be, but not anymore. That's why my name's Masters again."

"Who is President of the United States?"

"Jimmy Carter."

"Who is governor of Texas?"

"Ralph Bridger. Now it's my turn. What kind of an accident was I in?" she asked.

Gar raised a hand to attract the doctor's eye. "Doctor, do you mind if I ask Miss Masters a few questions first?"

"I suppose not," the doctor said. "I'm satisfied that she's going to be all right. We'll leave you alone, and complete our tests later." He touched the nurse's elbow, and the doctor and nurse left the room.

"I'm Texas Ranger Gar Garcia, Miss Masters," Gar said, and motioning toward the other two, continued, "This is Chief of Detectives Roy Sherman, and this is Lieutenant

Sylvester Karn."

"I know you, Roy Sherman," Bernice Masters interrupted. Like a drunk during a sobriety test, she spoke slurred measured words. "You played football at San Marcos High. You probably don't remember me, but I had a crush on you."

Sherman smiled. "Sure. I remember you."

Gar stepped to the side of the bed and closer to the patient. "We're conducting an important investigation. Please tell us everything you can remember as near to the accident as you can, and then we'll answer any questions you want."

"Okay." She closed her eyes a moment. "Let's see." She opened her eyes again. "My sister-in-law, Clara, invited me to go with her to Clearwater Springs. Oh, yes, now I remember. We were on the sky ride. The view was beautiful. Then the sky ride stopped." A startled expression came on her face. "That's the last thing I remember."

"Before that, Miss Masters. Why were you on the sky ride?" Gar asked.

"Well, Clara invited me to go with her. My brother, Burke, Clara's husband, had just bought her a new car, and arranged for her to take a holiday there. They hadn't been getting along well, and it seemed that they were doing better. Anyway, they were to meet at the hillside terminal snack shop with a lawyer at one-thirty. It was either take the boat across the river and climb up the hill, or take the sky ride directly to it. We naturally took the sky ride. We were just exactly on time to meet Burke and the lawyer. Burke hates people who are not punctual." She paused and her eyes widened. "But the sky ride stopped. I was under water. Did the sky ride fall?" she asked with alarm.

"Just a few more questions, Miss Masters. Believe me it is important. Then we'll answer all your questions," Gar said. "Now let me see if I understand this."

The officer held the microphone toward Gar.

Gar continued. "Your brother had asked his wife to meet him and a lawyer at the hillside terminal snack shop at one-thirty. Is that right?"

The officer moved the microphone back and forth from Gar to Bernice.

"Yes," she answered fearfully.

"Do you know why they were to meet?"

"Clara said it was to transfer some of their holdings into her name so she could be financially independent, and she and Burke wouldn't need to have any contact. She could go her way, and he could go his."

"Did your brother invite you to go with your sister-in-law?"

"No. He didn't know I was coming. Clara didn't want to go to visit the park alone, so she invited me. Why? What happened?" she insisted.

"Someone cut the cable. All twelve cars fell. The one you were in fell into the water."

"Oh. What about Clara?"

"She drowned," Gar answered

"Oh," Bernice put a hand to her mouth.

A man was killed, and several others injured. Do you have any enemies that might want to kill you?"

"No, of course not."

"Do you know of anyone who might want to kill your sister-in-law?"

Bernice's hand again went to her mouth, but she remained silent.

"Do you?" Gar insisted.

"No," she said in a barely audible voice.

"We're certainly glad you're awake," Gar said.

"How long was I out?" she asked in a slurred voice.

Gar looked at his watch. "It's seven. . ." Startled, his head jerked toward Sherman. "Another night gone. It's seven A. M."

Gar turned back to Bernice. "Excuse me. It's seven Monday morning. You've been unconscious for five and a half days."

"I can't believe it," she said with astonishment.

The doctor and nurse stepped back into the room. Bernice spoke to the doctor. "He tells me I've been out for four days. How can that be?"

"You very nearly asphyxiated, Miss Masters," the doctor said. "We don't understand all we know about it, but your body reacted automatically to the cold water, and closed your larynx, keeping water out of your lungs. Also, what is called the mammalian diving reflex, apparently took over, slowing your heartbeat. Those areas of your body that could get by with little oxygen received little, and most of the oxygen in your blood went to your brain. This is something that takes place routinely in seals and porpoises, but not always in humans. But it worked for you, probably because the water was so cold," the doctor said.

"Did I make history?" She asked, with a little girl smile.

"No. This has happened many times before. In one case the victim was submerged for thirty-eight minutes, but it was in colder water. You did make local history. It had never happened before in San Marcos," the doctor said.

"Something else I'd like to know," Bernice began.

"The first person I saw was this policeman." She pointed a thumb toward the young officer who still held the microphone toward her. "Am I under guard, or arrest, or is this guy writing a book?"

"You're under police guard," the doctor answered. "There was an unfortunate incident. Someone pulled the plug on your respirator. You didn't need it. You were breathing on your own. But a layman perhaps wouldn't have known."

"So a layman tried to do me in?" Bernice said.

"We believe someone doesn't want you to recover," Gar said. "Probably the same person who cut the cable on the sky ride. He's probably afraid of what you might say that would incriminate him. Do you have any idea who that might be?" Gar paused a moment, then asked emphatically, "Who would want to kill you?"

"I don't know." Tears filled her eyes and she covered her face.

"I think we'd better leave her alone for a while," the doctor said. All, except the officer with the microphone, left the room.

Bernice put both hands over her face and wept. "Poor Clara. Dear Clara. . . ," her voice trailed off.

Chapter 41

Closing In

Gar pulled a cord on the window's blinds allowing morning sunlight to streak into Gar's small office. He sat in the squeaky old wooden swivel chair. Syl sagged down in a wood side chair, and Sherman sat on a corner of the desk.

"I'm for seeing the DA now," Sherman said, with a weary sigh. "With this new stuff, we should get the restraining order lifted and get into Masters' house before he destroys any more evidence."

"I imagine it's destroyed by now," Gar said. He leaned back in the squeaky chair and folded his hands behind his head. The sunlight glistened on his black hair.

"I know what the DA will say," Syl speculated. "He'll say, 'Hearsay. All you got is hearsay. Wait until Monday morning and get corroboration from the bank,' he'll say."

"Then we can tell him what Bernice Masters told us," Sherman added. "And he'll say hearsay again."

"I think Bernice's testimony will stick," Gar said. "She was the last to talk to Clara Masters before she died."

"That is if Bernice will stick to what she said when she gets on the witness stand," Syl said.

A uniformed sergeant with a belly and a cigar walked by the door. He lifted a clip board in greeting to Sherman, grunted, and blew out a mouthful of thick, blue smoke. Sherman nodded a greeting. After the sergeant passed, Sherman stood, picked up a newspaper from the desk, fanned the smoke back into the hallway, and closed the door.

"And if she'll testify against her own brother," Gar said.

"And you can bet Burke Masters will have the smartest lawyers money can buy," Sherman said, resuming his seat on the corner of the desk. "Joann Rainey has a way of changing her mind about talking too."

The phone rang. Gar picked up the receiver. "Garcia. . . okay. Be right there." He hung up the phone and stood. "That was communications. There's a teletype coming in to my attention from DPS in Austin."

The three scrambled into the communications room and huddled over a teletype machine as it rhythmically clicked out capital letters on a continuous roll of paper. Two uniformed officers strained to see over the trio. From his shirt pocket Sherman withdrew a pair of amber reading glasses that matched his red hair and whisker stubble.

Syl began paraphrasing the message. "Block from stump of ironwood tree 'B' from Masters Ranch in Hidalgo County: Chainsaw marks perfect match to ironwood block found at scene of Diaz homicide." His voice grew more excited. "Forest Service Lab in Madison, Wisconsin, advises that dust samples six and eight from Masters shop in San Marcos came from same tree. Wow. That locks it."

The machine resumed clicking. "Here's more," Syl said. "Hairs from subject Masters, matched hair on false eyebrow found at the scene."

Sherman stood and removed his glasses. "I'm going to call the DA." He hurried out of the communications room. Syl followed.

Sherman shouted to a sergeant. "Charlie, get your crew ready to roll out to the Masters house. Then stand by.

I'll get back to you as soon as we hear from the judge. And Charlie, be equipped to read some fireplace ashes."

Sherman lingered giving more instructions to officers and picked up the phone.

Syl followed Gar into his small office. "Here's more," he said, holding up a sheaf of reports.

"Let's hear it." Gar sat down on the squeaky chair.

"The Navy Department has transmitted to the DPS computer the requested information on men over six-feet-two who had served since Nineteen Forty-Five. They're analyzing the data, along with other data received from the Texas maritime industry, yacht clubs and the oil industry. They should have some results for us Monday." Syl pulled another piece of paper and continued. "Thomas has been interrogated again, but still wouldn't talk."

"So far, that's no help," Gar said.

"Here's something that might," Syl said, bringing another sheet of paper to the top of the sheaf. "Our investigators checking Masters' background learned from a tenant in the Masters Building that a dark blue van had been parked in Mrs. Masters' parking place in the underground parking garage all day Tuesday."

A uniformed officer tapped on the half open-door of the office. "Ranger Garcia, there's a guy who wants to see you." Bearl Blitzboggen, carrying his overstuffed, leather briefcase, followed directly behind the officer. The officer turned and ran into him. "You were supposed to wait."

"It's okay," Gar said.

The officer shook his head and left. Blitzboggen hurriedly entered the room. Syl straightened the sheaf of papers by tapping their edge on the desk, and motioned to a chair. "Thanks, I'll stand," Blitzboggen said. Syl sat on the chair.

"My research paid off," Blitzboggen began.

"Good. What've you got?" Gar answered.

Blitzboggen set the briefcase on the desk and fumbled through the many papers. "Here it is." He withdrew a yellow legal pad. "There was a lawsuit three years ago that involved the 'homicide exclusion.'" The harried lawyer sweated so much his glasses began to fog up. He put the legal pad under his left arm, withdrew a crumpled handkerchief from his pants pocket and began to wipe his glasses. The briefcase fell to the floor, spilling its contents.

"Sorry," Blitzboggen said, continuing to wipe his glasses.

"Let me help," Syl volunteered. He laid his papers in his chair, got on his hands and knees, and began shoving papers back into the leather briefcase.

Blitzboggen finished wiping his glasses and continued. "It was MYT Ranch versus TRFI, the Texas Ranchers and Farmers Insurance Company. A woman shot at her husband, apparently intending to kill him." Blitzboggen shifted his weight and stepped on Syl's hand. Syl grunted in pain.

Gar wanted to say, "I know about it," but didn't. He didn't want to dampen Blitzboggen's enthusiasm. Then too, maybe Blitzboggen had something more than Joann Rainey.

"Sorry," Blitzboggen said, looking at Syl's injured hand.

"It's okay," Syl said, obviously pained. Syl sat back in his chair, leaving half the briefcase's contents on the floor, and rubbed his hand.

Blitzboggen tapped the legal pad with a finger, and continued. "The man who was fallen on was covered by *key man* insurance. The company refused to pay because his death was the result of a homicide, and their policy had homicide exclusion." Excitement filled his voice. "The court ruled that the insured was not the intended victim of the killer, that the killer did not gain from that death, and therefore, the death was technically accidental rather than a homicide."

"They paid off?" Gar asked.

"They paid off," Blitzboggen said.

"They paid off," Syl said, still rubbing his injured hand.

"Another thing," Blitzboggen added triumphantly, "Burke Masters was and is the owner of the MYT Ranch, the beneficiary of the *key man* insurance."

Blitzboggen got to his knees and shuffled through the papers on the floor. He withdrew a file folder and handed it up to Gar. "Here's the case information you can share with the DA."

"Thank you, Mr. Blitzboggen. You have been very helpful," Gar said, standing. Blitzboggen quickly shoved the rest of the papers into the briefcase and stood. Gar extended a hand. Blitzboggen shook it vigorously, grinning widely. He extended his hand to Syl, who continued to rub his injured right hand.

"Oh, I'm really sorry about that," Blitzboggen said, and dropped his hand. The big smile left his face.

"No problem," Syl said.

"See you later," Blitzboggen exited, carrying the even more disheveled briefcase. The big smile returned.

Sherman entered the office. "That was Blitzboggen, wasn't it?"

"That was Blitzboggen," Syl answered.

"He had some interesting news," Gar said. "It backs up what Joann Rainey told us. This is the biggest insurance scam that's come along in a long time." Gar then told Sherman what Blitzboggen had reported and what Syl had learned about the dark blue van.

"The DA's calling Judge Black now," Sherman said. "He'll call right back. The lab boys will be ready to roll as soon as we get the all clear from the judge." He paused. "Do you think the blue van might tie in with the missing key to the back gate of the park?"

"Sure. Thomas filched the key out of Bradshaw's office and gave it to Masters so he could get in the back gate. If Masters slipped down the back stairs, he could have put on a disguise, but how did he look to weigh a hundred pounds more?" Gar asked.

"He could have put on the disguise in the blue van," Sherman said.

"Does he own one?" Gar asked.

"No. We found no such record."

Syl spoke up, "I see. You think Masters could have gone into his office to establish an alibi, then slipped down the back stairs and into the van. He could have changed clothes there, and put on a wig and mustache. . ."

". . . and a hundred pounds," Sherman interrupted.

". . . and slipped out of the parking garage," Gar continued Syl's speculation, "opened the back gate of the park with the key Thomas stole out of Bradshaw's office, walked on down through the woods, and through the Inn to the restaurant where he was seen with Hawk Nose and their victim, Diaz. Then after the killing, Masters could have slipped back out the back gate, still in his disguise, and into the parking garage, and back into the van to change from mysterious Mexican giant to skinny Burke Masters again."

"Sure could be," Syl said.

"Probably so," Sherman agreed.

"Syl, get on the phone and call every rental agency in New Braunfels. Sherman, you call San Marcos, and I'll call Austin. Let's see if they've got a dark blue van, and if someone had it on Tuesday," Gar ordered.

Gar chose an Austin telephone directory from among a shelf full of phone books.

"Hello. This is Texas Ranger Garcia, calling from San Marcos. May I speak to the manager, please . . . Yes, assistant manager will be fine . . . Hello. Do you have a blue van?" He paused. "Thanks. That's all I wanted to know. Good-bye."

Similar conversations repeated over and over. Suddenly, from the other room, Syl's voice boomed, "Bingo."

As Gar finished the conversation on the phone and hung up, Syl reached Gar's office door. "A Don Thomas rented a dark blue van in New Braunfels on Monday, and brought it back on Friday. Even the mileage fits," Syl drawled excitedly.

Gar jumped to his feet. "We got it. I'm going to have another go at Thomas

"Okay," Sherman said, "But before you go, here's something that might fit. San Antonio PD has a bulletin out for a man with a bandaged arm driving a blue van. He shot a taxi driver in the airport parking area, robbed him and left him for dead."

"Sounds like Thomas," Gar said. "The puzzle pieces are fitting."

Gar went back to the interrogation room where officers had Thomas ready for questioning. After a few preliminary questions, to which Thomas refused to respond, a gentle knock pecked on the door. Sherman stepped in. "The District Attorney had agreed to talk to Judge Black to try to get the restraining order lifted."

"Chief, would you go out and get some coffee or something while I get serious with this maggot here?" Gar asked.

Thomas sat up straight as if his back had become unstrung. "Wait a minute," he demanded.

"Hey, he speaks," Gar exclaimed.

"Whatever you say," Sherman said, starting for the door. "You're the Governor's man."

"No. You gotta stay here. I want a witness. This Ranger is planning to hurt me," Thomas pleaded. Sherman sat back down.

"Why should I want to hurt you? Just because you killed a fine officer, the second one in a week," Gar's voice got louder, "and besides that a taxi driver in San Antonio you shot in the face is alive and can finger you. I don't just want to hurt you. I want to kill you. But I don't have to do that. The State will do it. You've had it. The wheels are in motion," Gar shouted into the suspect's face. "There is no way you're going to avoid that hot shot. They're going to tie you down to a gurney, and stick your arm. . . ," Gar grabbed the bandaged arm. Thomas winced. ". . . through a hole in the wall, so you can't see who's giving you the hot shot." Gar held the bandaged arm to the table top. "Then they're going to stick that needle in this arm. That drug is going to go through your veins until it hits your maggot brain, and you're going to be dead."

Gar stood to his feet, knocked on the door, and turned to Thomas who now held his bandaged left arm with his swollen right hand. "And the world will be just a little cleaner." Gar stood, waiting for the officer outside to open the door.

Thomas looked down at a large vein in the crook his bandaged arm. He began to shake. He looked at his swollen hand that had been bitten by Steve Pierce.

"I'm through with him," Gar said to the officer who opened the interrogation room door.

"Wait a minute," Thomas shouted.

"Yes." Gar paused in the door.

"Did the Governor really put you on this case?"

"Yes."

"Can you make a deal?"

"What did you have in mind?" Gar closed the door and sat down opposite the suspect.

"Guarantee me I don't get the death penalty and I'll give you the big man, the guy who planned the whole thing."

"You know the rules by now, Thomas. We can't guarantee you anything. We can make a recommendation. You give us Peters and anyone else involved in this thing. You testify in court, and be straight with us all the way, and we'll put in a good word to the DA and judge," Gar said.

"Okay," Thomas said with a sigh. Sherman bounded out the door and returned in seconds with a stenographer, a panting young woman carrying a small black machine.

"Tell us," Gar said.

"Okay. This guy Peters, Hawk Nose and I met in a club in Dallas a couple of years ago." Thomas nervously shook a cigarette out of a half-empty pack, put the cigarette in his trembling lips, and scratched a paper match to flame. "We tried to work a little con job on him but he was wise to us. Anyway, he said he wouldn't turn us in, but instead had a little job for us to do for him." The cigarette bounced as he talked, but he finally got it lit. He took a deep drag and exhaled a cloud of blue smoke. Sherman backed up.

"Peters?" Gar asked. "What did he look like?"

"He's about six foot six. Skinny. Has short gray hair, big hands. Looked tough as tire rubber."

"Any distinguishing marks?"

"Yeah. He's got three dimples, deep dimples, one on his chin and one on each cheek."

"Where did he live?"

"Told us he lived in Dallas."

"Where?"

"Don't know."

"What was the job you did for him?"

"Well," Thomas paused and put a hand on each cheek and rubbed his whiskers. "He had some kind of case against a couple of punks. One of them had been selling Peters' kid dope. The other had taught Peters' other kid to sniff paint thinner. We came here to San Marcos, 'arrested' them and took them to San Antonio. Peters told us how to do it. We took them to a motel. We got each one of them a big milk shake. Peters gave us a blender to use. We blended in about three-hundred aspirin tablets into each milk shake. The kids drank them. Didn't suspect a thing. When they passed out we left them in a motel room there in San

Antonio, the cops thought they'd just OD'ed."

"Go on."

"Peters gave us five thousand apiece for the punks. He called me in Dallas again a couple of months ago and hired us to help him do this Diaz job. He gave us twenty thousand apiece for this one. Said he wanted to hit Diaz because he was a big time dope dealer. There was another one, a woman in one of the cars on the sky ride. We had to watch for her to be over the water when Peters cut the cable, so he could kill two with one stroke, so to speak."

Sherman interrupted. "He told you the woman was a drug dealer?"

"Yeah. But there were two women in the car, not that it made any difference to us."

"Had he pointed the woman out to you earlier?" Gar asked.

"He showed us her picture."

Sherman opened a file and took out a picture of Clara Masters. "Is this the woman?"

"That's her. Peters also pointed her out to us in the restaurant just before the job so we'd know her for sure. Peters was careful to not let her see him. No one would have known him anyway in that disguise."

Sherman fished out a picture of Burke Masters. "Is this Peters?"

"Looks like him. Can't be sure," Thomas said. After a pause, he said, "I feel sick."

"I'm not surprised," Gar said.

He answered another knock on the interrogation room door. Syl announced, "The DA got hold of Judge Black. We're in."

Chapter 42

Body of Evidence

Within a few minutes Gar, Sherman, and Syl hurried out the front door of Police Headquarters. "It took the DA a while to convince Judge Black, but we've got the restraining order lifted, a search warrant, and an arrest warrant," Syl reported. "Charlie and his lab crew will meet us at Masters' place."

The three climbed into Gar's white Dodge and with red lights flashing through the grille, sped toward Masters' home.

"You think Peters and Masters are the same person?" Sherman asked.

"Sure fits. The description fits. One son's suicide, connected with drugs, and the other with a fried brain because of glue sniffing . . . those circumstances can't fit many people. What do you think?"

"Sure could be Masters okay."

The car stopped in the circular drive squarely in front of the door of Masters' home. Syl went around the house to the right; Sherman went to the left, and Gar rang the front doorbell. No answer. Gar waited, and listened. Otherwise quiet, splashing water from Cupid and the birdbath played a pleasant tune.

A black police van entered the circular drive and stopped behind Gar's car. Several officers emerged from the van, carrying cases of equipment.

"Nobody here," Gar said.

"We'll get it open," the sergeant said, motioning to

one of his men, who opened a small, black, leather case of tools and began picking the lock.

Sherman came around the house. "Masters left about a half hour ago," he said. "Our man watching the front followed him. Our man in back tells me Masters went to his office, and is still there. His partner's watching the Masters Building, but he's sure Masters made him."

The officer working on the door lock swung open the heavy wood door. Cool air rushed outside as the men entered. Gar hurried to the stone fireplace in the white-furnished living room. He opened the brass-trimmed glass screen. "It doesn't smell like wood or paper," he mused. "More like something synthetic." A heap of black char filled the iron grate. The lab men set a four by four-foot square of plywood on the floor, and gently set the iron grate and its contents on the plywood.

"That's paper underneath," the sergeant said.

"What's that above? Looks like a pillow, or a blanket," Sherman said.

"It's not burned totally," Gar said, reaching with a lead pencil into the heap, and lifting a layer to peer under it. "Look here." The men craned their necks for a view. "The labels are still intact. Looks like sweat shirts, or t-shirts." Gar paused a moment, studying the charred remains. "No. It's thermal underwear. Looks like about six or eight thermal undershirts all together, like they'd been worn one on top of the other."

"That's how he gained a hundred pounds," Sherman said excitedly.

"It's why he sweated so much too," Gar added. "Probably had on several thermal underwear pants too. It's a wonder he didn't pass out in the heat while he was chopping that cable. Let's see if he burned a large dark suit. Any sign of that?"

"Doesn't seem to be," the sergeant said.

"Check the closets," Gar said. "Maybe he kept it."

Gar searched a closet, but it contained only women's clothing. In a few minutes Sherman appeared at the bedroom door. "Found something," he announced.

Gar rushed into another bedroom where the sergeant peered through a magnifying glass at a coat on the bed. "What is it?" Gar asked.

"There's a tiny bit of black hair on the neck of this coat. I think it's from a wig," the sergeant said.

"Take a sample. Let's see if it matches the hair on the artificial eyebrow," Gar said. "What size is it?" he asked.

"Oh, tiny," the sergeant answered.

"I mean the suit," Gar said.

"Oh, it's a fifty-eight, extra-long," Sherman answered. "He's got several of them in there," he motioned to a large walk-in closet. "Ranging in size from forty-four extra-long to fifty-eight extra-long. I guess he kept his big suits after he lost weight."

"Most people are smart to do that, seeing how they sometimes gain it back again," The sergeant said.

"He shouldn't have kept this one, if he hoped to get away with murder," Gar said. "He did a performance, but it didn't play well."

Syl ran excitedly in the front door. "Come see what I found in the garage."

Gar followed him to the garage. "You told me to look for brass coat hangers. Well, I found some more," Syl said. He led Gar to a corner of the garage where narrow shelves contained a variety of paint cans. Next to them a small shelf about six inches wide, rested on two brass coat hangers? A single plastic bottle, incongruous among the displayed tools and paint, stood alone on the shelf. The label showed it to have contained 1,000 aspirin tablets but it now held about 300.

"He's a compulsive trophy maker, isn't he?" Gar said. "Let's go get him."

"Carry on here, Charlie," Sherman said to the Sergeant, and pointed to the empty aspirin bottle display. "This is evidence. I want pictures."

The phone rang before Gar could get out the front door. He turned quickly and walked across the room to the phone. "Hello."

"Who is this?" the voice asked.

"Texas Ranger Garcia," Gar answered.

"This is Judge Black. I thought you ought to know. Burke Masters just called me. He called to complain that a policeman has been watching his house and following him." The judge paused a moment, then said, "I'm afraid I let the cat out of the bag. I didn't intend to tip him off, but I guess I did."

"Thanks, Judge. We're on our way to arrest him now."

Chapter 43

Desperation

Red lights flashed through the grille of Gar's car as he Sherman and Syl sped across the city to the Masters Building.

Sherman and Syl quickly got out and rushed into the front of the building. Gar sped on around the block toward the back entrance. With the long chain-link fenced back of the amusement park property on his left, Gar turned right into the drive, and drove quickly down into the basement parking garage.

A silver blue Mercedes sports convertible with the top down, sleek and low, crouched in a parking place marked in yellow letters, "Reserved for Burke Masters."

Gar parked in a "No Parking" zone near a plain steel door marked "Stairs." After trying the locked door he stepped back and surveyed the entry area and elevators, both empty and quiet as a dry cave.

Gar walked back through the parking garage and up the inclined drive. At street level, he looked up to the building, and in each direction down the streets. Then peering to the elevator entry area, he saw the Mercedes' brake lights light up bright red. The sleek car backed up. Then it lurched forward, tires squealing, and sped toward the drive that rose to the street. Gar stood in the center of the drive and waved both hands in wide arcs.

The Mercedes gained speed, bounced, and almost flew as it topped the rise. Gar saw the grim and determined face of Burke Masters behind the wheel. As the car reached him, Gar jumped straight up. The top of the shiny, chrome grille hit his airborne feet, and sent him tumbling over the hood. The top of the chrome-lined windshield gouged into Gar's back.

Masters ducked. Gar's right-hand pistol fell out of its holster and onto the seat beside Masters. Gar's body bounced off the back of the seat and onto the trunk. He landed on his tail bone on the concrete street behind the lurching car.

A big Buick squatted to a stop a foot from Gar. "Are you hurt?" the man from the Buick asked.

"Not bad, I think," Gar said, wincing with each word.

Two more cars stopped. The three drivers had a committee meeting and decided Gar should go to a hospital. Gar struggled to get to his feet, but intense pain in his tailbone put him back down on the hot pavement. "I'll call an ambulance," one driver said and ran into a store.

Two burly medics loaded Gar onto a stretcher and into the ambulance. *I'll be the first Texas Ranger to die of terminal tail bone injury,* he thought. "Hey. Turn off that siren and yelper," he shouted to the driver. "I'm not critical, just bruised up." The screaming ambulance made the rest of the trip to San Marcos General Hospital quietly but with red white and blue lights flashing.

In the ER the medics rolled Gar onto a gurney. The pain in Gar's lower back intensified. When he lifted his head off the pillow it hurt all the way down to his tailbone. "This'll make you feel better," a male nurse said, and stuck a needle in Gar's arm.

Day Six

Gar gradually awoke to the rude sound of a ringing telephone beside the hospital bed, and wondered where he was and how he got there.

"Is this Ranger Garcia?"

"Yes." Gar's memory returned along with pain.

"Gar, this is Captain Summers. I hear you were hurt in an accident."

"Yes."

"I also heard that you lost a weapon to a perpetrator."

"Yes. When the car hit me . . ."

"I don't want to hear any excuses," Captain Summers said. "You know my rule: you never give up your weapon to a perp no matter what, even if he's threatening your mother."

"But, Captain . . . ," Gar began.

"This is a serious matter, Gar."

"Captain, I tried to tell you . . ."

Again Captain Summers cut him off, saying accusingly, "I said no excuses," and hung up.

A doctor came in and reported, "The x-rays are clear. No broken bones. You just have a really bruised area in your lower back. You should get better on your own."

"I feel better already," Gar said. "I can lift my head without it hurting."

Liz burst into the room. "What happened?" She ran to the bedside and kissed her husband on the forehead.

"Doc here says I'm just bruised."

"He should be able to go home when he feels up to

it," the Doctor said.

Late in the afternoon, although every movement caused pain, Gar got out of the bed, took off his hospital gown with no back and got dressed. As he buckled on his cartridge belt with two holsters but only one pistol, Captain Summers came in the room followed by G. W. Posey.

"There's no excuse for losing your weapon to a suspect. You may be suspended," Captain Summers said. "But Posey insists that we hear your explanation."

Gar explained in detail what had happened. "While I flew through the air after being hit by the car's windshield, I had no control over anything. I did not give up my weapon to a perpetrator. The weapon fell out of its holster. It wasn't on the scene, so I assume it fell in the suspect's car."

"Didn't give it up," Posey echoed.

Captain Summers looked hard at Posey, then at Gar. "Didn't give it up, you say."

"I'd say that's the way it happened," Posey said.

"Okay," Captain Summers said, "but you need to take measures to be sure it never happens again. A perpetrator with an officer's gun is doubly dangerous, and an unarmed officer facing such a perp is useless and usually soon dead."

Gar sat painfully on the old squeaky chair in his office at police headquarters. The rude telephone ring shot up his spine. "Garcia," he answered.

"Enrique."

Gar recognized his father's voice "Yes, Dad."

"Enrique, Joe is in jail, and they've impounded my van."

"Why?"

"Possession of a controlled substance."

"Marijuana?"

"Yes. They found it under the seat. I sure didn't put it there. The cops said they could confiscate my van."

"There's nothing I can do, Dad. I can't interfere. But you can. Call B. D. 'Bulldog' Barker. He's a sharp young lawyer who has been winning cases."

"Okay. I'll call him."

"Did Joe say what happened to Santiago's family?"

"Yea, her sister came out from Fredericksburg and got her and the kids."

"I'm sorry about Joe. This'll make him grow up, the hard way."

Sherman pecked on the glass door of Gar's office and entered. "I see you're still alive."

Gar hung up the phone. "Alive but sore. I never realized what a pain a tailbone can be."

"I stationed officers at every highway and farm road leading into San Marcos. That Mercedes will be easy to spot."

"Assuming he's still driving it."

"I don't think Masters is an accomplished car thief, so he might have trouble getting another set of wheels." Sherman resumed his usual seat on the corner of Gar's desk. "In the old days before the interstate highways, we could put up roadblocks on all the highways. If we did that now, I-35 would be stacked up with angry drivers from San Antonio to Waco. So our guys are watching the entrance ramps."

Gar's mind kept going back to his baby brother in

jail on possibly a felony charge. *I've got to keep my mind on business. There's nothing I can do for Joe anyway.*

As Farm Road 12 entered the city from the west two officers in a marked car watched the road on which Masters lived. Suddenly from behind them a silver blue Mercedes convertible passed from the west going into town. The startled officers gave chase. "We've got the Mercedes convertible, headed east on twelve," the officer said into the microphone.

"Be careful. He's armed," the dispatcher said. "I'll send some help."

Within five minutes three police cars blocked Farm Road 12. The Mercedes came to a panic stop. The chase car stopped at the Mercedes' back bumper. Six officers with drawn guns surrounded the driver.

A white-haired old man raised his hands high. "I didn't steal it. I bought it. I've got the title."

The officers holstered their weapons and learned that this Mercedes, identical to the one Masters drove, had been his wife's. Masters had sold the car to the old man.

"I always wanted a convertible, but couldn't afford one until now. You guys scared me to death."

Chapter 44

Chain Reaction

After Masters bounced Gar off the top of his car, Masters sped across I-35 and a mile down State Highway 80 to a garage with a faded sign, "Mueller's Auto Repair." The Mercedes bounced over the concrete floor of an empty stall. "Shut the door," Masters demanded.

A man in greasy overalls ran out of the office. "What's the matter?"

"Shut the damn door, Alfonse," Masters shouted.

"Oh, it's you Mr. Masters." Alfonse hurried to close the garage door. "The other two stalls are full, and I've got a customer coming in this one in an hour. What can I do for you?"

"Call your customer and tell him to come back another day."

"Oh, I can't do that."

"Sure you can." Masters opened his wallet and took out five $100 bills. "I want to rent this stall for a while."

"Well, okay," Alfonse said pocketing the money.

"And you're to keep quiet about it."

"I'll go call."

"No, wait just a minute. I want to borrow a car. I see you've got a lot full of them out there."

Masters bargained with Alfonse and struck a deal to rent a 1968 Dodge Hemi for $100 a day. Alfonse stuck the bill in with the others and handed Masters the keys.

"I need something else too."

"What's that?"

"Some clothes and a hat." Soon the usually well-dressed giant had on greasy overalls that came down only to his ankles and a greasy baseball cap. Masters rubbed black grease off of an engine suspended on a chain hoist.

"Looks like you're ready to wade water with those pants so short. Of course you wouldn't do it in those shoes," Alfonse said with a chuckle.

"You have to keep this quiet," Masters said as he rubbed the black grease on his face and hair.

After Masters drove away in the Dodge, Alfonse went into his office and turned on the television. The news anchor gave a report every few minutes on the manhunt with pictures of Masters and his silver blue Mercedes convertible.

Alfonse dialed the phone. "This is Alfonse Mueller, out on eighty. I can give you some information . . ."

Masters burst into the office. "Hang it up." Masters held Gar's single action revolver with the hammer back.

Alfonse hung up the phone. His face turned pale and he sagged down in his chair.

"I thought you might turn me in, so I doubled back to check on your loyalty. It turns out you have none," Masters shouted and his face turned red in contrast to Alfonse's. Masters pulled the trigger. The hammer struck the .44 cartridge. Gunpowder exploded, sending a lead bullet into Alfonse's head. He folded to the floor with a hole between his eyes and the back of his head blown away.

Masters dug Alfonse's keys and the six $100 bills out of his pocket, put a closed sign in the window, and locked the door behind him.

Meanwhile in Masters' home two police officers strung yellow "Crime Scene" tape around the house. "I don't know why we use 'crime scene.' This wasn't the scene of the crime."

"We just have to do what we're told," the other officer said.

As they drove down the lane a black Dodge met them. "Did you get a look at him?" Officer One asked.

As Masters met the police car he filled his mouth with air until his cheeks bulged.

"Yea. He looked like he was either black or filthy. Couldn't have been Masters. This guy's face was round and fat."

At his house, Masters ducked under the yellow tape, fished keys out of his pocket and entered the front door. He took a shovel from the fireplace and went to the large patio by the pool. He removed the grate from a brick charcoal cooker and started shoveling out ashes. He pulled out a steel plate the same size as the grate. He set the steel plate on its edge and ashes slid off. Masters reached into the cooker and brought out a steel tool box, opened it and examined the bundles of $100 and $50 bills. Masters left the ashes mess, hurried to the black Dodge, stowed the tool box in the trunk, and drove away.

He stopped at a convenience store gas station and filled his tank. Three young men, a Black, a Hispanic, and an Anglo, lounged around the entrance. Masters entered the store, paid for the gasoline, and picked up several items of groceries.

"Did you see that guy?" the Anglo asked

"I seen him. He's filthy," the Hispanic said.

"His clothes don't fit too good," the Black

interjected.

"I'm not talking about that. It's his shoes. Them shoes cost over a hundred bucks. They just don't go with the rest of his outfit."

"So what?" the Black said.

"So, he must have money," The Anglo said. "Let's take him."

"Want to do the back seat surprise?" the Hispanic asked. While the other two went into the store and tried to engage Masters in conversation, the Hispanic opened the rear door of the Dodge slipped in and concealed himself.

As Masters drove away, he opened a bag of potato chips and began to munch. An old red Chevrolet that had been dolled up and brightly shined approached from behind. Suddenly the man in the back seat threw a rope around Masters' neck and drew the rope tight. Masters fought the rope. The car went into a ditch and stopped. The other two men jumped out of the red Chevy, opened both front doors of the black Dodge and drug Masters, weak from being strangled, out of the car. One held a knife to Masters' throat while the other two tied his hands and feet.

"Okay, tell us where's your money," Anglo demanded.

"Okay. Okay, just don't hurt me please," Masters spoke in a falsetto voice and feigned terror.

"So where is it?" Anglo said.

"I've got six hundred in my pants pocket. You can have it just please don't hurt me," Masters said.

"What a pansy," Anglo said.

Black dug into Masters' pocket and pulled out the crumpled bills. Hispanic dug into Masters' hip pocket and withdrew his wallet. "Betcha there's more in here." He opened the wallet and pulled out another $1,000 in cash along with four credit cards.

"I told you he had money," Anglo said.

"You've got what you want. Please don't leave me here tied up like this," Masters continued in frightened falsetto.

The three young men had walked half way to the red Chevy when Black said, "Divvy up the money."

"Okay." Anglo stopped, took the money out of his pocket and counted out $500 to each of his partners.

"Wait a minute," Black said. "You're getting more than us."

"It was my idea. You guys would have got nothing if it hadn't been for me."

Shouting turned to shoving. Shoving turned to punching with clenched fists. The other two beat Anglo down to the ground.

Meanwhile, Masters wriggled loose from his bonds, quietly slid into the floor of the Dodge, reached under the driver's seat and pulled out Gar's .44. He cocked the hammer, and walked slowly to the three men. He shot two. They fell on dead on Anglo.

"No, man. You don't have to do this. I'll give you your money back."

"Hand it over," Masters spoke in his natural deep voice.

Anglo shoved the bodies off, reached into their pockets, and presented the crumpled $1,600 and several credit cards to Masters.

"Where's the wallet?"

"We just took the money and credit cards. The wallet's over there," Anglo said, pointing to a stand of weeds near the car. Okay. I'll just leave now. No hard feelings?"

"No hard feelings," Masters said, and shot the man in the head. Masters removed Anglo's athletic shoes. He struggled to get them on, but couldn't. He cut a semicircle around the front of each shoe, put them on and wiggled his toes sticking out of the hole.

Masters threw his designer shoes into the trunk of the Dodge, found his wallet in the weeds and drove away.

Alfonse Mueller's wife knocked on the shop door. She beat on the glass. "Alfonse, open up. What's going on?" She listened to the quiet a moment, then stuck a key in the lock and opened the door to see her husband with the back of his head blown away and his body surrounded by a bloom of splattered blood.

An officer pecked on Gar's door and opened it. "We found Masters' car."

"Where?"

"In a garage on the edge of town on Highway Eighty. And there's a homicide. The guy who owned the garage, Alfonse Mueller, was shot dead."

Gar sped code two, parked behind a squad car, and hurried into the shop office. Alfonse's wife held her face in her hands and sobbed.

"Mrs. Mueller, I'm Texas Ranger Garcia. May I ask you some questions?" Gar asked as gently as he could.

Mrs. Mueller never looked up, but answered, "Yes."

"We found Burke Masters' car in your husband's garage. I suspect he took one of Mr. Mueller's cars off his used car lot. Would you know if one is missing?"

With tear filled blue eyes in a field of red, Mrs. Mueller looked up at Gar for the first time. "He had five cars out there for sale. I'll look and see if one's missing." She tried to stand on shaky legs. Gar reached down and helped her up. He stepped ahead of her, opened the door, and held her arm as she slowly made her way to the cars parked in front of the shop.

"There were five. The best one we had was a Dodge Hemi. I don't see it."

Back in the office Mrs. Mueller found a file on the car that included a title with the vehicle identification number, the license tag, and a picture Alfonse had used in advertising.

Again Gar had difficulty concentrating because his heart hurt for Joe. Like trying to arouse from a bad dream, he forced himself to get his mind back on track.

Syl entered the office from the garage. "We found some really nice clothes that would fit Masters. He apparently changed clothes."

"There were no clothes here except work clothes. You know how dirty and greasy mechanics can get," Mrs. Mueller said, dabbing a tissue to her cheek.

"Get this information and picture out in a bulletin. Masters may be dressed as a mechanic," Gar said, handing the file folder to Syl.

Gar's beeper vibrated. He went to Mueller's phone and dialed Police Headquarters. "Chief Sherman, please." He listened a moment. "What's up?"

"Three dead bodies out on Farm Road Twelve, all shot with a large caliber, maybe a forty-four."

Gar and Sherman examined the bodies at the crime scene.

"Must have been robbery. Their pockets are turned inside out," Gar said.

"I can't imagine these guys having much to rob."

"This one's shoes are gone. I can't imagine anyone killing three men for a pair of shoes. Hey, just a minute, there's something still in this one's pocket." Gar pulled out an American Express card with Burke Masters' name on it.

One of the detectives questioning neighbors, radioed to Sherman. "A lady here in the convenience store says three punks were in her store today harassing a tall man in filthy clothes."

Gar rushed to the store and interviewed the clerk. "Can you describe what the man was wearing?" Gar asked.

"Yes. He was filthy with greasy old overalls. He had black grease on his face and wore a dirty baseball cap."

"How tall was this man?"

"Oh, real tall. We have a gauge by the door so in case we're robbed we can tell how tall the robber was. This guy was six feet four. He looked like he had grown out of his pants."

"What do you mean?"

"His pants only came down to above his ankles. His socks looked good." She paused. "Oh yes, what caught the three punks' eye was his shoes, real expensive leather."

"How did they harass him?"

"Two of them came in and asked him for a light. He said he didn't have a match. They asked him where he lived and all kinds of stuff. The third punk stayed outside where the guy had just filled up his car. Listen, I know these three punks. They hang around here a lot. I think they steal from the store, but I haven't been able to catch them. They're all the time showing off, taking off from our drive like it was a drag strip."

"Did you notice what kind of shoes the three young men wore?"

"They wore what they always wore, dirty white athletic shoes."

Again, worry took over Gar's mind. *Oh God, please don't let Joe turn out like these guys.* Gar realized that subconscious worry about Joe had been causing him to feel uneasy. With Joe facing jail time and a record, *uneasy* became squared.

Gar's beeper vibrated and displayed his father's telephone number. At a pay phone outside, Gar said, "What's up, Dad?"

"Well, I've got some good news for a change. You were right about Bulldog Barker. He's a sharp lawyer. Anyway, Joe is free and the charges have been dropped.

"How so?"

"The officer searched the vehicle without permission, so all the evidence was thrown out. Joe just got home in my van."

Chapter 45

The Scalding

Johnny Diaz, with a garment bag draped over his shoulder, stood at the registration desk of the Clearwater Inn, and spoke to the clerk. "I'd like Ranger Garcia's room number please."

"Sorry, sir, I can't give you that information. Would you like me to ring his room?"

"No. It's his birthday, and I've got a surprise for him," Johnny said, raising the garment bag.

"Well, he's not in, and I can't give you his room number. You can leave the item for him if you'd like."

"No. I want to give it to him personally. I'm his brother. Can't you give me his room number, and I'll take it to his room and leave it for him there?"

"Sorry, sir."

"Okay, call the room. Tell his wife his brother, Joe, is here to see her."

"The line's busy."

In Room 124 Liz talked on the phone. "Joe, I'm so glad to hear from you. Gar told me he saw you at dinner at your folks' house."

"Liz, I need to talk to Gar," Joe's voice came over the phone. "I saw on the TV that he says Reynaldo Diaz wasn't guilty. Gar was big enough to admit he'd made a mistake. I think I made one too, and I want to talk to him."

"I'm expecting him any time."

"Would it be okay if I come over?"

"Sure. We're in the Clearwater Inn, room one-twenty-four," Liz said.

"The line's clear now," the desk clerk said to Johnny. The clerk punched 1-2-4 on the phone. Johnny craned his neck to see the numbers on the phone out of sight under the counter. The clerk handed the phone to Johnny.
"Hello," Liz answered.
"Hello, this is Joe, Gar's brother; I've got a surprise for him. Okay if. . ."

Alarm covered Liz's face. She hung up the receiver.

". . . if I bring the surprise to the room," Johnny continued to talk to the dial tone. "Okay, thanks. I'll be right there." Johnny handed the phone back to the clerk. "She says it's okay."
"Mrs. Garcia?" the clerk spoke into the phone. "She's hung up." He punched the number 1-2-4 again.

In the room, the phone rang. Liz stood back away from it and looked as if the ringing phone had become a rattle snake.

A man and woman came to the registration desk. "We're the Watsons. We have reservations."
"Yes, Mr. Watson," the clerk said, then turned back to Johnny. "I guess it'll be okay. It's room one-twenty-four."
Johnny hurried down the hall, carrying the awkward garment bag. Finding 124, he knocked gently on the door.
In the room, Liz froze in silence. Johnny knocked

again louder. Liz picked up the phone and punched "O."

At the reservation desk the switchboard buzzed, but the clerk busied himself registering the Watsons.

Johnny knocked again. Liz held the phone to her ear and looked toward the door with terror-filled eyes.

The desk clerk, annoyed by the buzzing, picked up the phone, pressed a button and said, "One moment please," and laid the phone down.

Johnny stepped back as far from the door in the hallway, ran and hit the door with his shoulder. Liz screamed into the phone, but no one heard. Johnny hit the door again and the lock broke. Held now only by a chain lock, he kicked hard, the chain lock burst out of the door and the door opened. Liz bounded into the bathroom and locked the door behind her.
    Johnny withdrew a Winchester, lever-action, hunting rifle from the garment bag and rushed into the room.

Johnny Diaz sat on the edge of the bed with the rifle on his lap and watched the door. The sound of running water and steam came from under the bathroom door.
    "Go ahead and take your shower, lady. I'm not after you. I'll just wait here for your husband."

    "Which way's one-twenty-four?" a young man with a two-inch cut on his chin asked the desk clerk.
    "Can I help you, sir?" the desk clerk asked.

"Yes, I'm Joe Garcia. Want to see my brother, Ranger Gar Garcia in one-twenty-four."

The desk clerk looked skeptical. "A man calling himself Ranger Garcia's brother Joe went to the room a few minutes ago."

"Call the police. Which way's the room?"

"To your left."

"Call the police."

"I'm calling." The desk clerk grabbed the phone and searched an emergency list for the number. "I can't find it." With a trembling hand he dialed "0" and asked the operator to send the police.

Joe ran to 124. He pushed on the broken door. It opened half way, heavily scraping the carpet. The sound of water running in the bathroom and steam filled the room. Johnny ran to the half-opened door, opened it the rest of the way, and pointing the rifle at Joe, said, "Come in." He took a step back. "Shut the door."

Joe leaned back on the door and it closed.

"Where's Gar?" Johnny motioned Joe toward a chair, and stood, with his back to the bathroom door, and ordered, "Sit down."

Steam billowed out as the bathroom door suddenly opened. Liz, wet with sweat, and her hair in strings, held a steaming ice bucket. She lifted the bucket high and dumped hot water on Johnny Diaz's head. He sucked in a deep breath, dropped the rifle, grabbed his scalded head with both hands, and screamed an expletive.

Like a football blocker, Liz hit the scalded man in the back with her shoulder. He lurched forward. Joe jumped up from the chair and hit Johnny squarely in the face. Johnny fell to his knees and grasped the rifle just as

Joe jumped and landed on the rifle with both feet, pinning Johnny's fingers to the floor. Johnny screamed and jerked his hands free. Liz hit him again with her full weight behind her shoulder. Off balance, Johnny stumbled to the side.

Joe picked up the rifle, and cocked the hammer. "I'll shoot."

Johnny held up both hands, and backed to the bed. "Don't shoot." He sat on the floor, leaned back on the bed; put his face in his hands. For a full minute he sat still and quiet. Then suddenly he began to weep. "Ben." Between great sobs, he moaned, "Ben, Ben. Oh, God, what have I done? Oh, Ben." He continued to sob, and then shouted into his tear-filled hands, "I killed Ben, Reynaldo. Oh God, I'm sorry. I killed you Reynaldo. I wanted to be the big shot."

Johnny's soul, like a heavy bag of lead shot, continued to pour out. "Daddy. Daddy, can you forgive me? . . . They're all dead." He continued to sob long, mournful, unrestrained cries. Then he began to call for his mother with the voice of a little boy.

Chapter 46

Doubling Back

Masters parked the black Dodge in the farthest and darkest corner of the Masters Building underground parking lot. He climbed four flights of stairs to the private entrance to his office. He hurried into his private bathroom, shed the dirty clothes and got in the shower.

Joann Rainey looked up from her work, turned and listened to a faint spewing sound coming from Masters' private office. She tried the door. The knob wouldn't turn. She used her key, and opened the door. The sound became louder and more like running water. "Who's there?" she shouted.

Burke Masters came out of the bath with only a white towel around his waist.

"Burke. What are you doing here? The police are looking for you."

"Not any more. I've been cleared of all charges, so I need to go back to work."

"Really. According to the television you're sure to be convicted of murder."

"You know how they blow things out of proportion. I'm back and a free man. But the word hasn't gotten out on television yet, so I need you to keep quiet about me being here until my being cleared is announced."

"Sure, Burke."

"Now go back to work. I anyone calls for me say I'm out.

A few minutes later in the break room Joann Rainey

sipped a cup of coffee. A news bulletin interrupted the television program. "A garage owner was murdered today. Police believe it was at the hand of fugitive Burke Masters who has been charged with the grisly murder of Reynaldo Diaz and Masters' wife, Clara." The news anchor touched a tiny earphone. "Just a moment. There's more." He listened a moment. "Yes. Bodies of three young men were found in a ditch on Farm Road Twelve, all shot. The authorities believe Masters is involved in that as well."

The gorgeous receptionist got a coke out of a machine and sat at the table with Joann Rainey. "Looks like our boss is in deep trouble," the receptionist said.

"I promised to keep it quiet, but he's here in his private office. He told me he had been cleared. I don't know what to do," Joann Rainey said.

"Do you want to be charged with harboring a fugitive and accessory to murder?"

"Goodness no," Joann Rainey began to weep.

"You'd better call the police."

Back at her desk, Joann Rainey wept some more, shook her head, and picked up the phone. "This is Joann Rainey at the Masters Oil Company office. Burke Masters is . . ."

Two big hands formed a giant fist and slammed down hard on the back of Joann Rainey's head. She sprawled unconscious over the desk. Masters hung up the phone. "Bitch."

Led by Chief Sherman, police officers swarmed into the fourth floor offices of Masters Oil Co. "Are you the one who called?" he asked the receptionist.

"Yes."

"We also got a call from Joann Rainey, but she was cut off."

"Oh. I hope she's all right." She jumped up and hurried back to Joann Rainey's desk and found her there unconscious.

"Call an ambulance." Sherman swung open Masters' office door. Inside he found the dirty and greasy clothes. "Get this message to Ranger Garcia," Sherman said into the walkie-talkie radio.

After receiving the message, Gar drove to the parking lot entrance to the Masters Building.

Gar parked his white Dodge on the curb, and walked down the sloping drive that led to the underground parking garage. Tires burning rubber shrieked a warning. The black Dodge sped toward Gar. He had a feeling of *déjà vu* as he dodged right, and the car followed. *He's trying to hit me.* Gar jumped the other way. The car bounced out of the drive. *It's Burke Masters.* The fender hit Gar a glancing blow and knocked him down.

Cars from both directions screeched to a stop just short of the Black Dodge as it sped erratically across the street. Having swerved to hit Gar, Masters lost control of the car. The car's front tires flattened as they hit the far curb. The car bounced high over the curb, across the sidewalk, across 20 feet of grass, and hit a section of eight-foot chain-link fence with barbed wire on top. The fence collapsed and the car ran over it. The black Dodge came to rest with its front bumper against a black oak tree.

The edge of the flattened fence, now free of the car's weight, sprung back up three feet and continued to spring up and down. Masters jammed the gearshift into reverse and stomped the accelerator. The car lurched backward. The barbed wire atop the downed fence tore into the shiny paint on the rear of the car. The end of a downed galvanized steel pole gouged into a tail light. The rear wheels of the car spun in the dirt, sending clouds of dust flying, but the pole, set in concrete, and leaning into the rear of the car, prevented it from backing farther.

The car jerked forward and hit the tree again. Then it jerked backward and hit the top of the leaning pole again.

Gar stood painfully to his feet, instinctively brushed off the seat of his pants, and limped across the street. His tail bone still hurt and now he had other places hurting. His bloody tattered shirt sleeve covered a four-inch bloody abrasion on his right arm just below the elbow.

Across the street he saw the black Dodge, jerking back and forth in panic between the downed fence pole and the tree. Gar limped across the street.

Masters jumped out of the car, and disappeared into the woods, running downhill on the backside of Clearwater Springs Park.

Gar hurried and stepped over the bouncy fence. When he reached the barbed wire, he jumped. He groaned with pain as he held on to the rear of the car to steady himself. The fence sprang back up as if to continue guarding the car. He looked in the car for his lost revolver, but didn't see it.

Gar ran unsteadily into the woods, limping with every step. His wounded right arm hung at his side. Blood ran down from the wound on his arm and dripped off the ends of his fingers. He dodged trees and brush as he ran down the steep hill toward the river.

He stopped and listened but heard only the rustle of breeze through the trees, and insect and bird sounds. He continued.

Emerging from the woods near the water's edge, Gar walked on level, manicured grass, and onto an asphalt sidewalk. Five hundred feet ahead he saw two men on the bank beside a motor boat. The shorter man wore a bright, red and white Hawaiian shirt. Suddenly a gunshot shattered the silence and the shorter man fell to the grass. The bird and insect sounds abruptly stopped. The taller man scrambled into the boat and cast off the bow line.

"Stop. Police," Gar shouted as he ran limping toward the man and boat. Another shot came from the boat, and Gar dived to the ground. Lying on the ground he pulled his left Walker Colt .44 from its holster. He could see Masters, who stuck Gar's other pistol into his belt, and hastily pulled the start cord on the outboard motor.

Gar got to his feet again and ran toward the boat. The motor sputtered to life. Blue smoke and a stream of water shot out from the rear of the motor. Masters flipped the reverse lever and the boat backed out into deeper water. Gar hurried down the river bank carrying his heavy, Walker Colt in his left hand. He cocked the hammer.

Masters pulled the shift lever on the outboard motor into *forward* and turned the boat toward the center of the river. The motor buzzed louder. Gar reached the bank where the boat had been tied. Jim Bradshaw lay on his side writhing in pain. Tender green grass stained his shirt. Blood oozed up through red flowers on his shirt and through his fingers as he clutched the stomach wound.

The boat carrying Masters made it to 100 feet from shore. Gar leveled his gun toward Masters. "Stop. Police. Stop or I'll fire," Gar shouted.

Gar fell prone on the grass, and aimed his left pistol

at Masters. Masters turned his body toward Gar, and pulled the pistol from his belt.

Masters' face flushed with anger. He threw his head back and screamed in rage as he raised the pistol.

Gar squeezed the trigger.

The heavy bullet entered Masters' open mouth and exited through the back of his head. Brains, bone, and blood showered down on the crystal clear water as Masters' body, limp as a wet sock, folded to the bottom of the boat. As he fell, his body hit the tiller of the outboard motor, sending the boat into a tight circle.

The pink cloud of blood in the water grew lighter in color as it grew larger and moved deeper. Silver, little bubbles trailed the outboard motor's propeller as the boat circled forty feet above old Felix's hole. Felix the catfish treated this as he did almost every other disturbance. He ignored it.

Chapter 47

Resolution

That evening at police headquarters Chief Bryan presided over a press conference. The large assembly room buzzed with news reporters as thick as bees in a hive. Several took turns to corner Gar and ask him about the bandage on his arm.

Gar and Chief Bryan stood behind a lectern. Television cameras pointed toward him from several angles. Still photographers took flash pictures. Before Chief Bryan could open the news conference, a television anchor woman shouted, "Have you heard from Dallas?"

"Well, yes," the Chief said. "They asked an assistant chief from Los Angeles to take the job of police chief."

"Are you disappointed?" the anchor woman asked.

"Who wouldn't be? Now, that's old news. This is new: We just received word from the hospital that the subject, Donald Thomas Harmon has died." A murmur rose from the assembled news people. "He died of toxic shock syndrome brought on by a human bite."

"Who bit him?" a young man with a notebook asked.

"Steve Pierce," the Chief answered. "Steve Pierce helped to subdue the subject so he could be arrested. In the process Pierce bit him."

"More deadly than a snake bite," the young man said.

"Guess so," Chief Bryan said. "Actually this young

man, Steve Pierce, was responsible for the apprehension of, Giovan, alias Grimes, also known as Hawk Nose.

"How did he do that?" a young woman reporter asked.

"Well Hawk Nose and Thomas apparently tried to kill Steve Pierce with an overdose of heroin. In the process, Steve Pierce got away from them and threw Hawk Nose into the path of an eighteen-wheeler," the Chief explained.

"So, this young man killed both suspects?" the young woman asked.

"It appears so, but unintentionally," the Chief said. He lifted a note sheet and continued. "Jim Bradshaw, who was shot by Burke Masters this afternoon is in surgery now and is expected to recover."

"Did you find out who shot at Larry Wilkins?" another reporter asked.

"We believe it was Burke Masters," Chief Bryan said. "The spent bullet matched one of Masters' hunting rifles."

"What about the three guys out on Twelve?" a reporter asked.

"Gar is more familiar with that one," the Chief replied.

Gar stepped to the mike. "The evidence we pieced together indicates that they tried to rob Masters and he killed them."

"Did you have any physical evidence, or just your theory?" the reporter asked.

"We found one of Masters' credit cards in one victim's pocket. Ballistics shows that all three were killed by the same gun, a forty-four we knew to be in Masters' possession."

"What made you so sure Burke Masters was responsible for the murder on the sky-ride?" a young woman with red hair called from the back of the room.

"According to the evidence," Gar began, "Mr. Masters hired Thomas and Hawk Nose Giovan to help him assassinate Reynaldo Diaz in a spectacular way in order to cover up the murder of Mrs. Masters whom he killed for more than six million dollars in insurance money. He tried to make it look like his wife was not the intended victim to get around a 'homicide exclusion' in the insurance policies," Gar continued.

"Isn't there a law against a person benefitting from murder anyway?" the young woman asked.

"Yes. That's true. However, if he had succeeded in making the insurance companies believe that Diaz was the target of the killers and that Mrs. Masters was killed technically by accident, he would have collected the money. As it is, he gets nothing."

Gar left the press conference with Chief Bryan and hurried to the motel anticipating a passionate reunion with Liz.

When Gar entered the Inn lobby, he saw Blitzboggen standing near the entrance talking on a pay phone. He smiled and waved at the Ranger, and continued talking into the phone.

"Yes, my dear," Blitzboggen continued. In his always perfect pronunciation as if giving a classroom report. "I'll get at least a sixty-thousand bonus." He paused and listened. "Yes, my dear, at least sixty-thousand dollars. After all, I saved these companies over six million." He listened a moment. "Well, yes I do. I have an opportunity to buy an entire railroad carload of towels and wash cloths at ten cents on the dollar." He listened again. "Wrong? No, there's really nothing wrong with them. It's just that they're all orange."

Gar quickly stepped toward his new room where Liz had moved after Johnny Diaz destroyed 124. Inside, Liz watched the six o'clock News on television. A news reporter interviewed Steve Pierce and Anita Ramirez.
"I didn't intend to kill anybody," Steve said. "I was just trying to get away from those guys."
The camera zoomed in to show Anita squeeze Steve's hand. "The cops thought Steve was in on the murder, but I never had any doubt about Steve," Anita said, and then added, "My mother says 'He's not that kind of person.'"
Steve turned from the interviewer to face Anita. "She does?"

Gar pushed the key into the lock and winced with pain from his injured arm. He pushed the door open to see Liz sitting before the television set. She jumped up. Her white, low-neck nightgown flowed gently over her shoulders to the floor.
"Hi, hero. I just saw you on the tube. The good guys won," she said, stepping quickly to meet him. "Oh, your arm," she exclaimed as he put both arms around her.
"My arm's fine." He pushed the door shut with a foot and held her tight.
"The Governor called for you a few minutes ago. Said he'd send his plane here and take us back to the lake so we could resume our vacation. He said they'd send it

tonight if you want."

"Tomorrow will be soon enough."

"Did you see Joe?"

"Yes. So did the Chief of Police. He wants to send Joe to the police academy and give him a job."

"What about Johnny Diaz?"

"He's locked up in the county jail, raving about killing his brothers. He's to have a psychiatric exam before the Judge sets bail. That's enough of that," Gar said and pulled Liz to him.

Gar held her tight, and kissed her long on the mouth. "We're still married aren't we?"

"Yes. Did you forget?"

"It's been so long, I thought I'd check." He kissed her quickly, and released her. Opening a drawer, he took out a "Do Not Disturb" sign and hung it outside. He hurried to the telephone, took off the receiver, and covered it with a pillow. He turned to his astonished wife, swept her up into his arms, and carried her to the bed.

-------------------------------END-----------------------------

CPSIA information can be obtained at www.ICGtesting.com
Printed in the USA
BVOW02s0008190516

448694BV00017B/165/P

9 781481 183178